OUTLAW WOMEN

Outlaw Women

Prison, Rural Violence, and Poverty
in the American West

Susan Dewey, Bonnie Zare,
Catherine Connolly, Rhett Epler,
and Rosemary Bratton

NEW YORK UNIVERSITY PRESS
New York

NEW YORK UNIVERSITY PRESS
New York
www.nyupress.org
© 2019 by New York University

References to Internet websites (URLs) were accurate at the time of writing. Neither the author nor New York University Press is responsible for URLs that may have expired or changed since the manuscript was prepared.

Library of Congress Cataloging-in-Publication Data
Names: Dewey, Susan, author.
Title: Outlaw women : prison, rural violence, and poverty in the American West / Susan Dewey [and four others].
Description: New York : New York University Press, [2019] | Includes bibliographical references and index.
Identifiers: LCCN 2018042920| ISBN 9781479801176 (cl : alk. paper) | ISBN 9781479887439 (pb : alk. paper)
Subjects: LCSH: Women ex-convicts—West (U.S.)—Social conditions. | Women prisoners—Deinstitutionalization—West (U.S.) | Female offenders—Rehabilitation—West (U.S.) | West (U.S.)—Rural conditions.
Classification: LCC HV9305.W35 D49 2019 | DDC 364.3/74097809034—dc23
LC record available at https://lccn.loc.gov/2018042920

New York University Press books are printed on acid-free paper, and their binding materials are chosen for strength and durability. We strive to use environmentally responsible suppliers and materials to the greatest extent possible in publishing our books.
Manufactured in the United States of America
10 9 8 7 6 5 4 3 2 1
Also available as an ebook

CONTENTS

Introduction

"You're not from around here," surmised an expressionless, deep-voiced local woman in a flannel work shirt as one of us silently counted eighteen different kinds of beef jerky hung alongside a vast array of hunting equipment for sale at the gas station. "You workin' at the prison?" After gauging the silent nod she received in response, she stoically intoned, "Every one of them women is in there because of a man." Whether uttered in the small Wyoming town that houses the state's only women's prison or as part of national debates on criminal justice reform, such sentiments reflect the fact that many incarcerated women have struggled throughout their lives with poverty and abuse from family members and intimate partners who made them fear for their safety, eroded their self-worth, increased their likelihood of self-medicating with drugs and alcohol, and caused them long-term damage, sometimes in ways that further isolated them from potential sources of social and economic support.

Women in prison have also made choices that deeply hurt others, including their children, friends, and neighbors, thus perpetuating a cycle of violence, harm, and blame that they may or may not have been previously subjected to themselves. Once released from prison, women throughout the United States encounter socio-institutional expectations that generally fail to account for their caregiving obligations to children and others, relegation to the feminized ghetto of low-wage and uninsured service-sector work, and reduced access to credit, all of which are intensified forms of challenges many women without criminal records also face.[1] The material and sociocultural realities of life in the rural Mountain West further compound these difficulties in the form of limited social services, significant gender wage gaps, severe weather conditions that often make travel between small towns treacherous, and rigid expectations regarding women's appropriate social roles. As one of the women whom we interviewed for this book succinctly put it, "People kinda expect males to screw up, but us women are the ones s'posed to hold it all together."

An Architecture of Gendered Violence

This book argues that unique cultural dynamics shape women's experiences of incarceration and release from prison in the rural, predominantly white communities that many Americans still think of as "the Wild West." Together, these dynamics comprise *an architecture of gendered violence*, a theoretical lens that focuses on how addiction and compromised mental health, poverty, fraught relationships, and felony-related discrimination work in tandem with the women's decision making to construct their life worlds. The architecture of gendered violence is a multivalent force that profoundly shapes the lives of currently and formerly incarcerated rural women, many of whom have mightily struggled to make ends meet. This account of Wyoming women's experiences with incarceration and its after-effects is designed to offer clear and concrete suggestions for untangling the dynamic knot that ties so many women to circumstances, relationships, and patterns that figuratively or literally imprison them.

Arguments presented in this book provide a much-needed rural-focused contribution to the extensive body of published research on urban women's gendered pathways to incarceration. On the basis of her study of a New Haven, Connecticut, felony court, criminologist Kathleen Daly originally articulated these pathways as being comprised of strained family relations, limited job skills, substance abuse, compromised mental health, and violent victimization (Daly 1992).[2] Subsequent research on women's pathways to crime has emphasized the nexus of interpersonal violence (DeHart 2008), limited socioeconomic opportunities and social services (Ajzenstadt 2009), a gender-stratified street economy that, like its licit counterpart, relegates women to lower-paid, lower-status roles (Miller 1998), and a social order that demonizes nonconforming women (Chesney-Lind 1986). Such work indicates that women who have more extensive experiences with violent or grief-generating events are more likely to commit crimes for which they receive life sentences (Leigey & Reed 2010) and that some "late onset" women may not become involved with the justice system until well into adulthood (Nuytiens & Christiaens 2015). Pathways to women's long-term criminal justice system entrenchment feature a combination of individual characteristics and sociostructural factors that account for important differences with respect to age, mental health, addiction, housing, neighborhood, experiences with abuse, and responsibilities for children (Brennan et al. 2012).[3]

The architecture of gendered violence that comprises the primary pathway to incarceration among the Wyoming women in our study reflects how the suite of concerns facing currently and formerly incarcerated women manifests in a rural context far from the coastal metropolises that dominate the production of discourse and scholarship on mass incarceration and criminal justice reform. The women construe this violence as instrumentally productive of circumstances that result in their incarceration and, like a chronic pathology, continue to stalk them after their release from prison.

Theoretical Frames: Conceptualizing Women's Pathways to Prison from Rural Precarity

Our theoretical-analytical enlistment of the architecture of gendered violence that so powerfully emerged in currently and formerly incarcerated women's accounts of their lives derives primarily from engagement with work pioneered by feminist, rural, and narrative criminologists as well as studies, from a range of academic disciplines, on rural poverty and economic precarity. We hope that naming and disarticulating the specific components of this violence and its operations will provide academics and practitioners with a fuller understanding of how criminalized rural women navigate the considerable constraints that shape their lives both before and after their time in prison. In so doing, we make a contribution to a rich body of existing literature that offers evidence-based assessments of criminal justice policy and practice.

Feminist Criminology

The first criminological studies to incorporate women generally portrayed them as criminal deviants whose innate inferiority made them even more dangerous and unpredictable than their male counterparts

(Lombroso & Ferrero 1893 [2004]). Girls and women involved in crime—particularly prostitution—were regarded as psychologically damaged individuals in need of rescue, which often took the form of involuntary treatment that state-endorsed providers regarded as therapeutic (Thomas 1923).[4] Since at least the widespread social reform initiatives of the Progressive Era (1880–1920), prevailing criminal justice and social services solutions to addressing women's criminality have focused on changing lawbreaking behavior among the poor and working-class women who, then as now, constituted the majority of jail and prison populations irrespective of gender. Progressive Era criminal justice and social services reformers promoted women's caregiving roles in ways that were largely irrelevant to such women due to their need to work outside the home in order to economically support their families (Agustín 2007).

Such measures originally focused on teaching incarcerated women how to sew, clean, cook, and otherwise prepare them for life as servants to wealthier families or as wives to men who could economically support them (Dodge 2002). In the contemporary era, such solutions focus largely on cognitive approaches due to the prevalence of addictions and other mental health issues among correctional populations, most notably through programming that positions lawbreaking as the product of individual cognitive dysfunction, typically termed "criminal thinking" (Samenow 1984 [2014]). Yet, critics have pointed out that focusing on individual dysfunction as the cause of crime fails to account for social forces that contribute to higher rates of incarceration among poor and working-class people and people of color relative to their more privileged counterparts (Heitzeg 2015).

Women's historically and culturally mandated economic dependence on men, relegation to unpaid or low-wage work, and infantilized social status, for some early criminologists, was thought to protect them from detection of, and prosecution for, crimes they committed (Pollak 1950). Most early research with incarcerated women considered questions about the women's lives in relation to the experiences described by their male counterparts, in sharp contrast to studies of men's criminal justice system involvement that focused exclusively on issues of relevance to the men themselves. From the earliest criminological studies until quite recently, men's experiences with crime, incarceration, and reentry have provided the standard for scholarly and practical approaches to women's experiences. Consider, for instance, two midcentury studies that examined the then-current question of whether prisons constitute culturally distinct entities or reflect the normative structures and practices prevalent in the society of which they are a part: Gresham Sykes's *Society of Captives* (1958 [2007]) and Rose Giallombardo's *Society of Women: A Study of a Women's Prison* (1966).

Sykes's book, which is still widely regarded as a classic criminological text, posited that the social structure governing the men's maximum-security prison where he conducted his research reflected dominant cultural norms as well as strong social bonds among prisoners. These bonds, Gresham argues, subvert authorities' attempts to control all aspects of the men's lives. In contrast, Giallombardo's now-out-of-print book argues that women, unlike men, respond to the deprivations of prison life by forming quasi-familial and marriage-like bonds as a result of gendered social norms that value women's relational caregiving. One cannot help but wonder how Giallombardo's analysis might have taken a different route had the midcentury context in which she worked allowed her to examine the women's experiences as something other than an ancillary component to studies of their male peers.[5]

Feminist critiques of these prevailing criminological approaches began to emerge in the wake of second wave feminist movements that paved the way for then-unprecedented numbers of feminists to enter professional fields, including academia, where they had an opportunity to critically examine the criminal justice system's treatment of women (Klein 1973; Belknap 2014). These early feminist criminologists emphasized the need to theorize crime as a gendered social construction, interrogate criminal justice responses to violence against women, and advance gender equality more generally (Daly & Chesney-Lind 1988). They also critiqued what they viewed as a social construction of crime that disproportionately penalized girls and women for sexual and status-related offenses, such as prostitution or "promiscuity," and inappropriate criminal justice responses to these and other crimes (Smart 1977; Worrall 1990).[6]

Feminist criminologists directly confronted the role of public perceptions in perpetuating fears about dramatically increasing rates of crimes committed by women (Chesney-Lind & Rodriquez 1983; Heidensohn

2012), some of which arose from the publication of Freda Adler's *Sisters in Crime* (1975), a book that notoriously predicted an impending surge in women's criminal activity as a result of widespread workplace and socio-sexual shifts.[7] Women did indeed begin to funnel through the criminal justice system in far greater numbers beginning in the late 1970s, but not for the reasons that Adler had predicted. "Tough on crime" approaches, which enjoyed popular support in the wake of widespread sociopolitical upheaval, began to systematically target those involved in the illicit drug economy for criminal prosecution. Such initiatives prompted a massive upsurge in incarceration rates for women struggling with addiction and/or living in neighborhoods dominated by the illicit drug trade (Girshick 1999; Gottschalk 2006; Richie 2012; Rierdan 1997; Sudbury 2005).[8]

From 1977 to 2010, the number of female prisoners has increased by over 700% (Tapia 2010) with simultaneous, albeit less dramatic, increases occurring in the number of adolescent girls under the oversight of the juvenile justice system or tried as adults (Chesney-Lind & Irwin 2008; Johnson 2003; Miller 2008; Schaffner 2006). The subsequent efflorescence of research conducted with incarcerated women has emphasized the widespread effects that women's incarceration has on children and communities. A majority of incarcerated women are mothers whose struggles with the extreme stress of poverty and addiction-related issues often significantly contribute to the circumstances that surround their crimes (Enos 2001; Ferraro & Moe 2003; Golden 2005). For some women, however, motherhood coincides with an end to their drug-related or other forms of lawbreaking (Kreager, Matsueda & Erosheva 2010), and, as Michaelson and Flavin (2014) note, certainly not all women are mothers.

Incarcerating mothers has historically presented challenges to both correctional facilities and the women's families, including difficulties with custodial arrangements, relationships to children's caregivers, restrictions on visiting, and coresidence with infants in facilities that permit it (Baunach 1985; Craig 2009). Women often play a central role in maintaining incarcerated men's ties to their children and other family members, sometimes in ways that transform women with incarcerated intimate partners into "quasi-inmates" forced to navigate the justice system's complexities while living in the free world (Comfort 2008). Yet the fathers of incarcerated women's children rarely perform similar roles.

Children with parents in prison are far more likely to live in poverty (DeFina & Hannon 2010), and those with mothers in prison face particularly significant socioeconomic instability (Kruittschnitt 2010; Siegel 2011). Incarcerated women with children routinely face social erasure of their identities as mothers through pervasive stigma and pathologization due to their perceived maternal "unfitness" (Eldupovic & Bromwich 2013; Flavin 2009; Haney 2013). This erasure can prompt a pattern whereby untreated chronic substance abuse and addiction result in incarceration, which prompts child custody loss followed by a pervasive sense of guilt, shame, and hopelessness that discourages women from making life changes (Allen, Flaherty & Ely 2010).

Research by feminist criminologists has reached far beyond academic confines by prompting the implementation of a set of policies and practices designed to acknowledge that incarcerated women generally have different needs than their male counterparts. Collectively known as "gender-responsive programming," such policies and practices revolve around the principles that women fare best in supportive environments that strengthen their relationships with children and other loved ones, offer mental health treatment that considers histories of violent victimization, foster self-sufficiency, and ensure holistic postrelease services provision (Caputo 2014: 8–9). Gender-responsive programming requires that staff and facility culture comprehensively align with these goals (Covington & Bloom 2006; Bloom, Owen & Covington 2004). Yet gender-responsive programming's feminist critics express concerns that such programs can reinforce stereotypes about incarcerated women as psychologically damaged deviants by disregarding the gendered social contexts that shape their decision making (Haney 2010; McCorkel 2013).[9] Likewise, the "gender" in "gender-responsive" remains a synonym for "women," and it remains unclear why gender-specific programs that uniquely pertain to men have not also been implemented in men's facilities, given their potential benefits.

Feminist criminological research with incarcerated women has also provided unique insights into prison as a gendered and intensely bureaucratized social organization with multiple masters. Such work illuminates how prison social organization both reflects and is constructed by a combination of penal administrative philosophy and prisoners' own navigations of the totalizing structures that shape their lives (Kruittschnitt & Gartner 2000; Lempert 2016; Owen 1998). Examinations of women's concentration in lower-paid, lower-status professional roles in prisons (Britton 2003; Britton 1997; Zimmer 1987), where they perceive greater risks to their safety than their male counterparts (Gordon, Proulx, and Grant 2013), likewise illuminate the means by which correctional facilities replicate existing gender inequalities. By exploring carcerality as an increasingly globalized system that reflects complex modes and forms of governance (Barbaret 2014), such work offers significant insights into its manifold impacts on a wide variety of actors and contexts.[10]

Rural Precarity

The analysis presented here engages with a wide array of work by sociologists, economists, anthropologists, philosophers, and others concerned with the increasingly profound and widespread nature of precarity. Originally articulated by economist Guy Standing as the generalized absence of labor market security that has come to characterize almost every type of employment since the global implementation of post-Fordist economic policy beginning in the 1980s, precarity comprises a lack of stability in work, skill reproduction, income, and representation (Standing 2011).[11] In rural contexts, precarity is especially evident in the significant transformations agriculture and food production have undergone in recent decades. While the U.S. agriculture and food-production sector still employs an annual average of 2.5 million workers, it does so through heavy reliance on poorly paid and often undocumented or temporary workers with limited community ties and few legal rights to protest their working conditions (Martin 2009).

Wyoming's economy relies almost exclusively on mineral-extractive industries and is accordingly subject to a boom-and-bust cycle in which the state's fortunes are precariously tied to global coal, oil, and gas prices. Energy-related mineral extraction provides a significant proportion of state revenues, as twenty of twenty-three Wyoming counties produce one or more major energy sources from coal, crude oil, and/or natural gas (U.S. Energy Information Administration 2016). Agriculture, ranching, and tourism follow mineral extraction as major generators of revenue. Wyoming has the lowest population density in the United

States, with a great deal of its vast expanses—18.4 million acres of public lands and 41.6 million acres of federal mineral estate—owned by the federal government's Bureau of Land Management, which provides lease rights to ranchers, farmers, and companies engaged in mineral extraction (U.S. Bureau of Land Management 2018). Tourism attracts an estimated 4.2 million visitors annually to Yellowstone National Park in the state's northwest corner (U.S. National Park Service 2018), but, like mineral extraction, this source of income is rather precariously tied to the amount of disposable income households across the United States have to spend. Agriculture and ranching, the third largest revenue generator in the state, focuses on the production of beef cattle, hogs, sheep, hay, sugar-beets, and barley, with nearly half of Wyoming's 11,600 farms and ranches generating less than $10,000 in annual income, with 3,700 of those operations earning $10,000–$99,999 annually, and much smaller numbers earning more (U.S. Department of Agriculture 2016: 6–9).

As is the case in Wyoming, rural precarity takes especially dramatic forms in areas economically dependent on world market prices for natural resources such as oil, natural gas, coal, and other minerals, with workers in these sectors accordingly vulnerable to widespread layoffs when prices are low. These industries play a significant role in the social dynamics of communities in which they operate, including residents' perceptions of cohesion and other indices of well-being, such that the mine, oil field, or other extractive labor site comes to constitute area residents' shared sense of identity (Bell 2009; Brown, Dorins & Krannich 2005; O'Connor 2012). People who live in resource-dependent areas may also face strained community ties and social issues that they perceive to be caused by the presence of a transient workforce that will move elsewhere when the demand for labor diminishes (Goldenberg et al. 2008; Carrington & Pereira 2011; O'Connor 2015). They may also confront what criminologist Kerry Carrington and colleagues, in their studies of frontier masculinities in Australian mining towns, identify as the cultures of violence that can arise in some resource-extraction settings (Carrington, McIntosh & Scott 2010).

Despite these pressing rural socioeconomic realities, prevailing U.S. political, academic, and popular discourse about poverty tends to center on blighted urban neighborhoods economically dominated by the illicit drug and sex trades and subject to structural racism and other forms of social exclusion. Some scholars of rural poverty contend that the focus given to race and racism in dominant academic and national discussions of poverty underscores the uniquely American discomfort with acknowledging the existence of social class (Duncan 2015; Maharidge & Williamson 2011). Sociologist Kathleen Pickering and colleagues, in their extensive study of welfare reform's impacts on four historically impoverished rural U.S. regions, demonstrate this point. The authors argue that the significant amount of academic attention paid to the impacts of these reforms in urban areas among people of color elides the significant problems poor white people face in rural areas characterized by limited or no public transportation, inadequate schools, and constrained social services (Pickering et al. 2006).

This academic focus on "urban problems"—a phrase that often serves as cultural shorthand for challenges facing neighborhoods of color—is part of a problematic longstanding academic tradition that one prominent sociologist of color privately described to Susan as "the jungle trope, in which a white researcher enters the ghetto and emerges miraculously unscathed to tell the world about its brutality." Critics of the prevalence of such approaches, which contemporary social scientists term "outsider ethnography," note how white researchers' representations of problems within communities of color, including mass incarceration, can reinforce pervasive negative stereotypes about them (see, for example, discussions in and surrounding Contreras 2012; Goffman 2014). Controversies surrounding such "outsider ethnography" are somewhat puzzling given that most researchers, irrespective of their ethnic or racial identity, do not live permanently in the communities in which they conduct their studies and so hardly can be considered "insiders" regardless of how they self-identify. Even more puzzling is that such controversies surrounding ostensible insiders and outsiders have entirely elided social class differences among whites. This is particularly evident in studies of incarceration that focus on race, ethnicity, and/or national origin, often by applying these foci to the exclusion of poor whites, who make up a significant majority of those incarcerated. Yet perhaps this is not surprising at all given the realities of life in a profoundly class-stratified society that nonetheless champions the universal possibility of upward socioeconomic mobility, which sociologists have critiqued for decades as "the hidden injuries of class" (Ryan & Sackrey 1996; Sennett & Cobb 1973).

Such limited academic representations of both social class and rural life are likewise replicated in rural communities themselves, where explicit discussions about precarity seem to be muted or completely silenced in the interests of maintaining a rural status quo that heavily relies on a dominant U.S. cultural belief in equality. Sociologist Jennifer Sherman argues, in her ethnography of a remote Northern California community decimated by the loss of the timber industry, that many of her participants actively deny the class oppression they face at the hands of corporations that outsource working-class people's jobs to countries with fewer labor regulations. Instead, they favor cultivating a particular type of moral capital that enables them to position themselves as superior to those they regard as lazy, unpatriotic, or selfish (Sherman 2009; Sherman 2006). Such mobilization of moral authority vis-à-vis dominant U.S. cultural norms that prioritize financial self-sufficiency is also evident in a study of low-income Appalachian mothers who remained financially insolvent when they rejected paid work in favor of maintaining a valued stay-at-home mothering identity they viewed as incompatible with welfare-to-work requirements (Manoogian et al. 2015).

Anthropologist Kathryn Dudley notes that, among the rural poor white Iowans in her study of widespread farm foreclosures, "a blanket of silence falls over the obvious disparities of wealth that underwrite a banker's 'retirement' on a lakeshore resort and a farmer's compulsion to work until he dies," such that residents "are universally mum about the structures of inequality that give some families an advantage over others" (Dudley 2002: 18). Such silence includes models of masculinity that, according to one study of frontier masculinities, prizes public stoicism and emotional control in ways that result in numerous private harms, including high rates of suicide and self-harming behaviors such as substance abuse (Carrington et al. 2013), while naturalizing anger as a normal expressive mode for men (Pease 2010). Limited economic prospects, combined with even less cultural capital ascribed to rural life, results in a brain drain when even local residents begin to regard their rural communities as futureless wastelands from which young people must flee in order to make a living (Carr & Kefalas 2010).

Rural Criminology

Our work responds to critical criminologists' calls to explicate and better theorize the unique forms that crime takes in rural contexts (Donnemeyer 2016; Donnemeyer, Scott & Barclay 2013; Websdale 1998). The field of criminology has focused on urban areas as a result of a widespread idealization of small towns and rural communities as idyllic places free of discord (Carrington, Donnemeyer & DeKeseredy 2014). Such idealization occurs in sharp contrast to popular cultural representations, particularly in horror films, which one study found to frequently depict rural white people in a violent and depraved manner that reinforces dominant cultural stereotypes of their general backwardness (DeKeseredy, Muzzatti & Donnemeyer 2014). It could be argued that in North America these popular cultural portrayals have deep social roots in early-twentieth-century eugenics movements that sought to eradicate social inequality through forced sterilization, birth control, and segregation of all people living in intergenerational poverty, including both people of color and poor rural whites (Dyck 2014). Eugenicists promoted legislation, research, and representations that emphasized how birth control, sterilization, and related measures were practical antidotes to what was then widely regarded as the innate inferiority that resulted in impoverishment among both North American whites and people of color living in both rural and urban areas (Sanger 2007). With titles like "Mongrel Virginians" and "Hollow Folk," eugenicist-sponsored projects were used to justify the forced sterilization of poor rural whites and people of color as well as other harmful practices under the guise of stemming what was then termed "feeble-mindedness" and "human rubbish . . . incapable of producing 'normal offspring'" (Currell 2017: 498). Such practices are hardly confined to the distant past in their evocation of the "pathology of place" that often features in popular cultural representations of rural areas as replete with mental illness, addiction, and criminality (Corner 2006: 293). Examples include a number of enduringly popular cultural works featuring poor rural whites as murderous degenerates, most notably *Wisconsin Death Trip* (Lesy 1973), *Texas Chainsaw Massacre* (Bernard 2011), and *Deliverance* (Creadick 2017).

Despite the prevalence of such representations, rural criminology remains undertheorized, and studies of crime in nonurban areas tend to focus on violence against women (Donnemeyer & DeKeseredy 2008; DeKeseredy et al. 2007), substance abuse, and addiction.[12] Scholarly explorations of rural criminal justice systems are somewhat more varied and emphasize the generalist nature of rural policing. Police in less-populated areas must respond to a much greater array of complaints and situations than their urban counterparts, who have far more specialized training and resources at their disposal (Payne, Berg & Sun 2005; Sims 1990; Weisheit, Feisheit & Wells 2006). That rural police face such pressure is particularly concerning in light of the widespread moral panic surrounding methamphetamine use in rural areas (Linnemann & Wall 2013). In such cases, a feedback loop exists between folklore about the drug's supposedly lifelong impacts on the brain, national legislation, state and local policing initiatives, and methamphetamine users, who in rural areas are often poor and white (Omori 2013). Anthropologist William Garriott (2011) documents the vast carceral expansion such paranoia about methamphetamine enabled in a West Virginia town where rural residents and local law enforcement colluded in policing methamphetamine users and manufacturers. Rising white incarceration rates have likewise been attributed to the fact that heroin use and addiction are now far more prevalent among rural and suburban whites nationwide than among inner-city people of color (Cicero et al. 2014; Subramanian, Riley & Mai 2018).

Rural criminology's relative underdevelopment in comparison with urban-derived theories and studies of crime has led some researchers to question the utility of mobilizing the generally vague and subjective "rural" and "urban" categories. For instance, sociologist Barbara Rockell, in her work with drug-involved women who live in what she terms "the rural-urban fringe" of central and western New York State, demonstrates the interplay between these geographic locales, emphasizing that small towns and rural areas are interconnected with urban illicit drug and other criminalized economies (Rockell 2013). Other researchers regard rural and urban crime and the contexts in which it is committed as fundamentally different, with one comparative study of rural and urban crime rates cautioning researchers against applying "empirical truths" from urban criminological studies to rural settings because of fundamental urban-rural differences, including the greater likelihood that rural crime will go undetected due to greater privacy, underresourced police officers spread over long distances, and rural people's propensity for dealing with illegal activities through extrajudicial mechanisms such as in-person problem solving (Deller & Deller 2011). Rural policing varies tremendously by location, with the general public's fear of crime and community relations with police appearing to play determining roles in rural perceptions of public safety (Nofziger & Williams 2005).

Special challenges arise with respect to rural policing in resource-extraction areas undergoing the rapid population and infrastructural growth that undergirds the social organization of areas colloquially characterized as "boomtowns," particularly with respect to violence (Carrington, Hogg & McIntosh 2011). Rural police can quickly feel overwhelmed as the population outpaces infrastructural and policing resources, as occurred in 2008 in western North Dakota's Bakken oil formation as well as in the simultaneous boom in Canada's Fort McMurray (Dahle & Archbold 2015; Ruddell 2011). Yet a study that contrasted crime-related fears among native, long-term, and recent migrant boomtown residents in Wyoming and Utah found that long-term migrants who moved to the town during a period of rapid expansion expressed the greatest fears of crime. This finding indicates that such towns may change their character over time and develop a culture of accommodation to large numbers of transient migrants (Hunter, Krannich & Smith 2002). A similar study from an Australian mining town determined that "crime-talk" had an important community-building role, with longer-term residents using it as a means to establish social cohesion (Scott, Carrington & McIntosh 2012).

Narratives and Narrative Criminology

In focusing on currently and formerly incarcerated women's own accounts in this book, we enter into a dialogue with narrative criminology as well as a long feminist tradition of giving voice to women who may not otherwise be heard in a book-length format. Culture, context, and individual personality coconstitute the storytelling modalities available to those asked to provide narrative accounts, which often carry moral weight for both their tellers and their interlocutors (McAdams 2013; Marshall 2009). Narrative criminology takes an interdisciplinary approach to discursive and written forms of self-representation among justice system–involved individuals (Presser & Sandberg 2015). While relatively new to criminology, facilitating such self-representation has an extensive history among feminist researchers and practitioners (Bryne 2003).

Narrative criminology has explored the interpretive and explanatory mechanisms men use to recount their involvement in events that led to their incarceration and the futures they envision for themselves after their release. Identifying the various moral codes and identities currently and formerly incarcerated men use to interpret their experiences helps to contextualize their actions and decision making within the broader socioeconomic forces that shape their lives (Brookman, Copes & Hochstetler 2011). For instance, Andy Hochstetler and colleagues analyzed how men who have committed crimes that physically hurt others resist self-identifying as violent, raising important questions about the intersections of self-conception and action (Hochstetler, Copes & Williams 2010). Narrative criminologists have also identified the existence of "narrative hot spots," events that incarcerated individuals describe as pivotal in shaping their lives in conjunction with various social forces (O'Connor 2015). Narratives are distinctly gendered, and in one of the few studies addressing gendered differences in what the authors term "transformation narratives," Herrschaft et al. (2009) found that women generally attributed positive role transformation to a relationship in their lives, while men generally attributed such changes to status-related goals like employment. Narrative work with criminalized women often emphasizes relational aspects, such as in Kristin Carbone-Lopez and colleagues' work with women's descriptions of the contexts in which others initiated them into methamphetamine use. Such descriptions underscore the sociality of the experience, which often took place with family members or others to whom the women were intimately connected (Carbone-Lopez, Owens & Miller 2012). Jennifer Fleetwood, in her study of North American and European women incarcerated in Quito, Ecuador, as a result of their involvement in attempting to transport controlled substances, observed the frequency with which the women invoked dominant gender norms to justify their involvement in the international drug trade, particularly through their relational connections to husbands, intimate partners, and family members (Fleetwood 2015). In their examination of women's gendered narratives of addiction recovery from methamphetamine use, Jody Miller and colleagues document how the women "clearly situated their meth use in the context of a clearly articulated storyline of gendered conformity followed by destruction," whereby methamphetamine use prevented them from being the women they wanted to be (Miller, Carbone-Lopez & Gunderman 2015: 87).

In engaging with the ways in which rural women envision and reflect on their pasts, presents, and futures as they move through prison and the often further circumscribed choices available to them after their release, this book offers a significant contribution to the burgeoning literature on mass incarceration. Findings presented here are particularly meaningful in light of the political invisibility these women face as residents of an extremely rural region of the United States that depends on the volatile natural-resource-extraction economy. Exploring the intersections between the way these global economic forces impact criminalized women and their families in a stratified rural social order where women earn far less than their male peers offers unique insight into the intermingling of criminal justice and economic systems.

The women who participated in our study understand all too well the importance of providing their own accounts of their lives and themselves, as they must often do so as part of their encounters with police, judges, case managers, and therapeutic group facilitators. As a result of these encounters, the women know that the stories they mobilize to represent themselves and their choices have enormous creative and destructive potential. We accordingly remain carefully attuned to the women's accounts of their lives throughout this text, even when their self-representations appear contradictory. Criminalized women know that words hold inordinate weight in courtrooms and other criminal justice settings, where their use in particular ways can justify loss in almost every humanly conceivable form: of children, possessions, work, status, friendships, family, marriages, money, and, as universally occurred among the women in our study, freedom.

Situating a Wyoming Women's Prison in National Context

The number of individuals incarcerated at the Wyoming women's prison remained relatively stable over the three years prior to our writing this book, with the average daily population at 239 in 2016 and 254 in 2014 and 2015. Such a small number of women residing in a physically isolated location makes the prison, along with its North Dakota counterpart, the smallest and most geographically remote of the sixty-seven U.S. state women's prisons.[13] A prison's location matters significantly because it determines potential visitation, staff retention, programming, and public perceptions. Remote prisons discourage visitations from family members and loved ones and limit prison administrators' abilities to recruit and retain highly qualified staff. Most volunteers, including those who enjoy significant university or other support, cannot easily devote several hours of travel time in addition to the services they provide at the facility, which results in remote prisons having fewer classes and programs than those in close proximity to metropolitan areas. Prisons that are largely hidden from public view by location in rural areas also diminish public awareness and concern about such facilities.

While nearly half of all U.S. states have prison systems housing one thousand or more women,[14] only ten states have more than one state prison for women.[15] Eight state prison systems, in addition to Wyoming's, house fewer than 260 women: those in Maine, Montana, Nebraska, New Hampshire, North Dakota, Rhode Island, Vermont, and West Virginia. State prison systems in Alaska, Connecticut, Delaware, Hawaii, Idaho, Indiana, Iowa, Minnesota, and South Dakota each incarcerate 261–500 women, and those in Alabama, Kansas, Kentucky, Maryland, Massachusetts, Nevada, New Jersey, Tennessee, Washington, and Wisconsin each house 501–1,000 women. Twenty-six women's state prisons are within fifty miles of their respective state capitals,[16] thirty-eight state women's prisons are less than fifty miles away from a town of sixty thousand or more,[17] and seven state prisons for women are located from fifty to a hundred miles away from such a town: those in Arkansas, Hawaii, Illinois, Missouri, South Carolina, Virginia, and Washington. Only Wyoming and North Dakota have prisons that are more than one hundred miles away from a capital city or a town of more than sixty thousand people.

Size and geographic location also influence prison social dynamics, which continue to be a subject of great interest to numerous parties. These include researchers who seek to understand the worlds prisoners create and navigate, practitioners and other professionals tasked with maintaining order in correctional facilities, and a general audience that avidly consumes popular cultural representations of prison life. Prison social dynamics are shaped in significant part by the previous life experiences and expectations of those who are incarcerated there, such that conceptions of social order, safety, and disorder can vary dramatically between prisons (Carrabine 2005). Hence Susan could not resist asking a senior staff member at the Wyoming women's prison, as we idly conversed during count, a quiet time when the women must return to their cells until correctional officers have registered the presence of all prisoners, "Does it bother you when the women call this prison 'Camp Cupcake'?"

Our research team had puzzled over some of the women's propensity to refer to the prison in ways that seemed to dismiss or mitigate the totalizing nature of their surroundings, including phrases like "Camp Cupcake," "Barbie Bootcamp," and, Susan's personal favorite, "Little Prison on the Prairie." Sometimes women used these phrases in conjunction with a statement along the lines of, "This isn't a real prison," which was sometimes followed by a speaker's assessment of the kinds of violence, gang activity, and abuse that they believed to occur, or, in some instances, that they had themselves experienced, in a "real prison." Hence it should have come as no surprise when the staff member laughed at the naiveté of Susan's question and explained, "They use terms like that because they feel safe here."

Our goal in emphasizing the facility's safety relative to other prisons is not to minimize the considerable pain and isolation from loved ones felt by incarcerated women. In fact, on numerous visits to the prison, some of us have been struck by how differently individuals might view its small physical size and population relative to those of other prisons and its considerable distance from a town with more than one grocery store. An urban woman transported to the facility to serve her sentence may see a brick structure that looks like a rural public school surrounded by a chain link fence amid a vast prairie. A Wyoming native, conversely, may see a rare manifestation of state power set in a small town. Important differences between women's perceptions of the prison also arise from experiential and demographic factors, such as age, race, drug involvement, and sentence.

Demographic information that the Wyoming Department of Corrections shared with our research team indicates that as of 2017, over two thirds of women in the prison were in their twenties and thirties, with approximately 15% over fifty. The vast majority of women, like most Wyoming residents, self-identify as white, with smaller numbers of women identifying as Hispanic (8.7%), Native American (7.6%), Black (2.9%), and Asian (0.7%).[18] Women were serving sentences for seventy-nine distinct felony offenses, most of which fall into two broad categories the women categorize as "drug crimes" and "money crimes." Thirty-eight percent of the women received drug-related convictions, including possession, manufacturing, delivery, and child endangerment related to substance abuse or involvement in the illicit drug economy; 5.8% of women were convicted of driving under the influence of alcohol or drugs. Of those who committed "money crimes," 15.6% were convicted of burglary, larceny, or shoplifting and 10.5%, of forgery and credit card offenses. A smaller number, about 20%, of the women were convicted of violent crimes: 10.5% of murder, 5.1% of assault and battery, and 4% of sexually abusing a minor. Ten and a half percent of women received other conviction types, including robbery, accessory, arson, property destruction, interference with police, child abuse, and abuse of a vulnerable adult.

Cheyenne, the state's capital and the town with a population of over sixty thousand closest to the prison, is nearly 150 miles away. Cars enter the prison parking lot through a single unattended gate undergirded by a set of steel pipes, known as a "cattle guard," that prevent livestock from wandering onto the premises. The prison is a relatively small, nondescript building constructed in 1977 and surrounded by a chain link fence topped with loops of barbed wire. Visitors enter through a small and usually empty reception area with a single metal detector and a wall of small lockers with clear plastic doors for storing belongings. Incarcerated women use a different entrance into the facility subsequent to their arrival, after which they stay in a separate unit for newcomers before being assigned to a housing unit.

The control office consists of a small room inside which sits a single uniformed officer watching a small set of black-and-white closed-circuit cameras monitoring different areas of the prison. From the officer's vantage point, the main areas of the prison materialize within the tiny boxes that hold images of women working, talking, reading, playing cards, eating, sleeping, sitting in group, getting haircuts, and otherwise going about their daily lives. The officer will also see some women in restrictive housing, which the women term "down east" due to its location. Like most prisons, the facility is brightly illuminated with artificial light that can make it difficult to determine the time of day despite the structured routines women follow depending on their security classification, place of residence, job, and personal preferences. Where windows do exist, such as in the hallway outside the sewing workshop, classrooms, and the chaplain's office, they organize the brilliant Wyoming sunlight into orderly shadow boxes on the floor and, while spotlessly clean on the inside, bear external traces of mineral deposits left by massive snowdrifts that have melted.

An intensely bureaucratized system derived from federal, state, and local legislation as well as institutional culture governs the women's treatment as they move through arrest, sentencing, incarceration, and, for many, parole supervision. While it is self-evident that every woman in prison is unique, the prison's socio-institutional order provides some discretionary latitude with respect to structuring their daily lives. Women's choices regarding everyday life in prison generally depend on how long they have been incarcerated, the length of their sentence, their conviction type, where they reside in the prison, and their attitudinal orientation to incarceration and life more generally.

A new arrival to the prison typically spends approximately thirty days isolated from the general prison population and under observation by prison staff while undergoing a battery of screenings and paper-based tests. In conjunction with the woman's conviction type, these assessments will determine her housing unit, case plan, uniform color, and other aspects of her everyday routine. The amount of time a woman spends in isolation may vary by type of offense and criminal history, such that an eighteen-year-old incarcerated for the first time and unaccustomed to the stress and social norms of a correctional setting might spend more time under observation compared with a mature woman who has served multiple prison sentences. Prison staff assess new arrivals in isolation—colloquially referred to for generations in many U.S. prisons as the "fish tank" because of the twenty-three hours per day of observation it involves—by attempting to determine their mental health status, including their likelihood of being aggressive or dangerously depressed, as well as to predict how they will interact with others in a new environment.

Most women will move from the observation period to general population where, as in other prisons nationwide, their security classification and other staff assessments will determine their place of residence, job, and participation in programming. Women in general population reside in one of two separate residence areas that refer to their shape: halls and pods. Halls, which house women with higher security classifications, feature two-person cells along a narrow corridor, while the pods, for women with lower security classifications, consist of two-person cells situated along a high-ceilinged, two-story rectangle featuring a large open area with immobile tables in the middle. All cells have neatly made bunk beds, a toilet, and, often, photographs of children and other loved ones fastened to the cinderblock walls. Women shower in a separate area located within each housing unit.

Women in general population keep busy with a variety of social activities, individual hobbies, classes, and jobs for which they receive a small amount of money that they can spend at the commissary, which sells snacks, personal hygiene products, and a limited selection of entertainment items, including a single type of television. The prison's most competitive and well-paid jobs are at the indoor tilapia farm, which raises the fish in massive tubs supervised by a full-time ichthyologist and delivers them for sale to a distributor from neighboring Colorado. Women may also work at the library, at a sewing workshop that makes uniforms and other items by order, and in the kitchen. When not at work, women may sign up for classes or groups that focus on crafts, religion, addictions treatment, exercise, reading, or education, with many women forming interest-based social groups among themselves around these activities.

Keeping busy while residing in general population provides a way for women to pass the time in a highly structured social context where they otherwise have limited decision-making opportunities. For many women, choosing among the admittedly limited ways to create a routine for themselves in prison is an important aspect of self-actualization while incarcerated. Women may find that these activities, and the self-reflection, routine, and responsibility they attempt to foster, can help them to envision new possibilities for themselves following their release. In many ways, structuring their time around a set of activities and spending it with women who have shared interests keeps women connected to community and helps them to cope with difficult circumstances.

Yet other women spend their time in general population unmotivated to make changes or to form a routine for themselves, choosing instead to spend their time sleeping, watching television, and participating in as few activities as possible. Such individuals often isolate themselves by socializing minimally, spending a great deal of time alone, and only interacting with others during mealtimes in the cafeteria. Women who do actively work and participate in programming sometimes speak about such women with a mixture of scorn and pity due to their perception that they have limited interest in making changes to their lives despite the fact that they may be struggling with depression or other mental health issues.

The prison's third housing unit, situated separately from the halls and the pods, is the Intensive Treatment Unit, which prison staff and the women most often refer to by its acronym, ITU. Women who reside in ITU score highly on the Addictions Severity Index, an assessment screening administered to new arrivals, and must commit to a rigorous schedule of classes and expectations for conduct that are much higher than for the rest of the prison. ITU residents may not have any contact with women who live in general population and must adhere to the therapeutic community model that emphasizes personal and social responsibility. Women in ITU cannot work due to their busy schedules, which involve spending almost all of their time with their coresidents in classes, program-related writing and other exercises, and self-reflection. All women agree that ITU's highly scheduled routine makes time pass quickly, but, as with any addictions treatment model, women's opinions of the program span a continuum from those who praise its focus on accountability to those who feel traumatized by its emphasis on processing one's painful past experiences.

Women from all three housing units can be sent to restrictive housing ("down east") if staff deem them a danger to public safety or themselves because of serious rule violations, such as fighting, or a debilitating mental health episode. Like new arrivals to the prison, women in restrictive housing spend most of their day in complete isolation, with only an hour for exercise. Being sent into restrictive housing can extend the amount of time a woman spends in prison by adding to her record of disciplinary infractions and removing or invalidating a positive record, or "good time," that may result in fewer days or months served in prison. A minority of women, particularly those who struggle with being surrounded by so many women at all times or who suffer from severe mental health issues, will deliberately act out in order to be sent to restrictive housing and experience its associated privacy.

In Wyoming, as nationally, women serving very long or life sentences play an enormous role in setting and maintaining the overall tone of prison life, communicating to newcomers that the prison is not just a holding cell but their actual home for a long time. These women serve as essential role models who teach other women how to successfully navigate their sentences while also preserving institutional culture. Many women who have been in prison for more than a decade take leadership roles in various groups and envision themselves as responsible for maintaining the prison's social order. Staff and administrators are well aware of these women's important social role, and for some women with lengthy or life sentences, the higher standards to which they are held can be burdensome. For some women, this social role is a point of pride, whereas others may simply perceive it as part of their responsibilities as women serving lengthy sentences. The situation is quite different for women who are preparing for release from prison.

Women preparing for release from prison do so in one of three ways. Some women choose to serve their entire sentence, colloquially referred to as "killing [my/her] number," in prison and then be released without any obligations to parole, mandatory drug testing, or related requirements. Others appear before the Parole Board, which is comprised of volunteers appointed by the governor, and, if recommended for parole, after release must report on a regular basis to parole officers who may stipulate a significant number of restrictions on the women's movements, relationships, and other important aspects of their lives. Women may also serve the remainder of their sentence at an Adult Community Corrections facility that privately contracts with the Wyoming Department of Corrections, and where the women must find a job and pay rent. Although the women live in the free world in such facilities, they are still prisoners completing a sentence.

Taken together, these various ways that women navigate their time in prison underscore the nuanced complexities inherent to life in a totalizing social institution that, in more instances than not, continues to impact the women throughout their lives. This is particularly significant given that most of the women incarcerated in Wyoming come from, and will return to, rural areas characterized by a gendered rural social order that positions them as fundamentally suspect and deserving of heightened scrutiny. Our research team's recognition of these unique rural dynamics prompted special methodological and ethical considerations in a state that Wyoming natives often refer to as "a small town with long roads."

Methods and Ethics in a Rural Research Context

We situate this text within a wealth of innovative feminist work with incarcerated women that eschews the hierarchies imposed by the academic research, writing, and publishing enterprises. These hierarchies are most readily apparent in socio-institutionally enforced divisions between university and community, professor and student, and, of course, the free and the imprisoned.[19] The project that forms the basis of this work began at the University of Wyoming in 2014 when sociologist Catherine Connolly introduced anthropologist Susan Dewey, literary and social justice scholar Bonnie Zare, and graduate student Rhett Epler to Rosemary Bratton, founder and director of the Hilde Project, a Wyoming nonprofit organization that helps currently and formerly incarcerated women prepare for self-sufficiency. Rosemary has served as a volunteer at the Wyoming women's prison for many years, during which she has taught courses on personal financial management, career empowerment, and skill development.

Keen to conduct an action research project with positive direct potential benefits for our community, we mobilized our respective skills as researchers, activists, and people with intergenerational local ties to design a qualitative interview-based needs assessment that sought to determine community reintegration challenges faced by women who have been incarcerated at the prison. Between December 2014 and August 2015, Cathy, Bonnie, Susan, and Rhett interviewed seventy-one women, forty-three of whom were incarcerated at the time of the interview and twenty-eight of whom were on parole and residing throughout the state, about their perceptions of their life experiences prior to, during, and subsequent to imprisonment. We used two open-ended interview guides, one for currently incarcerated women and one for formerly incarcerated women, to elicit responses regarding the participants' perceptions of their support systems and their abilities to be economically self-sufficient.

The research team organized the interview guide around three central sets of experiences: life before incarceration, experiences in the Wyoming women's prison, and actual or anticipated postrelease experiences. The interviews consisted of open-ended questions about the women's aspirations, education, decision making, support systems, and daily activities, and included numerous prompts that encouraged women to discuss aspects of their lives that they regarded as significant. Each interview lasted approximately one hour and was transcribed verbatim, resulting in approximately two thousand pages of transcripts, which the research team members deductively and then axially coded to determine the project's most significant findings. This data, which undergirds the arguments presented here, indicated that many women expressed a desire for more classes and programming; in response, Susan initiated Wyoming Pathways from Prison, which provides college credit to incarcerated women at no cost through remote technological and in-person instruction by University of Wyoming faculty, staff, and supervised students.[20] Susan also subsequently conducted over one hundred additional interviews in the summer of 2017 with parole officers, as well as with men and women under their supervision, and findings from that work also inform the analyses presented here.

We attribute a great deal of this action research project's success to a strong, mutually respectful relationship with the Wyoming Department of Corrections (DOC), which supported this work from its inception. DOC leadership allowed us to record interviews in the prison, which enabled us to analyze verbatim transcripts rather than messy and incomplete handwritten notes. DOC staff members read and fully considered the findings presented in a report submitted shortly after the research was completed and continued to support higher education in prison initiatives despite the fact that doing so meant adding to staff's already significant workloads. Simply put, this work would not have been possible without such generosity from the DOC, and we continue to be humbled by the genuine concern evinced by DOC staff for the incarcerated women under their supervision.

We conceptualized this book as the collaborative product of our respective skill sets after jointly defining the arguments presented here in a series of meetings. While the collaborative process was nearly effortless as a result of our shared feminist values, concern for the women who participated in the study, mutual respect for one another, and a long history of successfully working together as colleagues, we remained mindful of the ethical challenges raised by the unique research and social context in which we worked. Aspects of Wyoming's dominant sociocultural norms and the general social structures that govern everyday life played a significant role in our research design, its implementation, and the decisions we made in writing this book.

In Wyoming, as everywhere, these normative structures impact individuals in different ways depending on who they are and where they are, such that gendered rural cultural practices that may strike some people as archaic or excessively restrictive are defended by others who regard them as normal because they constitute the only way of life familiar to them. Our research design consciously engaged with these norms by tightly attuning our modes of inquiry and analysis to the physical, cultural, and socioeconomic realities that surround us in our daily lives. A number of these realities resemble dynamics at work in other parts of the rural United States, where limited prospects for work or social mobility prompt many young people to migrate, the interests of intergenerational landholding families hold powerful sway, and the cultural beliefs that make life possible for some are intolerably oppressive for others.[21]

Weather governs everyday Wyoming life in a totalizing manner difficult to explain to outsiders because of the ways in which snow, wind, hail, fires, and other natural occurrences frequently combine with very limited state infrastructure to make interstate highways and local roads impassable for days. During such storms, the state becomes an American Siberia, with an undulating lunar landscape snow-blanketed and whipped by ferocious winds that can violently twist tractor-trailers into heaps of obliterated roadside steel within seconds, with temperatures plummeting to twenty degrees below zero. A heavy snowstorm, particularly when accompanied by gale-force winds, will often leave the streets of even populated areas covered in ice and snow for weeks until warmer temperatures melt it away. It is not atypical for interstate highways to remain minimally plowed relative to other parts of the United States that experience heavy snowfall, necessitating, for those who can afford them, the purchase of studded tires, chains, or other forms of snow protection unknown (and typically illegal) in the Midwest or Northeast where snowplows regularly clear the roads. Road closures that ensue after a major snowstorm render virtually all travel impossible and make the often-lengthy driving distance between one town and the next especially apparent as grocery store stocks dwindle and town streets become treacherous or impassable.

The state, with its vast geographic space, has a population less than that of Des Moines, Iowa, and a quarter of the Denver Metro area (or of Brooklyn and Queens put together), although most residents live and work in, or within a short driving distance of, a small town. While Wyoming has one of the shortest commute times in the nation, most Wyoming drivers travel longer distances with a sleeping bag, nonperishable food items, and water at all times of the year, and many are proud of the personal responsibility and self-reliance created by the sometimes-hostile climate. Long driving distances from one town to the next, a lack of public transportation, and difficult travel conditions also create a situation in which many areas of Wyoming are considered "food deserts" because they lack grocery stores and access to fresh produce.

Small-town life is the norm in Wyoming, where the capital city, Cheyenne, has just over sixty thousand people. Many local people see the state's wide-open spaces as emblematic of a personal freedom that consists of being left alone and unencumbered by city life. Those who live in small Wyoming towns or in the countryside entirely without neighbors take pride in their belief that they do not have to lock their doors to protect against intruders or theft, and many highly value what they regard as a supportive, close-knit community. These dynamics also involve what some city dwellers might regard as gossip or intrusion into personal life, as small-town Wyoming residents often comprise one another's entire social worlds.

Wyoming has a remarkably homogeneous ethno-racial composition, with many locals descended from Protestant German homesteaders. As one woman of color from another state explained to Susan and Rhett during an interview at a halfway house where she was residing after her release from prison, "I never seen so many white people in my life." An urban visitor to Wyoming from the East Coast or a major midwestern city is likely to be struck by how most residents are monolingual English speakers who do not express strong affinities for the European countries from which their ancestors migrated to the degree that many people do in cities with larger populations of European immigrant groups through the maintenance of language, celebration of national cultural heritages, and related practices. It could be argued that this is the case because many European migrants who moved west chose to leave these cultural and linguistic practices behind, or had no one to share them with, unlike in more densely populated areas where early European migrants, as many migrants still do today, settled in communities with shared cultural affinities.

This relative homogeneity was also evident in the absence of discussion regarding ethnicity, race, or cultural identity in our interviews with women, the vast majority of whom were white. The research team is also white, which may have impacted discussions about race with women who participated in our study, given that whiteness is a majority identity in Wyoming and an assumed cultural category that does not lend itself to critical interrogation in the absence of the kind of ethnic and racial diversity found in many other U.S. states. Since many people are from predominantly white towns of eight thousand people or less, it is fairly common for these residents to have rarely or never met a person of color or a person who speaks a language other than English. The few times when discussions of race did occur, notably, were either with white women who had lived in other states (including in prisons in other states) or with the very small group of Latinas, Native American women, and African American women interviewed, and then only after the person doing the interviewing mentioned her home state of, depending on the interviewer, New York or California.

Despite the conformity one might expect to ensue from such homogeneity, many Wyoming residents regard themselves as fiercely independent. A local person familiar with the hard, and sometimes dangerous, physical labor of mining, ranching, or oilfield work may resent the commodification of its associated cowboy culture by wealthy urbanites who own ski vacation homes in Jackson, a resort town in Wyoming's northwestern corner. This negative perception of outsiders deemed insensitive to local ways extends to state and federal regulatory oversight, which many Wyomingites perceive as burdensome because they are subject to metropolitan policy, standards, and legislation without reaping its benefits. Hence someone who owns a ranch may object to a state oil and gas inspector's right to examine an oil well on his or her property, which he or she regards as sovereign despite the potentially significant negative impacts that an oil or gas leak has on groundwater and air quality shared by all state residents. Such sentiments stem from a landowning system generally maintained across generations through gradual land acquisition of neighboring properties, often at prices reduced by the desperation of those who could no longer make a living.

A Fraught Historical Context

Our research team remained highly conscious of the fraught cultural and historical terrain in which we carried out our work in a region long mythologized in U.S. popular culture as the fearlessly independent "Wild West," where gun-slinging cowboys, Native Americans, sheriffs, and outlaws battled for control of a region characterized as the frontier because of its distance from the East Coast centers of federal government power that were already well established by the time leaders began to promote Manifest Destiny in the mid-1850s. Historians generally attribute the origins of this widespread myth of the frontier to the work of historian Frederick Jackson Turner (1893), who, following then-contemporary prevailing political sentiments among most white Americans, argued that the frontier was "the meeting point between savagery and civilization," demarcated by the "existence of free land," and thus "furnishe[d] the environmental conditions under which Americans come into being" (Turner 1893, cited in Redding 2007). Turner wrote during the post–Civil War Reconstruction era, a time when dominant U.S. cultural and government powers alike had a vested interest in promoting a sanitized version of colonial conquest and genocide in which white settlers heroically brought civilization to previously unsettled or "savage" lands (Slotkin 1992; Chapple 2008). This myth, as originally promulgated by Turner, would not be nearly as disturbing if not for its enduring power in both national politics and the dominant cultural imagination, as cultural studies scholar Arthur Redding notes:

> The struggle between federalism and libertarianism virtually defines our national elections. . . . When a presidential candidate wants to "get big government off our backs," he dresses up like a cowboy, as did Ronald Reagan, who twice ran successfully on an anti-federalist platform. In the west, "tax-and-spend" liberals are demonized as east-coast Washington insiders and ignorant bureaucrats, as tax collectors, and, ultimately, as effeminate. Libertarian values are strong in the heartland. We think of ourselves as self-reliant, fiercely independent, and competent. We like guns and we like settling things for ourselves. (Redding 2007: 316)

The myth of the frontier, as numerous scholars and activists have argued for decades, largely erases the fact that Native Americans, including the Arapaho, Shoshone, Lakota, Cheyenne, and Crow, inhabited the western states, including Wyoming's Wind River Valley, for at least five thousand years prior to the arrival of white settlers (Bishop & Plew 2016). Yet this history of contact between Native Americans and Europeans is more nuanced than any single history can convey. While the Shoshone and other Native American groups began using horses acquired through trade with European missionaries, fur trappers, and travelers as early as 1700 (Stamm 1999), large-scale contact between Native Americans and white settlers did not occur until after Lewis and Clark's 1804 expedition into the western region of what is today the United States, after which fur traders began to arrive in much larger numbers, followed by gold prospectors, ranchers, miners, and others (Cassity 2011; Hughes 2000; Sanderson 2011).

Socioeconomic relations between Native Americans and white settlers were profoundly impacted by two major initiatives promoted by the U.S. federal government: the Homestead Act of 1862, which turned over nearly 10% of the total land area of the United States to settlers, including women and people of color, for ownership to those willing to build a home and reside there for at least five years; and the increasing push to resettle Native Americans onto reservations, which took very different forms across the United States in terms of violence, coercion, and resistance (Deloria 1992). Some scholars have argued that such colonization continued into the twentieth century through Native American people's overrepresentation in prisons relative to population size, as has historically been the case in Montana and other Rocky Mountain states (Ross 1998).

Reservation life, for Arapaho and many other Native American communities, undermined cultural systems that previously provided community support and a positive sense of shared identity (Fowler 2001). These difficulties were further compounded by the facts that many reservation areas were located on parcels of land deemed least desirable for agriculture, ranching, and other forms of settlement and that Native Americans had limited opportunities either for wage employment or to practice their traditional ways of life on reservation lands due to early government efforts to "assimilate" Native Americans into European-derived ways of living and working (Massey 2004). Native Americans demonstrated resistance to these considerable constraints, including through creolization of Christian missionary texts in ways that respected Arapaho and other religious traditions (Anderson 2001a; Anderson 2001b) just as Native Americans continue to do today through defying the unfortunately persistent nature of racism and injustice (Deloria 2004).

Despite the complexities inherent to these historical encounters, it is important not to focus exclusively on a version of history that only tells the stories of Native Americans and white settlers. African Americans, Latinxs, and individuals from many other ethnic and racial groups also relocated to Wyoming hoping to begin new lives for themselves free of the socioeconomic constraints of their original homes (Patton & Schedlock 2012). Wyoming granted women suffrage in 1869, a full fifty years before the rest of the United States, although historians continue to debate whether suffrage was a bid to increase voting power in a low-population-density state, an effort to attract more women settlers, or evidence of a then-progressive mindset (Morris 2017). Women played a particularly significant role in establishing schools as well as in other forms of work that were stigmatized or off-limits to women in other parts of the United States and necessary in the West due to labor shortages and, among women married to men, long periods of separation as men searched for or performed work in resource-extraction fields that, then as now, are segregated by gender (Rankin 1990). Western women also practiced entrepreneurship through prostitution, including its management in brothels, sometimes becoming quite wealthy in the process in areas where men dramatically outnumbered women (McKell 2009; Butler 1997).

These western histories and identities have remained enshrined in the dominant U.S. cultural consciousness from Turner's time until today and are evident in the way contemporary Wyoming tourism—the state's third-biggest industry—continues to profit from widespread fascination with the myth of the frontier. Buffalo Bill Cody, for whom the tourism-reliant town of Cody, Wyoming (near the famous Yellowstone National Park), is named, created a "Wild West Show" that toured the United States and Europe in the late nineteenth and early twentieth century after the entrepreneur failed to profit significantly from obtaining the water rights to Wyoming's Big Horn Basin (Bonner 2002). Today, most visitors to Yellowstone National Park will also visit the large tourist-oriented historical center memorializing Buffalo Bill Cody's legacy. Across Wyoming, numerous small towns annually enact local celebrations that likewise embrace the myth of the frontier, sometimes in ways that emphasize Euro-American versions of history that exclude or replicate stereotypes about women and people of color, particularly Native Americans (Rommie 2018; Shalinsky 1991).

Contemporary Wyoming remains a fraught context, with relations between local people of various communities, state governments, and the federal government subject to the vicissitudes of national and international prices for commodities derived from its extractive industries. "Ghost towns" formerly home to residents who mined for gold, minerals, and uranium are a testament to Wyoming's complex and contested relationship to the world (Amundsen 1995). This fraught history and context, combined with tightly knit sociofamilial ties and suspiciousness of outsiders, is by no means confined to any one particular group in Wyoming. For instance, it could be argued that negative sentiments toward the federal government and other forms of state control among descendants of white settlers is just as prevalent as is resentment toward ongoing neocolonial forms of oppression among Native Americans. Land ownership and the rights to use of land and water continue to be points of contention in this region, as despite what a visitor to Wyoming would likely regard as vast expanses of wide-open, empty, and generally arid land, the majority of it is owned by either private citizens or the federal government.[22] Law enforcement officers and other state agents, who are also products of their cultural context, can likewise evince a complex relationship with state authority that closely resembles the ethos of ranchers and others who genuinely believe in their sovereign right over their land. One particularly striking example of this near-feudal belief occurred several years ago when Susan sat with a county sheriff and attempted to review the standard informed-consent script that notifies an interview participant of his or her rights, the purpose of the study, and the study's funder, which in that case was the Department of Justice's Bureau of Justice Statistics. "Well, darlin'," the sheriff intoned before indicating that the interview was over before it even began, "you were doin' pretty good there until you mentioned the Feds."

This unique cultural and geographical context informs the lives of the women who participated in our study in complex ways that, of course, vary depending on each individual woman and the socioeconomic resources available to her. Women from "outlaw families," a term we heard used to describe kinship networks with extensive histories of criminal justice system involvement, often felt profiled and disproportionately punished by rural police officers. Since most rural police officers grew up in the same communities as those they professionally engage with in a law enforcement capacity, sometimes women from outlaw families feel that arrests and other negative police encounters are a result of their relatives' reputations. This dynamic is strikingly different from that of most urban contexts, where it is relatively uncommon for most officers to live in the neighborhoods they police.

Once women are released from prison, Wyoming's rural context challenges them because small-town residents are more likely to learn of their peers' criminal histories than would be the case in a city, where ex-offenders enjoy greater anonymity. Yet, for some women, the familiarity induced by such high-density social ties could also create the possibility for increased interpersonal and community bonds rather than intensifying the stigma of a felony conviction. Likewise, some women look forward to the opportunity to start over in a small town where they know no one, whereas others feel intimidated by their probable exclusion from the established family or social networks that can lead to work and other forms of socioeconomic support in such contexts.

This tightly knit research context also presented challenges in terms of the most respectful way to protect the women's confidentiality without compromising the book's empirical accuracy. We carefully considered these challenges after dozens of meticulous transcript reviews, developing central themes in an extensive codebook, deductively and axially coding all two thousand transcript pages, and then determining the book's central argument and structure. Wyoming has so few people that any information about a woman's life is potentially identifying, and this is particularly true for women in prison, given that their stories, like those of their male counterparts, are often reported at length in local newspapers because of the state's very low crime rates. Our solution to this dilemma was to develop five composite characters—Tammi, Nedrah, Dakota, Itzel, and Janea—who serve as narrative anchors for the analysis featured throughout the text by representing the central issues of concern, as the women expressed them to us, among currently and formerly incarcerated women.

We recognize that our use of composite characters presents some ethical challenges, particularly with respect to the risk of imposing or projecting our research team's understanding of issues facing currently and formerly incarcerated women. Yet our alternative, which would expose the identities of our participants to others in Wyoming, would come at far too high an ethical price because it could potentially cause long-term harm to the women who so bravely shared their stories with us. All quotations derive directly from ideas expressed in the transcripts of recorded interviews, and all reconstructed scenes involve events one of us either observed occurring among the women or heard about during the course of an interview. Verbatim quotations have been used as often as possible in the chapter vignettes, where their use does not risk identifying any research participants.

We take creative license in chapter vignettes by developing points emphasized to us by the women in interview transcripts or observations. While some events described were observed, distinguishing those from events developed using our interview data risks identifying our participants. All expressions of emotion and motivation by the composite characters emerged from careful deductive analysis of transcripts and observations in ways that avoid identifying any of the women who participated in our research while emphasizing common sentiments among the women. All family members and intimate partners are non-identifying composites derived from women's descriptions, as are their friendships and other relationships. Women's interactions with these important figures in their lives likewise derive from our research team's data, although we depict these interactions in ways that cannot identify any of our participants.

We tried our best to ensure accurate and holistic representation of these complex issues by sharing the manuscript prior to publication with multiple individuals, including Department of Corrections staff members, formerly incarcerated people, and others who generously offered to read and comment on the manuscript. Susan discussed the approach taken in this book with numerous currently and formerly incarcerated women, all of whom universally agreed that the composite characters play an essential role both in protecting women's confidentiality and in emphasizing the dynamic nuances of their lives. We hope that we have done right by all concerned.

The Women: An Introduction

"Tammi" is nineteen years old and knows what it feels like to lose her mind; she also knows how to prepare a variety of controlled substances for ingestion and self-identifies as "very institutionalized" because of her lifetime trajectory through foster care, group homes, the juvenile justice system, and, after she turned eighteen, jail and then prison. "This is my normal," she says, tugging on the green uniform that identifies her and her peers as residents of the prison's addictions treatment unit. "I been in the system my whole life." Most of Tammi's milestones—her birth, passing her high school equivalency exam, trying and failing to maintain contact with a daughter she gave birth to in the free world—have occurred in state facilities, which is also true of her siblings and family members more generally. For Tammi, incarceration is a fact of life in ways that allow her to reflect on the differences between various Wyoming jails and prisons: "I visited my baby's father too many times when he first went away, and trust me, those officers are *mean*. It's not so bad here."

Tammi's extensive family involvement with the criminal justice system and social services means that they have "outlaw family" status that subjects her to intensified police scrutiny, which may be characterized as a form of rural police profiling. Both her parents struggled with addiction, leaving her to care for her younger siblings and successfully evade the Department of Family Services, which is tasked with the oversight of children who have parents deemed unable to care for them, until she was arrested as a young adolescent and subsequently resided at the Girls' School, Wyoming's detention facility for minor girls. Tammi's extensive criminal record, her youth, and her long history of substance abuse led to her placement in the prison's addictions treatment housing unit, where she, like many women who have resigned themselves to spending their lives under institutional surveillance, is familiar with the language and actions required to demonstrate program compliance. Yet, like a number of her peers, she also knows from experience how to evade or deflect questions or topics she regards as too personal for discussion in group.

"Nedrah" spent six years in prison after being convicted of conspiracy to manufacture methamphetamine and endangering the welfare of a child, the result of her peregrination from a decade of marriage to the son of her mother's best friend to life with "Wyatt," whom she met when he rented a unit in her family's apartment complex following one of his stints in county jail. "I grew up very sheltered," she explains, "and for all his flaws, Wyatt really knew how to live, and that made me feel alive, too. Everything we did together was an adventure." Nedrah and Wyatt quickly embarked on an itinerant life in which methamphetamine's frenetic pace dissolved the structure and order that characterized her marriage; they drove for days across Wyoming with little need for sleep or food, searching for ways to make money.

Once in prison, shunned by her family and forbidden contact with the man who had so obsessively occupied every minute of her time, Nedrah finds it difficult to form relationships with other women or to engage in therapeutic or addictions treatment groups, which she regards as formulaic, infantile, and designed to encourage acceptance of the structured and orderly life she voluntarily abandoned and usually characterizes as "settling." She feels exhausted just thinking about the effort it would take her to determine whom she might trust and consequently avoids other incarcerated women, most of whom she regards with contempt and scorn. "This is like living in a town of two hundred–some people," she says, "and just like in any little town of two hundred–some people everybody knows everybody's business." Once released, however, Nedrah finds her world even further restricted as small-town social mores and the additional burden of a felony conviction leave her even more dependent on the family she tried to escape.

"Dakota" has deep roots in Wyoming and, like many of the rural people she knows, regards herself as "middle-class" despite her family's intergenerational struggles to keep their ranch while they also work at a variety of semiskilled jobs in a town located about thirty miles from where their ancestors homesteaded. She was thirty-four years old when she went to prison, with two adolescent boys, an unemployed alcoholic ex-husband living in the same rural county that comprised her entire social world, a University of Wyoming accounting degree, and a poorly paid job at a medical office that she hated. Indebted, desperate, and unable to communicate her desires for a new and different life to those she loved due to fear of both their judgment and the unknown, Dakota started cooking the medical office's books to cover her phone bills and the minimum loan payments on the overleveraged family ranch. Over a three-year period, she embezzled fifteen thousand dollars, knowing that she would have earned at least this much more than her small salary if not shackled to the only place and people she ever knew before going to prison.

Sentenced to fourteen months, Dakota obediently does her time by working in the kitchen and occasionally attending support groups filled with women who share with her their accounts of addiction, abandonment, and other pain that reinforce her sense that she is different from them. She feels lucky that her parents took in her two boys, rather than sending them into the foster care vortex that snatches away so many other incarcerated women's children. Yet, just as other women in prison warned her would happen, her court-mandated restitution payments, coupled with difficulties finding someone to hire her, make life even more difficult following her release. "I thought I knew what hardship was before I went to prison," she says, "but that was nothing compared to now."

"Itzel" is twenty-one and from the Spanish-speaking neighborhoods around Federal Boulevard in Denver, where she spent the last year of her teens in prison after she assaulted a girl whom she suspected of sleeping with her boyfriend, "Dante," whose name is tattooed on her neck and whose baby she is carrying. She has seven months remaining on her sentence for aggravated assault and battery as a result of an altercation that took place when she and Dante attempted to collect on a drug debt owed by a small-time purveyor of controlled substances in Cheyenne, Wyoming's capital city; because she was the one who hit the man in the face with a tire iron, Dante faced no charges. While she was initially proud of her loyalty to her man, being incarcerated takes a toll on Itzel, who finds a small group of other women from Colorado who help her to mitigate the isolation she feels in the facility.

Lacking strong legal representation and without family members who can exert influence, Itzel faces constant roadblocks as she attempts to arrange an interstate compact that will allow her to complete the terms of her parole in Colorado. The thought of living in a halfway house in a state where she has spent only a few hours outside of prison terrifies her, and she is shocked at the significant differences between the conditions characterizing the two prisons in neighboring states. "In Colorado," she says, "we had a huge yard, we could take all kindsa classes, we could talk to our case workers and actually get an answer; here there's nothing and the women locked up in here don't even know no better. I get chills when I think about leaving here with nothing." For Itzel, familiarity with the criminal justice system as a result of her neighborhood, family members, and friends provides little comfort as she attempts to find ways to create a future for herself and her baby.

"Janea," who is fifty-five, grew up in Texas, where at age twenty-two she met and quickly married "George," a charismatic drill rig operator, and spent the next ten years as a stay-at-home mother to their two sons outside of Dallas. Early on in their marriage Janea's husband always seemed to have trouble controlling his anger, which she regarded as a normal byproduct of his very dangerous occupation, just as it seemed to be among most of the men in her family. In Texas she could always go stay with relatives after a bad fight, but everything changed when he took a better-paying job in the Wyoming oilfields, where their closest neighbors lived in a town located across twenty-five miles of poorly plowed and badly maintained roads. The night she shot him in the head is a surreal blur of images, from the cottonwood limbs thrown into stark relief by the full moon to the sudden shocking sound of a single bullet leaving the hunting rifle.

"The judge told me 'I'ma make an example of you' and, boy, he sure did," Janea says. "I'll probably die in here." Numerous chronic health problems, some of them caused by years of physical abuse by her husband, compound the difficulties of everyday prison life, and she has spent several nights in restrictive housing for refusing her assigned top bunk due to her fear that she could have a seizure and fall. Janea treasures the small privileges that mitigate the routine that will endlessly repeat throughout her life sentence: her job at the prison library, helping women prepare to take high school equivalency exams, and reading letters from her two adult children. She has little patience for trouble-making younger women serving short drug-related sentences, of whom she says, "We lifers, we set the tone of the prison, and that's not the tone we want in here."

Throughout the chapters that follow, these five composite characters interact with other, less central composite characters whose experiences likewise derive from patterns our research team observed in the life experiences of currently and formerly incarcerated women. These less prominently featured composite characters came to be representative of particular identities through the same process we used in developing the central composite characters. They feature less frequently and are chapter-specific because the experiences and circumstances they represent occurred less often in our transcripts and observations. These interactions between primary and secondary composite characters are necessary to accurately depict the sociality of everyday prison life, where women live, eat, work, and participate in groups and other activities in a totalizing environment that involves near-constant interaction with others.

Tammi's and Nedrah's respective experiences with addiction and treatment both in and after prison are discussed in the first chapter, where they variously encounter the secondary composite characters Crystal, Kat, and Deb. Crystal, a prisoner who serves as the addictions treatment unit's head of house, takes her prison responsibilities very seriously, particularly in terms of mentoring other prisoners and ensuring the enforcement of unit rules. For some women in our study, such a leadership role was extraordinarily meaningful because it granted them special privileges, accorded them status, and, in some cases, was the first time in their lives that they had some amount of formal responsibility over others. Kat, Tammi's addictions treatment unit cellmate from the Wind River Reservation, spent a year in prison waiting to get into the addictions treatment unit. Like Crystal, Kat finds great meaning in the unit's highly structured approach to drug treatment and puts its teachings into practice by clearly setting interpersonal boundaries with Tammi, who is accustomed to defining herself through her relationships to others. Deb, a former itinerant rodeo performer married to a woman who is a professional gambler, attacks a fellow prisoner in order to return to the general prison population when all her other efforts to be removed from the addictions treatment unit fail. Deb loathes what she regards as the psychobabble of prison groups and, like some of the women in our study, regards her socioeconomic and interpersonal circumstances as far more instrumental in events leading to her incarceration than her individual flaws and choices.

Dakota's and Itzel's unique experiences of incarceration and preparations for release are the focus of the second chapter, in which they have occasion to interact with Denise, KelliAnn, Lexi, and the less frequently featured characters DeeDee, Skylar, Alaine, and Maggie. Denise is Dakota's kitchen coworker and cellmate, who also committed a money crime; their relationship reflects the bonds that many incarcerated women make on the basis of perceived similarities. In the case of Dakota and Denise, this similarity is their shared belief that they are inherently good, hard-working, and fundamentally different from their incarcerated peers who have experienced lifelong struggles with poverty, addiction, and related social problems. We see this condescension expressed by Dakota and Denise as they watch their less privileged prison peers DeeDee, Skylar, and Alaine playing cards while talking about what Dakota and Denise see as the product of unrealistic plans and disjointed thinking. These prison hierarchies and distinctions women prisoners make among themselves are also evident as KelliAnn attempts to establish respect among her peers due to her greater knowledge of correctional facilities in the Denver area, the only metropolitan area for hundreds of miles in the Rocky Mountain region. Itzel, who is from a family intergenerationally involved in the justice system, ignores and dismisses these efforts as naïve affinities for "street life" expressed by a young woman from an affluent family. Lexi, like Itzel, isolates herself from women she views as coddled and emotionally weak and in the free world prefers a transient existence; as with some women we interviewed, long-term relationships and staying in one place feel like another kind of prison to Lexi. We see this in Lexi's barely disguised disdain for both Maggie, who placidly waits to be released to her family, and the kindly correctional officer who attempts to express hopes for Lexi's success in the free world.

The lifelong interpersonal and structural violence experienced by Janea, Itzel, and Tammi feature in the third chapter, which also discusses how such violence manifests in the lives of secondary and less-featured characters. Johanna, who was a reservation drug and alcohol counselor prior to her incarceration, is a mentor to Angela and Taylar, teaching them about Battered Woman Syndrome and the cycle of violence prevalent in the lives of many currently and formerly incarcerated women. Janea's informally organized group of intimate-partner-violence survivors demonstrates how survivors of abuse support one another in the absence of prison classes or programming related to such violence. Emma, Sadie, Grace, Alaina, and Adalynn gather to discuss the abusive relationships in which they lived prior to their incarceration and, in so doing, begin to come to terms with the long-term impacts of this violence on their lives. Gennessa, Lorna, and Alliana likewise represent a range of circumstances surrounding currently and formerly incarcerated women's custody arrangements and their attitudes toward them at a critical juncture when women are preparing for release into the community and the imminent prospect of a free-world life that may or may not involve family reunification.

The experiences of Dakota, Nedrah, and Tammi following their release from prison are detailed in the fourth chapter, where their struggles in attempting to establish new lives for themselves bring them into contact with secondary and less-featured composite characters. The parole officers tasked with the respective oversight of the three women are composites derived from interviews Susan conducted at all twenty-five Wyoming probation and parole offices in 2017. Nedrah's friends from her free-world Narcotics Anonymous group—Jenna, Leanne, and Randi—evince a range of attitudes and beliefs toward everyday prison life as expressed to us by women following their release from prison.

The women's diverse experiences coalesce around an architecture of gendered violence particular to their rural communities yet reflective of issues faced, albeit in context-specific ways, by virtually all of the approximately 1.3 million women under U.S. correctional supervision (U.S. Department of Justice 2016a: 19), 113,495 of whom reside in state prisons (U.S. Department of Justice 2015b: 3). Writing from and about a state most Americans know only as "the Wild West," we mobilize the fraught symbolic weight of the American frontier as a means to articulate the widespread family, community, and national damage wrought by mass incarceration. The American frontier's symbolism tightly binds historical events and ideals in the dominant cultural mythos: rugged individualism, seemingly endless vistas of possibility, the violence of genocide directed at Native Americans, and environmentally induced hardships. We consciously return to this quintessentially American symbol at a historical moment when an ever-expanding criminal justice system, continued disappearance of full-time, stable jobs that pay working people a living wage, and evisceration of community, healthcare, and social benefits function in tandem to compound rural people's political invisibility on the national stage, despite the results of the 2016 presidential election.[23]

Chapter Overview and Structure of the Book

Each of the four social problems that comprise the architecture of gendered violence—addiction and compromised mental health, poverty, fraught relationships, and felony-related discrimination—is the focus of a chapter in the book.

Chapter 1, "Hitting Rock Bottom," argues that the criminalization and medicalization of substance abuse, addiction, and other mental health issues work both with limited, far-away, or nonexistent treatment options and with gendered rural social control mechanisms to further stigmatize women's substance abuse and discourage help seeking for mental health problems. Addressing the addiction and mental health trajectories that led a significant number of women to prison elucidates how, for some women, incarceration offered their first real opportunity to receive therapeutic treatment for substance abuse and mental health issues. This chapter details the socioconceptual organization of available addictions treatment within and outside the prison, with particular attention to how the women maneuver within contexts that seek to align therapeutic treatment with punitive practice.

Chapter 2, "A Productive Member of Society," contends that most currently and formerly incarcerated women find themselves juggling competing narratives as they reconcile the realities of their lives with a prevailing moral-cultural ethos that denies the structural violence of rural poverty, sexism, and felony-related discrimination. Illustrating the types of training, education, and work the women complete before, during, and after their respective prison sentences illuminates the economic need, lack of social supports, and, for some women, interpersonal and other forms of chaos that precariously balance the rickety stage on which they enact their everyday lives. This chapter narrates how the women describe their attempts, successes, and failures at meeting their individually valued ways of working, living, and finding meaning in the world.

Chapter 3, "Violence Has Flow," analyzes how the women's family and other socioeconomic structures reflect rural patriarchy and discourage women in abusive relationships from seeking help. Many women were victims of interpersonal violence in their families of origin and, later on, with intimate partners and children, some of whom they also perpetrated violence against in various forms. This chapter discusses how women situate their understandings of these violent dynamics within the physically harsh, rural terrain in which they lived before prison, and to which they generally plan to return. It also explores the relationship-related perspectival shifts some women experienced during incarceration, including the symbolic weight with which a number of women described mothering as a lifeline to the future.

Chapter 4, "On the Radar," engages with the gendered cultural meanings associated with a felony conviction in rural areas where male-dominated resource-extraction industries offer women few options for economic self-sufficiency and judgmental small towns leave women feeling trapped and unable to begin a new life after incarceration. Exploring the various forms of state, community, and interpersonal surveillance women experience during and after their incarceration emphasizes how women actively manage prison's complex social worlds before transitioning to less intense, but still salient, forms of social scrutiny after their release.

The conclusion highlights the big-picture insights and contributions of the project. Foremost among these is the architecture of gendered violence, with its focus on the negative consequences of criminalizing/medicalizing addiction and mental health issues, poverty within a dominant cultural ethos that denies inequality, violence against women, and socioeconomic structures that exclude women from work. It then offers evidence-based alternatives to the architecture of gendered violence, including the need to assist currently and formerly incarcerated women with building the kind of community and systems of mutual support that many rural people pride themselves on fostering.

1

Hitting Rock Bottom

The low, steady whistle of the coal train stirs Tammi from the viscous cocoon of low-quality black-tar heroin and prescription opioids in which she has been suspended since her older brother Cody left her on the outskirts of an oil town. Cody refused to give her cash and appeared to be in a hurry to leave, twitchy with nerves as he paid for the motel room up through two extra days after her approaching court date, just in case she caught the judge in a generous mood and managed to get probation again. Shadowy outlines of objects in the room align and shift into focus as Tammi's body and psyche begin to jaggedly knit together, her growing awareness of where and who she is sharply conjoining with the pervasive ache emanating from her bones. Washed ashore on the cold, wet sands of dope-sick, she can still vaguely feel warm opiate waters lapping at her feet as the fibers of the polyester bedspread, sweat-slick and cold, hook into her skin as she tries, and fails, to avoid vomiting on the mattress.

As she starts to recognize the person-specific ringtone clamoring from beneath the bed, she regrets letting Cody borrow a run-down pickup truck from one of her regulars at the strip club where she hustles when money is tight, which is more often than not. Now the man will not stop calling her, which is understandable since he probably needs his pickup to get to work. Tammi knows that Cody probably used it to make the three-hour drive to Salt Lake City, the closest densely populated area to Rock Springs, Wyoming, where they and their siblings have spent their lives in arrangements that progressed as they aged from foster families to group homes to, once they reached eighteen, various rentals shared with other illicit drug users and intermittent stays in county jail and, for some, prison. They are part of what local people refer to as an "outlaw family," a term that consciously evokes the nineteenth-century Wild West and its associated disregard for the rule of law to characterize the substance abuse, addiction, and constellation of criminalized income-generation pursuits some poor people use to make it in the world.

While these pursuits are generally small-scale and highly localized, including the purchase and resale of relatively minor amounts of illicit drugs, theft, and disputes regarding both, they are subject to literal and figurative policing as a result of Wyoming's small size and the rural social-control mechanisms that dominate everyday life. Tammi has never been to Salt Lake City, but she knows that it is the source for at least some of the controlled substances in Rock Springs, which quite a few Wyoming residents call "Rock Bottom" due to their perception that the town's steady stream of itinerant and mostly male oil and gas workers creates a culture that normalizes substance abuse and other illicit pursuits. When she is hustling for money in the bar, Tammi often hears these itinerant workers, many of whom come from Texas, Louisiana, and other states with prominent—albeit more diversified—oil and gas extraction industries, comment that Rock Springs' nicest buildings are its strip clubs.

Tammi slowly props herself up against the headboard and searches for her cigarettes among the thin twists of stained bedsheets, fast-food wrappers, foil, rolling papers, and related detritus strewn across the bed. She finds the criminal court summons for a drug possession charge she received a few weeks prior, when Cody bailed her out of jail, and a single bent cigarette and pink plastic lighter stuffed inside a tattered cigarette pack with four worn ten-dollar bills. Exhaling deeply, Tammi tries to focus her gaze on several inches of the brightly lit outside world visible through the parted curtains and considers what she knows about her situation as the phone on the floor beneath her continues to issue what sounds like an increasingly ominous tone.

Tammi knows that there is a man on the other end of the line who is furious that he does not know the location of his pickup truck. She also knows that Cody, a frequent flyer in both Utah and Wyoming county jails, may not be coming back. The parking lot she can see through the window is still full of the heavy utility trucks loaded with equipment used by the oil workers who live at the motel while they labor at exhausting split shifts for weeks or months at a time before returning to their families in faraway states. Their presence indicates that it must still be very early in the morning, which means she may or may not need to leave the room soon since Cody only paid for a week's stay. Checking the date on her summons, Tammi stifles an involuntary sob as she realizes that she has no idea what day it is. She knows that another failure- to-appear charge, in conjunction with her pending drug-possession case, extensive history of short-term jail sentences, the possibly stolen pickup truck, her low social status as a strip club dancer who occasionally turns tricks, and her family's bad reputation may all combine in a vicious vortex to prompt the district court judge to send her to prison.

Lighting the cigarette and inhaling deeply, Tammi pulls herself onto the floor and reaches under the bed, silencing the phone with shaking hands as she clutches her summons and searches the printed page and the phone's small screen for the numbers that will determine her future. Tammi, who has been arrested on drug-related charges at least four separate times in the almost two years since she turned eighteen, knows how to do jail time and, at some points, has regarded jail as a respite from the intergenerational poverty and struggles with addiction that structure the everyday lives of almost everyone she knows. Yet the unfamiliar and intimidating prospect of prison has her unsteady with fear as she recognizes that the portentously mismatched dates on the summons and the screen mean that her court date was two days ago, well enough time for the judge to issue a warrant for her arrest.

Pulling a hood over her head as she fumbles for her shoes, she quickly gathers the foil and rolling papers with other trash into a tightly wadded paper bag and flings open the door, the rush of frigid March air and swirling snow hurling forth into the fetid motel room. Tammi strides as fast as she can across the parking lot without drawing attention to herself and shoves the bag deep into the trash can, hopefully avoiding another drug paraphernalia charge. Unsteadily making her way back to the room, she scans the highway for police cars, remembers that she only has forty dollars in her bag, and sinks with deep fatigue onto the floor, resigning herself to spending her last few hours of freedom in that position. She knows it is just a matter of time before the police come to arrest her again since this motel is one of only a dozen where they would be likely to search for her. As the phone starts to ring again, she uses all her strength to calmly but purposefully obliterate its screen on the corner of the bedside table, removing the SIM card and folding it into tiny pieces so as to make it impossible for police officers to review her call or message history. She wonders what Cody is doing, wishes she had another cigarette, and wonders if, this time around, she might get some help.

Addiction and Mental Health in Rural Areas

Like Tammi, Cody, and their peers, people use illicit drugs and alcohol for many different reasons and, for some, the pursuit and use of these substances is an all-encompassing preoccupation that supersedes other responsibilities and desires. Yet addiction is a fraught concept that derives as much from the cultural context in which it takes place as it does from the behaviors associated with it in various settings. The limited body of research on the rural dynamics of addiction and mental health issues tends to focus on four primary areas: rural-urban comparisons, illicit drug use's social organization, addiction and mental health trajectories, and available treatment. The first juxtaposes rural and urban data to ascertain potentially significant differences and similarities with respect to prevalence as well as the availability and utilization of addiction and mental health services. The second area focuses on the social organization of illicit drug use, with some attention paid to how rural gender roles impact participation in the criminalized drug economy. Rural addictions and mental health trajectories, including motivations for initiation and cessation of illicit drug use, constitute the third primary area, and the fourth addresses access and barriers to rural substance abuse and treatment.

The preponderance of substance abuse and addiction research concentrates on urban areas, which may stem both from the location of most research universities in large cities as well as from prevailing stereotypes that regard rural areas as devoid of urban problems. The vast majority of social science literature on substance abuse and addictions addresses urban "street cultures" that bear little resemblance to the way illicit drug use occurs in or impacts rural contexts, where mistrust of outsiders combines with pervasive stigmatization to make it difficult for researchers to gain an understanding of these practices (see Carlson et al. 2009; Draus et al. 2005; Weisheit 1993). Hence it is perhaps unsurprising that existing literature offers a mixed set of results with respect to the unique addictions and mental health dynamics facing rural populations, especially given the diverse cultural and geographic contexts that researchers may classify under the broad umbrella of "rural," which may be variously used to descriptively contain both remote Alaska and suburban Ohio.

Despite such diversity of context and geography, a significant body of work indicates that the prevalence of substance abuse, addiction, and mental health issues does not significantly differ on the basis of population density. Such problems are by no means confined to cities or large towns. This is the case across a wide swath of geographic contexts that may reasonably be termed "rural" because of their small population sizes, economic dependence on agriculture, and distance from a large city or town. Yet "rural" remains a sloppy federal, state, and local demarcation of areas derived from either census classifications based on population size and density or Office of Management and Budget designations of metropolitan or nonmetropolitan based on the presence of a nearby large city (Johnson-Webb, Baer & Gesler 1997). A survey of county commissioners in eleven western U.S. states, including Wyoming, revealed that population concentration is the most significant variable used in characterizing areas as "urban" or "rural," followed by a much more unevenly described set of attributes, including infrastructure, services, and recreational opportunities (Berry et al. 2000).

Distinctions between urban and rural areas are even more unclear with respect to illicit drug use across a wide range of areas in the United States characterized by small towns, lower population densities, reliance on agriculture, distances from major metropolitan areas, and other indices of rurality. Nebraska researchers, for instance, found that methamphetamine use rates among individuals arrested in four rural counties closely resembled those of their peers in Omaha, the largest city in the state (Herz & Murray 2003). Yet some studies suggest that substance abuse may be even more prevalent in rural areas. For instance, young people living on farms located in or near communities of fifteen hundred to forty thousand residents across the states of Washington, Oregon, Utah, Colorado, Illinois, Kansas, and Maine are more likely to use illicit drugs, including marijuana, inhalants, stimulants, and hallucinogens, than their counterparts who live in towns, although frequency of use does not vary significantly (Rhew, Hawkins & Oesterle 2011).

The synchronicity between rural and urban drug use rates appears to occur for almost all controlled substances, with heroin and prescription opioids perhaps the most striking examples of this reality. A nationwide study on changing characteristics among heroin users entering drug treatment demonstrates significant demographic shifts in recent decades from urban people of color to primarily suburban and rural whites in their late twenties (Cicero et al. 2014). Illicit prescription opioid markets and abuse in rural areas take unique forms arising from their cultural contexts, leading public health researchers to investigate possible reasons for particular types of use in specific areas. For instance, public health researchers hypothesize that widespread prescription opioid abuse in Kentucky, West Virginia, Alaska, and Oklahoma emerges from greater numbers of opioid prescriptions issued, high-density kin and social ties that facilitate drug distribution, youth out-migration that creates a general sense of limited future prospects, and the stress of poverty (Keyes et al. 2014). This finding is particularly significant in light of a rural Appalachian study that suggests a three-year mean from prescription opioid abuse to first injection of the prescription opioid, heroin, or other drug of choice (Young & Havens 2012). Most illicit drug users and public health experts would agree that injection drug use poses an additional health burden due to the difficulties rural people have, relative to their urban counterparts, in procuring sterile syringes and associated greater likelihood of reusing or sharing possibly contaminated injection equipment.

The lack of treatment services and highly qualified mental healthcare professionals increases the rural addiction and mental health burden. Such limited treatment options are worrisome given that nationally representative samples indicate that rural and urban people suffer from similar rates of most psychiatric disorders, trauma exposures, and substance abuse (McCall-Hosenfeld, Mukherjee & Lehman 2014). A comparative study of rural and urban treatment-seeking methamphetamine users observed that—relative to their urban counterparts—rural midwesterners reported much more significant complications related to their drug use, which they typically began at younger ages, and higher rates of intravenous use, alcoholism, cigarette smoking, and psychotic symptoms (Grant et al. 2007). Hence, while people appear to abuse controlled substances at similar rates in both rural and urban areas, the disproportionate lack of services renders rural substance use a much more life-threatening proposition; this reality is strikingly evident in rural opioid use and opiate overdose rates that are 45% higher than in cities and towns in at least forty-two U.S. states (Faul et al. 2015).

Poor-quality or nonexistent drug treatment services, ready availability of controlled substances, constrained economic opportunities, and limited social worlds are a "small-town vortex" that reduces or eliminates rural midwesterners' motivations to abstain from substance abuse (Draus & Carlson 2009). Such rural anomie is also evident in Appalachian Kentucky, where illicit drug users associate the prescription opioid oxycodone with greater social capital than other controlled substances, such that those who are able to procure it receive elevated social status in a very economically stratified region (Jonas, Young & Havens 2012). Illicit drug use is always a product of the context in which it occurs, and in southern farming communities, polysubstance users adjust their type and frequency of consumption in conjunction with physical demands created by seasonal agricultural cycles as well as the need to participate in arduous farm work that may require relocation (Bletzer 2009). In Wyoming, socialization into methamphetamine use, particularly (but not exclusively) among men whose first use is at a later age, has been found to occur in work settings and among family coworkers, particularly in physically demanding jobs that require long hours, such as those in resource extraction–related fields (Bowen et al. 2012).

As in other rural settings, Wyoming's social and geographic dynamics also influence access to substance abuse and addictions treatment across a wide spectrum of costs and approaches. Yet wait lists are often lengthy and unable to accommodate people in crisis; according to one Wyoming state legislator, at one point the entire state had less than ten available spaces for women in residential drug treatment. The capital city, Cheyenne, has a single recovery community center that, following the national model for such centers, offers a gathering site where people in recovery can convene for social events designed to assist individuals in making the transition from addictions treatment to long-term sobriety. Twelve step groups, which prioritize an individual accountability–based model of addiction recovery, are organized by volunteers at least once a week in most towns at no charge. Despite criticism of the model's limitations, the American Psychiatric Association recommends twelve step self-help groups as a method of addressing addiction, and this model remains the most common form of successful intervention with people who are voluntarily seeking to give up substances or are mandated to address their addiction (Moos & Timko 2008). Twelve step groups are also particularly attractive because they are free, offer confidentiality, enable one to share one's own story, and are open to anyone who has struggled with addiction.

Church-based groups that view practicing Christianity as the solution to substance abuse exist in several towns. Twelve step or church-based groups may or may not organize group meetings in county jails. Court-supervised treatment, popularly known as drug court, is also free of cost and available in fourteen of Wyoming's twenty-three counties, in addition to the Shoshone and Arapaho Tribal Substance Abuse Treatment Court on the Wind River Reservation. Counselors and physicians also provide substance abuse treatment at a cost, and just over a dozen residential addictions treatment programs exist across the state, with some charging fees on a sliding scale. Yet the relative lack of anonymity in Wyoming towns, all of which are small, impacts individual perceptions of the ability to access these services, even when they are low-cost or free, often in ways that relate directly to both small-town notions of propriety and the criminal justice system as a whole. A small-town sheriff, social worker, or other respected member of the community is highly unlikely to attend an addictions treatment meeting where he or she has to sit side by side with the people with whose supervision he or she is professionally tasked. Likewise, those from families with long histories of criminal justice involvement may mistrust the kind of disclosure required in such settings or dismiss them altogether as part of a system irrelevant to their lives.

This lack of anonymity in rural areas is further compounded by the fact that families and other social ties have been found to play an especially significant role in the social organization of rural illicit drug use. Some scholars have argued that this is particularly true in areas characterized by histories of intergenerational poverty and neocolonial or other forms of ethnic or racial oppression. In rural northern New Mexico, which has some of the highest rates of heroin addiction in the United States, intergenerational poverty, illicit drug use, and addiction are conceptualized as a form of inheritance associated with community loss (Garcia 2014). A study of rural drug offenders and recent drug use likewise demonstrated that Hawaiian youths, in comparison with non-Hawaiian youths, had significantly more drug offers from peers and family members as well as much higher rates of alcohol and marijuana use (Okamoto et al. 2014). Youth in a study conducted in rural southwestern New Mexico describe illicit drug use as a widespread practice that alleviates considerable boredom in a context offering youth very limited educational and employment options or hope for the future (Willging, Quintero & Lilliott 2014). Adolescents in rural Nebraska likewise attributed their prescription drug misuse to a lack of opportunities and activities (Park, Melander & Sanchez 2016).

Data from national studies indicates a lack of gender differences in rural substance abuse and dependence, in sharp contrast to urban areas, where women generally report lower rates of substance abuse. Researchers have attributed rural women's increased rates of substance abuse to "downward economic mobility, resulting in the loss of social cohesion especially among whites, who comprise about 85% of rural residents" (Chamberlain, Mutaner & Walrath 2004). The illicit drug economy, like its licit counterpart, is fundamentally gendered, with higher-status and better-paid roles ascribed to men. Yet women serve essential roles by providing housing, buying illicit drugs, financially or otherwise supporting men who are addicted, and participating in small-scale sales (Anderson 2005). Women employ creative strategies as they navigate the illicit drug economy, manage resources and relationships as they enter recovery, and contend with punitive sociolegal approaches to addiction (Anderson 2008). These patterns are also often evident in rural areas, particularly in analyses of gender differences characterizing illicit drug use.

Rural women who use illicit drugs manage a greater array of social roles and relationships relative to men, reflecting the cultural norms and expectations that shape their lives. For instance, a study of injection drug users in rural North Wales emphasizes the challenges women face in balancing their addictions and relationships with children, parents, relatives, intimate partners, and judgmental small-town communities more generally (Smith 2014). Researchers in rural north-central Florida found that women's greater caregiving responsibilities mean that they must conceal their illicit drug use activities from children by only using when children are away, or in places children are not allowed to go (Brown & Smith 2006). A related study, also conducted in rural Florida, indicates that drug-using women's social networks tend to include more men, but fewer drug-using peers, than their male counterparts as a result of the intensified stigma experienced by women substance abusers (Goldbarg & Brown 2010). Such increased reliance on or association with illicit drug-using men can, as researchers found in rural west-central Ohio, the Arkansas delta, and western Kentucky, foster or intensify a situation of dependency on men's greater earning power relative to women, with addicted women more likely than men to trade sex for money or drugs (Wright et al. 2007).

These gendered relational associations are also evident in differences between rural women's and men's initiation into injection, with an Appalachian Kentucky study finding women much more likely than men to be injected with a used syringe administered by a sexual partner (Young, Larian & Havens 2014). In Wyoming, girls and women reported beginning their methamphetamine use at younger ages than males in conjunction with social influences (Bowen et al. 2012), some of which may stem from girls' and women's greater sexual capital vis-à-vis men and their consequent reduced likelihood of having to pay for drugs. Incarcerated queer-identified Appalachian women reported experiencing violence more often and abusing substances at younger ages than their straight peers who were also incarcerated, although both groups of women were equally likely to engage in sex with acquaintances with whom they used illicit drugs (Otis, Oser & Staton-Tindall 2016).

Dual diagnosis, the co-occurrence of a mental health disorder and an addiction, is common among rural substance abusers, with 80% of incarcerated drug-using women in a rural Appalachian study reporting depression and 60% exhibiting anxiety and posttraumatic stress disorder (Staton-Tindall et al. 2015). The prevalence of dual diagnosis is concerning given that the absence of mental health court or other formal support structures that provide alternatives to adjudication to those struggling with mental health issues in rural areas can lead to the overincarceration of mentally ill individuals in county jails for crimes symptomatic of their illnesses, as has been identified by researchers in Kansas (Etter, Birzer & Fields 2008). Similarly, although alcohol, illicit drug use, and mental health conditions do not significantly differ across rural, isolated, and reservation areas in South Dakota, respondents in isolated and reservation areas report less access to primary healthcare, and knowledge of treatment options was significantly lower in isolated regions (Davis et al. 2016).

Stigma surrounding addiction and mental illness impacts treatment seeking, with rural Ohio stimulant users expressing a strong preference to avoid receiving drug treatment from a mental health or other medical professional. Fewer than one third of these stimulant users express comfort with the idea of talking to a physician about their drug use despite nearly half characterizing their health as fair or poor (Draus et al. 2006). Similarly, most methamphetamine users in rural Arkansas and Kentucky report cessation for health, legal, or family reasons, with most not utilizing formal substance abuse programs and instead relying on will power, self-isolation, staying busy, family support, or use of substitute drugs (Sexton et al. 2008). Researchers who led a rural California study noted that family responsibilities, the multiple forms of loss associated with addiction, and avoiding incarceration intertwine for people who wish to end their substance abuse, particularly in rural areas where smaller population sizes make it more difficult to keep these struggles from becoming public knowledge (Patten, Messer & Candela 2015).

Drug-using individuals' perceptions of barriers to substance abuse and related mental health treatment take gendered forms, with women more likely than men to acknowledge experiencing such barriers. In a comparative study of rural and urban areas in six southern states, women differed from men on measures of treatment affordability, accessibility, and acceptability, while rural women reported greater barriers to treatment affordability and accessibility as well as increased incidence of severe illness (Small, Curran & Booth 2010). A Kentucky study of rural and urban women's perceptions of contextual barriers to mental health services indicated barriers in the form of affordability, availability, accessibility, and acceptability, with fewer services available to rural women, especially those with victimization histories (Logan et al. 2004).

Another rural Kentucky study indicated that half of substance-abusing pregnant women reported barriers in accessibility and acceptability of treatment. A quarter of these women reported availability barriers, and even fewer women reported affordability barriers (Afton & Shannon 2012). Researchers in Washington State contend that these gender disparities in treatment extend to incarceration, where women are less likely than men to receive drug treatment in prison despite results strongly indicating that such programs reduce the likelihood of returning to prison (Mosher & Phillips 2006). Similarly, results of a gender-disaggregated study conducted in a California prison-based therapeutic community indicate that although men had more serious criminal justice system involvement than women prior to incarceration, women faced greater struggles than men in terms of employment histories, substance abuse, mental health, and sexual/physical abuse prior to incarceration (Messina et al. 2006).

Our findings build on this literature, not least by adding a new rural geographic area to research focused heavily on Appalachia, the Midwest, and the South. We argue that the criminalization and medicalization of substance abuse, addiction, and other mental health issues works in tandem with limited, far-away, or nonexistent treatment options and gendered rural social-control mechanisms to further stigmatize women's substance abuse and discourage help seeking. In so doing, we draw on descriptive accounts of how women who have struggled with substance abuse and addiction navigate the interpersonal and structural organization of the prison's addictions treatment unit, the socioconceptual underpinnings of self-help groups, and everyday life once released back into community and under parole supervision.

The Other Side

Tammi, like all new arrivals, spent her first thirty days immersed in a near-timeless netherworld of relative solitude while under staff observation designed to help determine where and with whom she would spend her fourteen-month prison sentence. Shapeless in a newly issued green cotton uniform that readily identifies her as a resident of the Intensive Treatment Unit (ITU), she is now sitting, consumed with anxiety's virulent slithering, opposite a likewise green-uniformed woman. Although the district court judge sentenced Tammi directly to ITU, thus guaranteeing her a space in the program, she still tried her best to emphasize her and her family's nearly life-long struggles with addictions in all the paper-based assessments and conversations with prison case workers she encountered in the prison's Reception and Diagnostic Unit during her first month at the facility. She spent her time there much like the other women waiting for a housing assignment: thinking, trying to read, and occasionally talking to other new arrivals.

Crystal, a fellow prisoner and ITU's head of house, is partially responsible for the program's administration, in conjunction with other
prisoners who lead it, and is charged with explaining to new residents
the classes and groups that will hungrily carve up their lives for nearly
a year. Tammi pretends to listen obediently as she silently scans the
white-walled expanse of the open-plan unit, where large mounted signs
bearing inspirational green-lettered phrases hang elevated above and between steel cell doors with oblong windows. "Face your fears," she reads,
trying not to move her lips so that Crystal, whom Tammi already knows
she does not like, will think she is paying attention. "Accept responsibility for your choices." "Talk to someone about you." "Think." "Try honesty." "Ask for help." "I may have failed in the past, I am not a failure for
I will succeed today." The sign to the left of 10J, her new home, reads,
"Freedom is not going back."

Crystal is ageless and quite pretty even without makeup, which ITU
residents must not use because it is thought to detract from the therapeutic work of addiction recovery by inhibiting women from coming
to terms with their core internal issues. She asks Tammi repeatedly if
she has any questions before she continues speaking while they sit at
one of the circular tables bolted to the floor in the center of the large
room. Tammi is still quite surprised by the fact that other prisoners—
rather than prison staff trained in counseling, social work, or related
fields of relevance to addictions treatment—are responsible for ITU's
daily administration, including issuing punishments that could impact
a program participant's ability to complete it, and accordingly be released from prison, on time. This fact makes her watch Crystal especially closely and makes her even more determined to observe the other
women of ITU as well. She knows that her success in the program will
depend on following the rules, but her ability to get along with the other
women will also play a crucial role.

Tammi does not know how to articulate the question of what it will
be like to spend the majority of her time with the fifty-two other women
who, at this late point in the evening, are sleeping, reading, or whispering in the cells adjacent to hers. Tammi has already heard the other
women dismiss as "the other side" those living in general population,
the halls and pods that comprise the prison's main residential units, and
wonders if what she perceives as Crystal's haughtiness is shared. She

is relieved when Crystal introduces her to Kat, whom, using program parlance, she describes as Tammi's "big sister," tasked with enculturating her into the program's schedule and overall structure, which relies on the premise that all residents will support one another in their shared journey toward addiction recovery while incarcerated.

Tammi knows, from multiple stays in county jails, how to quietly gauge the unspoken hierarchies embedded within incarcerated people's quotidian interactions, yet she is uncertain of how she will fit among the women of ITU. Her thick veil of anxiety parts momentarily and she sees Crystal's gravitas, which stems as much from her program responsibilities as from her relatively lengthy sentence, unshaken by Tammi's distracted responses or what Tammi regards as Kat's almost affectedly sincere welcome to her. In sharp contrast to Tammi's previous experiences of jail and what she knows of prison from her relatives' stories about it, Kat immediately introduces herself with striking honesty. "This program has helped me to overcome my past history of failing to be accountable for my choices," she says while making direct eye contact that makes Tammi quite uncomfortable, "but in three months I will go back to Wind River and be a mother to my daughter again." Before Tammi can respond, Crystal nods and praises Kat for her candor, while Tammi thinks of other women she has met from central Wyoming's Wind River Reservation. She wonders if she and Kat know some of the same people.

The lights dim slightly for sleeping as the women settle into their bunks and Tammi, trying to determine what kind of relationship she might have with her new acquaintance, thinks carefully about how to engage with her. "Hey, green-eyed Kat," Tammi strives for a mixture of playful and conspiratorial in the whispered greeting she sends toward Kat's upper bunk, "that's a fine-lookin' high horse Ms. Crystal got, huh?"

Kat, in her late thirties, immediately senses that this much younger woman is terrified and using her best jailhouse tactics to find someone, anyone, to protect her in much the same way that she probably has lived most of her life in the free world. She remains silent, hoping Tammi will just fall asleep, until she hears small choking sobs beneath her that will definitely draw a correctional officer's attention if Kat does not make her stop. She leans over the edge of the top bunk to keep her voice as quiet as possible as she tries to emphasize the importance of maintaining order before quickly withdrawing to her own bunk. "Listen," she slowly intones to indicate that her words will be the last spoken between them that night, "we can't be friends in here, and it ain't personal. This is your time to work on yourself. I cannot do that work for you."

Kat, who spent a year on a waiting list for the program and feels profoundly annoyed when new arrivals fail to appreciate their opportunity to receive addictions treatment, is proud of herself for setting this interpersonal boundary, a skill she learned in ITU. Telling people "no" is a newly acquired habit for Kat, which she regards as the best thing she will take back to the outside world, where the steady, crackling brushfire of hopelessness seems poised to continue its slow consumption of everyone she cares about. When Kat thinks about the women she knows back home, she is struck by how few of them know how to say "no" firmly, even when they need to; at first she thought this might just be life on the reservation, but she also hears white women in ITU regret the fact that no one ever taught them to say no, either. Momentarily shocked into silence and then tamped by her thin pillow, Tammi's keening descends to a low vibration while Kat, her eyes shielded from the ever-present fluorescent lights by the blanket she meticulously folds back into place every morning in an almost mindless routine, retreats into the free-floating abyss of memory that she hopes to transform into dreams. The prairie wind's mournful song surrounds her as she takes pity on the dying sage grouse pierced with her arrow and shuddering at her feet, its death rattle portending that her family will eat well that night.

When Tammi hears Kat's alarm shrilly sound at 5:20 the next morning, she is exhausted from spending most of the night crying. She is surprised to see Kat's nonchalance as she greets her before she leaves their cell, prison-issue soap and towel in hand, to shower. Tammi quickly gathers the same and follows Kat in a stupor of exhaustion, a glimpse of her face almost unfamiliar with tear-streaked swelling in the mirror Kat purchased in the commissary and hung on the wall. Tammi quickly catches up to Kat, who explains to her how the daily routine will unfold: after a quick shower, the entire unit goes on lockdown for count to ensure the presence of all prisoners; breakfast is in the dining hall at 6:30 a.m.; and then, from 7:30 a.m. until 4:00 in the afternoon, the women participate in classes on twelve step philosophy, relationships, parenting, and other topics Kat knows are thought to help them understand the paths that led them to prison. By engaging in this kind of reflection, the women are meant to develop new strategies for living that will reduce their chance of returning to prison. The women spend the remainder of their time before bed reading, playing board games, and cleaning their unit through a set of shared chores that, for at least some of the women, create a sense of familiarity and shared purpose.

"All of us in ITU have so much in common," Kat explains as she begins to informally introduce Tammi, whose hair is still dripping from her shower, to other women from ITU. "Just the way we were raised, like domestic violence, sexual abuse, all those things that led us up to being here," Kat continues as other women nod in acknowledgment, stunning Tammi with their candor around issues she has never before heard openly discussed.

A woman nearby smiles at Tammi, adding, her voice raspy from years of smoking, "And time flies by in here because we are scheduled all day long. I have been in this program for almost seven months and am getting out in just a few weeks. I can't even wrap my head around all the stuff we've covered, but I'll take it with me when I go and it'll make me stronger."

As they sit on their bunks during lockdown, Tammi asks Kat, "Is everyone in here so positive?"

"Look," Kat says honestly, "this is prison. Women are gonna gossip, they're gonna be petty, but it's up to you to stand your ground and hold your boundaries. Let it build up your self-esteem when they do that, because when people are hating, that means that you are taking up a lot of their mind because they can't express something to your face."

The women, workbooks in hand, welcome Tammi as they settle into chairs for morning meeting, where Crystal reminds the women about the importance of following ITU's chain of command in sharing concerns. Residents must first speak with her, as head of house, and then she relays their concerns directly to the fifty-four women's single shared case worker. One woman, who Crystal reminds everyone has been in the program for three months, sighs dramatically enough that it attracts several women's attention as Crystal continues talking about the program's unique rules and respect for confidentiality. "People open up and share things about their lives that doesn't need to be shared anywhere," echoes the ITU behavior coordinator, another prisoner whose name Tammi does not catch. "If you talk to general population, which we all know isn't allowed in ITU, how would we know that you're not gossiping of what's going on in the program?" Most women agree with this sentiment and thoughtfully nod, knowing that ITU participants routinely share very painful aspects of their past in a group setting as part of the broader goal of processing what led them to prison.

The same woman repeats her dramatic sigh and raises her hand to get attention. Once Crystal acknowledges her with the slightly raised eyebrows of a warning, the woman says, "Look, can we be real for a minute before we get into it for the day? I'm just as disappointed in myself as the next girl but for the life of me, I don't see what rehashing my past for the fifty-seventh time has to do with me staying clean. Don't sit there and tell me that that's how we need to cope with our problems in order to move forward. I know how to be an addict, I'm good at it."

Tammi anxiously watches the other women for their responses, which range from tacit nods to dismissive utterances. "You need a pull-up, sister," a woman firmly states from the back of the room, indicating that the sighing woman needs to publicly admit that she has done wrong by failing to respect the rules of group. In the worst-case scenario of a serious rule violation, such as showing repeated disrespect in meetings, she might receive "ghost status," a form of shunning in which all program participants must refuse to talk to the violator or face punishment.

As the program's newest resident, Tammi is increasingly intrigued but also troubled by these rules, and over lunch in the cafeteria she is relieved to overhear two experienced ITU residents discussing the program in a critical light. Serving as the site of socialization, gossip, and a bulwark against the monotony of prison life, meal times in the crowded, high-energy dining hall are the only times women from ITU can see prisoners from general population, although they are not permitted to interact with them. "Hey, you remember Deb?" one says in hushed tones as she drives her red plastic spoon/fork combination into the chicken and rice on the thick orange plastic tray silently handed to her in the line by one of the women from general population. The other nods sharply and follows the direction in which the speaker nudges her head toward a corner of the cafeteria where she can see Deb, a former ITU resident, in animated conversation with a group of women from general population.

"Man," she shakes her head and bites into a waxy red apple as she speaks to the other women in a low voice, "she probably got big time flat-lined after she went down east." They both closely observe Deb talking, trying to assess her inner state as they think about how her refusal to participate in mandatory ITU programming got her sent to restrictive housing, and possibly resulted in flat-lining, the removal of any possible sentence reductions that she may have previously accrued for good behavior.

Crystal determinedly shakes her head to chastise her peers: "You girls are bein' real negative and I think you know that criticizing the program undermines our integrity. Compared to the other side, our lives are so structured and different. When I hear them talking, they just sound so vulgar and chaotic and out of control. It really opens my eyes to how lucky we are."

Tammi exchanges nervous glances with the two women who had been speaking about Deb and all stop talking immediately and busy themselves with eating their chicken and rice, listening to the lively conversations going on among the women from general population seated at the other long metal tables. Tammi hears a woman seated behind her, whose face she cannot see, talk about her recent stint in restrictive housing, saying, "I'm there listening to people scream back and forth from cell to cell, but at least I didn't have to deal with people." Tammi, who hates being alone, suppresses a shudder; Crystal seems okay, but the idea of having other prisoners assess her progress in drug treatment still does not sit well with her.

As the women of ITU walk in an orderly single file back to their unit, Tammi looks through every window she can see, trying to get a sense of both the world outside and the everyday goings-on among women in general population. The last one she sees before returning to ITU's segregated space looks in on a classroom, where an energetic volunteer in street clothes is facilitating a group of ten women, and Tammi leans back a little to watch them even as she keeps up the steady march to her new home, where the women automatically arrange their chairs into a circle to discuss the deeply held self-perceptions, or core beliefs, that they regard as negatively impacting their lives, especially with respect to the ability to abstain from substance abuse.

"One of my biggest problems," says the woman sitting in the middle of a circle of her peers, pushing her hair back with her hands in exasperation, "that has always been there for me is taking things personal. I think that comes from the core belief that I'm basically a bad person and that I have to prove I'm worthy of anything."

A woman leans forward from her chair to speak directly to her peer at its center, prompting her to further explore this point by using her own experiences. "What do you think are your warning signs that you're gonna use? Like now that I've been in ITU, I've noticed that for me loss is the warning sign. I've lost my aunt to an overdose of pills, not meaning to, you know, I've lost my mom from an overdose, my dad was an alcoholic, and so it's a big issue in my family, loss."

The woman at the center of the circle bites her lower lip and nods as her eyes well up with tears. "I really don't know any other way to live, but I'm just so tired of getting fucked up. I'm tired of being locked up. I'm sick of—all this," she says as she gestures expansively toward the room's white walls.

Tammi silently recognizes the woman seated in the center of the circle as Joelle from the outside world, where she thinks they may have spent some time in county jail together, and she listens closely as Joelle says, paraphrasing language from the workbook they are currently completing, "I know I need to take accountability for my actions because others do not dictate the course of my life."

Another woman echoes this sentiment from the circle's periphery, applauding Joelle's honesty in speaking openly about her will to change. "That's right," her voice rises with emotion, "no shame in your game."

Eyes narrowed with concentration and arms crossed, Crystal encourages Joelle, whose posture is increasingly relaxed in the center of the circle, all eyes on her, "Talk to us about shame," and Joelle continues.

"When I first came here, I felt shamed, like when we get called out on certain things, like our behaviors. But I been shocked to learn that I'm passive aggressive. I use sarcasm as a weapon and think everything's a joke to cover up my emotions, because I don't want to feel my feelings. I numb them with substances so that person who is sarcastic all the time, that's not really me. I don't want my legacy to be that type of person because that's not who I really am."

"Who are you, really?" the woman from the circle's periphery says with an enthusiasm that sounds almost like parody, and Joelle immediately sits up straight and says, "I am a woman who is not afraid to let her walls down, to just be me, and feel my feelings. I'm going to find that balance, that happy medium."

"Can I go next?" the woman from the periphery jumps out of her chair after Crystal nods, and tells the group, "So, I want to talk about mental illness and how challenging it was on the outs, because I wasn't on meds before I came here, like on a regular basis." Settling into the plastic chair, hands like restless birds nested in her lap, voice lowered, she utters a heavily laden "Sooooo" before continuing in rapid speech. "Most of you know that I am bipolar, and I focus more on the manic mania when I have an episode and I can lose everything I worked hard for in a day. So for me, meds are part of my support system."

Another woman interrupts her, arms skeptically crossed. "Meds can't be a support system, that has to be people."

A petite redhead sitting near Crystal disagrees as she turns to look directly at the speaker in the circle's center, emphatically stating, "No, for people with mental illness, they need those meds so they can function. So maybe meds aren't a support system exactly, but they're necessary, like, definitely."

"Thank you!" the speaker asserts in frustration, eyes widened in her critic's direction. "It's hard for people who don't have mental illness to understand what we go through. Like with my bipolar, I had my daughter with me and my mom didn't want us living with her anymore, so we got ourselves a trailer and I couldn't handle it, so things went downhill pretty quick. Next thing I knew I was under arrest for assaulting a police officer."

Sympathetic sounds issue from the circle, but the critical woman continues to verbally push her. "But you are the one who did that. You need to take accountability for your actions."

"But she is," the redhead says, voice rising with emotion. "She's saying that she knows now that without her meds she can't make it on the outs."

"Yeah, that's what I meant to say," the woman who spoke about her bipolar disorder echoes, her voice rising in pitch. "Listen, I know that in here we have an obligation to go up to others and say 'I'm holding you accountable' and I appreciate all that, but sometimes I wish that people would be more understanding, like, when you're bipolar and not on meds, you can't have boundaries. In here we have structure, everything is clean, we don't have to worry that we're not gonna eat and we have groups like this to resolve conflict, but out there, it ain't easy, particularly with mental illness."

"No, it isn't easy, but you can do it if you really try. Listen, we did real good today, family," Crystal appraises, her expression momentarily souring as she beckons the critical woman into the circle's center for what ITU terms a "learning experience," in which a person must acknowledge rule breaking and ask for the group's forgiveness. The same woman had lashed out in frustration at morning meeting the day before, filled with rage after rereading the letter in which her sister intimated that their neighbor, her husband's high school girlfriend, is pregnant and no one is sure about the father's identity. She is supposed to share these frustrations with the group, but her own sense of propriety demands she keep some things to herself. Despite all the protests to the contrary about secrets keeping women sick, she suspects other women do the same. Clutching a sheet of handwritten paper, she stands in the center of the circle and stumbles over the words of her apology to the group, kicking her feet slightly with every mispronunciation and hating how this reminds her of being dyslexic and small in a rural school with teachers who she felt were mainly there for the guaranteed paycheck.

"Yesterday morning," she reads as slowly and deliberately as her anxiety will allow, "I expressed my feelings inappropriately and I apologize. I should not have said, 'why the fuck did I have to come to prison to get addictions treatment?' and thrown my workbook on the floor. I acted in anger and would like to ask for your forgiveness and ask ten of my peers to help process my poor decision-making with me."

Nine women automatically raise their hands, with Tammi hesitantly half-lifting her arm, still uncertain about the women's apparent lack of self-consciousness as they make these candid self-disclosures. The ten women agree to sit with her later that evening and discuss her learning experience with her as she quickly returns to her seat, leaving the center of the circle empty as programming finishes for the day and the silence dissolves into the buzz of fifty-four women's quiet conversations among themselves. Rising with purposeful solemnity to replace the chairs against the walls that hold them within the most rigidly structured environment of their lives, the critical woman turns to Tammi and asks, with great sincerity, "Hey, you wanna play Monopoly?"

The Shit We'll Need in the Real World

Deb tries to hide her self-satisfied smirk while unobtrusively watching the wall clock's show of thirteen more minutes until the end of the

Narcotics Anonymous (NA) meeting where she sits listening to twenty other women from general population get emotional about free-world drinking and drugging. Deb could really use a drink, preferably some bourbon so she could get right down to business, while listening to Ruby from Alabama pour the group yet another tearful cocktail of guilt, shame, and regret. Ruby, who wouldn't know a real problem if it punched her in the face, seems to really like crying and soon descends into gasping sobs that strike Deb as pathetic in ways that, if this were a real prison like the one in Colorado where Deb did a three-year bid in her twenties, would mark her as a weak-willed target for trouble. Back in the bright orange uniform that marks her as a resident of the higher-security halls, Deb spent lunch in the cafeteria with her NA friends pretending not to notice her former ITU coresidents whisper as they cast sidelong glances at her from the table.

Deb keenly remembers her final desperate attempt, after multiple requests to the head of house, to move back to general population. "Crystal," she pleaded, hoping that she could get the woman to see reason by speaking plainly, "I didn't come to prison to join a cult run by inmates. Just put in a request to our case worker and ask him to send me back to general pop."

Crystal, emotionless as ever, droned, "You know, Deb, I've seen a lot of women like you over the years. When ITU first opened, women were like 'oh, you go into ITU and you get out of prison.' Well, I can tell you from personal experience that that's not how it works. You can't skim the surface and skate through, wasting everyone's time. You're in here to work on yourself, and I'm gonna push you to do that work." Deb is unafraid of fighting after years of winning barrel racing competitions she proudly attended with her wife, who is waiting for her on the outside and whose shrewdness at poker tournaments financed their campervan itinerancy to rodeos across Wyoming, Utah, Montana, and Idaho. It disturbs her, at some deep-seated level she finds hard to articulate, that she cannot remember how Crystal ended up on the floor getting pummeled in the face by Deb's fists until two correctional officers pulled Deb off and dragged her down east, where she spent a month in restrictive housing. Nonetheless, she is content with the result: being thrown out of ITU after the fight means that she will not have to return to the program and, in fact, probably could not do so even if she wanted to.

Despite losing all of her good time, as institutional parlance terms the months she spent without causing any problems, Deb feels much better now that she is back in general population and can exercise some autonomy in structuring her days. She finds her own freedom in prison, casually attending groups like NA to help break up the time, just like she found it traveling with her wife from rodeo to rodeo with the money one or both of them would periodically win gambling or in rodeo competitions. Had Deb not misjudged as mere aspiring beauty queens her competitors in the big Montana rodeo, she never would have spent all nine thousand dollars of their money on a horse she named Ace, whose calm, earthy breath she could catch if she cupped her hand under his nostrils. She never would have had to cash checks from a closed bank account to get back to Wyoming, never would have jeopardized her marriage, and that was all bad luck as Deb sees it, not some fundamental flaw in her person.

"My life has pretty much been chaos since I was a kid," Deb hears Lacey, who lives three cells down from her, say as she drifts back into focus, checking the clock to see ten minutes remaining, "but I didn't get into dope until much, much later. I was forty-three years old when I got heavily into methamphetamine. Someone told me you could use it to lose weight and I worked the night shift, so I could stay up all night. It was the biggest mistake I ever made and then I got into selling drugs and by the time I got caught I was so tired. It was almost a relief when I got arrested."

McKenna, who plays cards with Lacey every night, follows group rules in waiting for Lacey to finish before echoing her account. "So, so tired," she says. "Before I got arrested on a sell and delivery charge, people I knew couldn't even believe it. I just hit rock bottom and so many times I told myself 'I can't keep doing this' and yet, here I am." Lacey and McKenna sigh in unison and Deb wants to roll her eyes but doesn't because she knows that she will hear about it once everyone is back in the halls.

"Don't I know it," McKenna says as she starts to recount the story of how she landed in prison for methamphetamine distribution, which Deb and almost everyone else in the halls already knows by heart because she tells it so frequently. "I tried to go into rehab. God knows I tried. I was ready to go, and so I gave someone methamphetamine, I didn't sell it, I gave it away, and still they counted it as being sold. I finally got into rehab in Ohio and they arrested me and brought me all the way back to Wyoming. Now tell me, how is that a good use of taxpayers' money?"

Deb finds it entertaining when the women complain about the costs of their incarceration as if they are frustrated public servants, when she knows full well that on the outside the vast majority of the women were too broke, too addicted, or too involved in a conglomeration of criminalized hustles to pay taxes. She knows that other women think she is cynical and so she is guarded about what she reveals in group or in the halls. Since Deb just wants to finish her last eight months in peace, she uses her best poker face when telling the others, who often encourage her to participate more fully in the prison's elaborate social world, "I'm just here enjoying the show." Deb is a solid, imposing woman and this alone usually does the trick when she wants to be left alone.

Five minutes remaining, Deb observes as she continues to feign interest in the other women's stories, even though she could practically recite them herself after hearing them so many times. A tall, broad-shouldered woman, whose first name Deb can never remember and who adheres with near-religious fervor to the twelve steps' power to heal addiction, attempts to draw attention to similarities among the experiences of the women in the room, as she frequently does in meetings. "We've all come from different places," she says, "but a lot of our stories are the same. It encourages me because I know I'm not alone but at the same time it's really sad. I am very similar to all of you, like most of us are mothers and we've all hit our rock bottom, we're all stuck in our addictions even if we're not currently using." Deb listens patiently, comfortable with small doses of hearing about sobriety because, unlike in ITU, she does not live at an NA meeting.

Silence immediately slices through the room as the crackle of the public-address system indicates the impending announcements that occur at least every hour to tell the women they are free to move from one scheduled activity to another. "Laaaaaadies," the deliberately exaggerated voice of a correctional officer trying to break up his, and perhaps the women's, monotonous routine, "open movement has started, open movement." The women must now reach their next destination in ten minutes or less, which is not difficult to do in such a small facility, or risk receiving a write-up that can further reduce their already limited menu of options for structuring their days. Deb plans to take a nap, read, write a letter to her wife, then eat dinner in the cafeteria with the other women from her hall, play cards, and then talk with her cellmate until she goes to sleep. Tomorrow she will wake up and start this routine all over again. She hears Nedrah, who is usually so withdrawn that she appears not to like anyone, express excitement about attending a financial management class taught by a volunteer from outside the prison immediately after NA, and this time Deb does not hesitate to roll her eyes. Deb has never had a problem managing money. Her problem has always been that there was very little money to manage.

With just a few days left until her release, Nedrah has no time for negativity even though she knows the other women actively dislike the way she isolates herself from others with a vague air of superiority. Nedrah does not particularly like or trust other women, not that she's had much luck with men. In fact, Wyatt, the man she left her son, husband, and entire community of friends and family for once he and methamphetamine took over her life, is serving time in the men's medium-security prison about an hour's drive away. Six years in general population, even in the lower-security and more comfortable pods, have her wondering what it will be like to handle money, which was never easy in the coal town where she grew up and to which she will return in a matter of days. Classes fill up quickly in the prison, with priority given to women based on upcoming release dates because of the perception that such women have a more urgent need for skills. For years Nedrah has watched other women file into classes like this one, the sparkling anticipation of release unmistakable in their every movement. Today she tries to walk more confidently than usual into the classroom, knowing that others are watching her animation.

The smallish room contains six grey plastic tables that fold into long rectangles for storage alongside thirteen stacked chairs the women must put out and then replace at the end of each class. Such close temporal proximity to the free world sharpens Nedrah's focus on those around her, who will continue the routine that has consumed her life after she leaves the back gate through which she entered six years prior. Their heavy cotton orange uniforms, like her own, are pilling and fading from harsh detergent in the laundry room's industrial washing machines, and many women are wearing the commissary's greying, long-sleeved synthetic thermal undershirts. Two of the twelve women have on hairnets because they have just come from working in the kitchen, and Nedrah can immediately see who can afford the commissary's better-quality shampoo and soap, which leaves the women's skin and hair less dry and lank.

Nedrah never had commissary money to spend on such luxuries. About a month after her arrival in prison, her sister Starla wrote to tell her that no one would visit her and that the family planned to tell everyone that Nedrah had a nervous breakdown and was in a mental hospital rather than a prison. "In fact," Starla had added at the end of the letter, "I think you probably would be better off in a mental hospital because only a crazy person would do what you did." Eyes drifting from the ceiling's beveled rectangular squares of perforated tiles to the well-shined grey floor, Nedrah tries to block out that memory by listening to conversation flow more freely than usual due to the presence of an empathic volunteer who does this work in her retirement and encourages the women to share their personal experiences as part of the class.

Nedrah begins to imagine what it will be like to walk in a world lit by brilliant mountain sunlight as she flips through the workbook the volunteer, Sarah, gives her and the other women, explaining how they will spend the next two hours together discussing their relationships to money. Sarah begins class by asking the women to talk about their experiences with money growing up, and Nedrah takes a deep breath, every minute closer to the catapult propelling her back into the fear of living paycheck to paycheck because she has never before held a job. Without a husband or much formal education, she knows that the feminized ghetto of low-wage service-sector labor will be her only real escape from her sister's place, where she will live until she finds a new man and, she hopes, a better life. Nedrah is especially grateful that, even if they refused to visit or have any contact with her while she is in prison, her family's good reputation means that she will have a place to land. She is well aware that many other women are not so lucky.

One of the women, whose parents' sending her the maximum allowable amount of money each month enables her to spread commissary goods across her bunk like an orange-clad empress, admits, "I think there was already a part of me that always thought because my family had money, if anything did happen then I wouldn't get into trouble.

But I was dating someone who, we had a terrible relationship and we were addicted to meth, neither of us were working. My grandma had a trust fund she left me and I was disqualified because of using. We had no income and we were completely invested in this addiction. So, I wrote checks that did not belong to me." Sarah notices some of the other women shifting in their seats and, well aware of the signs that women feel silenced, ashamed, or just plain left out, is about to add in something about her own life experiences with poverty when Sierra, a slim woman in the back row, speaks up. She is determined to get every last bit of information out of this class, since in a matter of months she will need to find a job and pay rent at a transitional housing facility where she will serve out the remainder of her prison sentence while living and working in the free world.

"I was in and out of foster care my whole life because my mother was an addict," Sierra says in the slow, practiced tone she favors in group, "and now that I'm healthy I see what I put people through for the past twenty years. This place has been a blessing to me and hopefully I take these tools with me when I go. All my friends were in the same boat: drugs, alcohol, the mental abuse, 'oh you're stupid,' so I never thought there was a different life. I got divorced three years after I got into prison."

Sierra's cellmate guffaws and interrupts, "That's nothing, sweetie, I just got a letter last week from the warden notifying me that someone has stolen my identity and law enforcement can't pursue it because it's not over six thousand dollars. Try handling that from in here." Sierra tightly folds her arms across her chest, holding herself, hurt but unsurprised that her monologue has gone unappreciated.

"Let's try to stay on track and speak one at a time, please," Sarah says politely, her years of working as an advocate in the anti–domestic violence movement showing through in the kindness with which she makes this statement. Sarah is deeply committed to making the women feel heard in her classes because she feels that they so often have been silenced or ignored; at least this is how she explains the propensity to interrupt that so many of the women seem to have in her classes. "Sierra, it sounds like you really accomplished a lot in here and have good reasons to be very proud. I think you were going to say something else, am I right?"

Sierra earnestly continues, with uncharacteristic unself-consciousness, and asks openly, "I want to learn how to budget and I really appreciate you being here to teach us about how to manage money, but my real question, if I ask it honestly, is how to budget with no money? Not that I'm not eager to leave, but I am scared to death about how it will be for me out there."

Sarah nods thoughtfully and opens the question to the room of women, who describe a range of budgeting strategies. Johanna, who is highly respected because she helps run the kitchen, says, "Usually I always pay my bills first and everything else is play money. Like in here I work in the kitchen and I save 20% of what I earn, instead of 10% like on the outside."

The woman sitting next to Johanna adds, "She's in the same boat as me, I don't have anything else but what I earn in here, so I take care of hygiene needs first, like soap and shampoo, and then I save the rest. It's not easy at thirty cents an hour, but it's something." She shrugs, her exhaustion from insomnia evident in the puffy circles under her eyes, before adding, "Out there, just like in here, I don't like to shop. If I buy coffee it's because I need that and I don't look around for anything else."

Sierra's cellmate, who manages to be constantly busy, says, "But you need a little something, in here, just to make things a little easier. I'm not a huge commissary fan but in here I have purchased yarn for crafts. If I don't have yarn to crochet, I feel antsy, that's kind of a need because it's a coping skill for me. I don't need a TV because there's one in the day room, but it would make me comfortable."

"For a lot of us," one of the women who is a relatively new arrival to general population says with great earnestness for someone new to prison, "this is an addiction issue. I have two really strong addictions. Alcohol, of course, is my drug of choice and the other one is shoplifting, and now I am trying to find out why I want to steal. I am starting to rub the surface of it, because I was molested as a child. My innocence was taken away, and it's like there is something deep down inside of you, that pain, and for me it was like when I went to a store, if I took something it's like I'm getting my power back. I'm getting control. I can do this and I have something now. You see what I mean?" Other women mutter affirmatively as the woman continues speaking. "It's this weird connection to molestation, it really is. I am just starting to catch it." Sarah nods sympathetically, accustomed to the way that the women's individual contributions to the class frequently dart from subject to subject like an electric current through water, and she likes to let them speak freely and openly. She knows that her classes have long waiting lists because she does not maintain rigid boundaries around what the women can discuss, and accordingly she often hears accounts of violence, poverty, and addiction. She does not push the woman speaking, or the others, to eschew what she or other people from the free world might personally regard as overly simplistic explanations for their crimes, because she knows that these sometimes hold great meaning for them. Instead, she waits for her to finish and is silent for a moment to ensure that no other women want to speak.

"Part of our curriculum," Sarah says to gently urge the class back to the day's subject matter, "is to recognize the signs of financial abuse, so that when we are making budgets we are able to make sure that we have control over them."

Johanna, who runs the kitchen, shakes her head. "See, now, I don't really agree with that because I think that in a marriage or in a serious relationship, we need to share money because sometimes there isn't a whole lot to go around. I was raised on a ranch and had six kids and ranch work is one hundred and twenty hours plus a week, and I can't like say, 'oh, I have my own separate money, sorry we can't fix the horse trailer to get them to auction, so we won't make any money at all this week.'"

"That is true," Sarah acknowledges, "and in a healthy relationship sharing a bank account or other finances is not an issue because both partners mutually respect each other and agree on how to spend the money."

Johanna looks unconvinced but continues to listen as Allie, who is sitting across the room, looks directly at her and volunteers, "I know what Sarah means because I was in a relationship like that with my old man before I came here. We weren't married but it was like a marriage because we lived together. He'd always find ways to get me fired, go in and cuss out the boss because he'd say, 'if you have nothing then you can't leave me.' He'd leave me and our kids with nothing and we lived far out of town, so I couldn't go anywhere."

Sarah continues, closely tethering Allie's example to the materials she distributed to the women. "On the first page, our workbook says that financial abuse is just one more way that abusers gain power and control."

Another woman adds, "I never want another relationship like that again. I want someone who is physically, mentally, and financially stable. My picker is broken because all the men I've chosen bought boy toys and never helped with groceries or bills."

"It can work both ways, though," Sierra cautions the group as she, like everyone in the room, remains unmoved by the current of violence and poverty that runs through the examples they share because they are so normalized for the women. "Part of the demise of my marriage was me making more money, and I really think that I was the financial abuser, because I had all the money. Like, I'd hide things I bought because of my shopping addiction but then I'd tell him, 'go finish the laundry and I'll buy you a six-pack.'"

"Yeah, both men and women can be abusive in a relationship," Sarah nods. "Sharon, how about you? You told me that you signed up for the class because you wanted to see your credit report."

This prompts the class in a new direction as Sharon smiles. "I'm excited to see my credit report because I spent a year in addiction where I didn't care. I lost my job of eleven years and didn't pay my medical bills and racked up credit card debt. I'm leasing out my house which isn't quite paid off yet. I'm $5,000 in debt and that's a fortune with a big house payment and my kids and my old man's in prison. I know I'm not going to get a job making twenty-five dollars an hour again, and this is my worst-case scenario, being right here."

Sarah, who has heard versions of Sharon's financial situation many times previously, pragmatically responds, "I'm sorry to say that bankruptcy will be the only option for some of you once you get out. You can begin the process in here, but the real work can't start until you are released."

Sierra, accustomed to needing to redirect conversations among the women and increasingly less concerned with what others think of her since she will probably never see any of these women again once she leaves in a few months, urges Sarah to help her. "I need to know what kind of disaster I'm walking into when I leave here, because I've been inside for a long time. Do you think anyone will really hire me?"

A woman who has been to prison multiple times insists that she has never had any difficulties finding work, adding, "There will always be jobs in motels, in restaurants, and other places, but the reality is that it's hard out there."

Johanna confidently states, "There's a sellable aspect to having been to prison because you can tell people how you've reformed yourself and changed your life. People get inspired by stories like that."

Sarah continues, "Yes, absolutely. It's true. There are so many ways to answer questions about the circumstances that brought you here, but ultimately it will be up to you to decide how you want to share that information with potential employers."

The public-address system issues its crackling call for open movement and the women gather their folders, thank Sarah, and begin to hustle out the door. Nedrah is already considering, as she has over the course of the past few weeks, what she might say about what brought her to prison if she even gets a job interview, knowing that many of her applications will simply go into the trash can when she checks a box to indicate that she has been convicted of a felony. "This is the shit we'll need in the real world, Sarah," Johanna tells her sincerely on behalf of the other women as Sarah packs her teaching materials into a roller-bag. "I hope you know how much this means to these girls."

On the Outs

Nedrah's sister Starla moves around the kitchen, still dressed in her night-shift nursing uniform, packing lunch for her husband and teenage daughters with the weighty confidence of someone who knows she is a family success story. Most of the women in their family do not work for pay, and so her nursing career, however modest, almost always garners women's envious furtive glances at holiday gatherings because of the controversial glamor surrounding the fact that Starla earns her own money. Starla's husband, still unaccustomed to his later reporting time as newly promoted shift supervisor at the mine, hovers uncomfortably on the periphery of the small kitchen bathed in low-wattage yellow light that turns the tile floors something like the color of bile, while her daughters silently fold their lunch bags and avert their eyes from Nedrah. Starla's aged terrier, wiry and perpetually shaking, arches its back and issues a long series of barks that no one seems to notice as the family says goodbye for the day and the pair of unnervingly modest teenagers follow their father outside into winter's morning darkness.

Starla, face partially obscured as she drinks from a coffee cup that reads "World's Best Mom," waits until she can no longer hear the soft sucking sound of the truck's tires carrying her husband and daughters down the street before starting to speak. Nedrah, shrinking in a chair she's positioned as close as she can get to the kitchen's back wall, is conflicted about sleeping in her sister's basement, but she knows that she needs to get used to it even though doing so seems just one small step up from prison. Her only other choice was to parole out to a transitional housing facility where she and a few other women would live in close proximity to numerous men also recently released from prison. "Nedrah," Starla intones while leaning her head slightly to the side, "I hope you know that I worked really hard to convince Barrett that you wouldn't be a bad influence on the girls." Though she has prepared for this moment for quite some time and knows that Starla only wants her to know how difficult it is to be the only member of their family on speaking terms with her, Nedrah is almost overcome by the resolve it takes to silently stitch together the ragged edges of her rage.

Using the most neutral and forgiving language she can remember from role playing in her Anger Management class, she begins, "Starla, I know I've made mistakes in my past . . ." but the high pitch of Starla's incredulous laugh quickly pierces its canned artificiality. Starla aggressively perches her hands on her bony hips as her upper body leans forward like a crane over cornered Nedrah.

"Mistakes, Nedrah, really?" Starla's jaw hangs slightly open between words. "In prison is that what they call abandoning your child and your husband for that no-account dope slinger who tried his best to ruin all our lives? Because I can think of a lot of other words for what you did, but 'mistakes' is not one that I would choose. A mistake is parking in a handicapped zone when the sign is hidden behind a snowdrift."

Not quite yet defeated, Nedrah measures her words. "Wyatt will be in prison for even longer than I was . . ."

Eyes widened, Starla throws up her hands as she tries not to shout at her sister. "I don't want to ever hear that thing's name in my house again. Ever. Nedrah, I mean it. Ever. In all honesty, I don't know what the hell you were thinking then and I can only hope that you'll have the ability to think more clearly now, because Barrett and I aren't going to tolerate any bull puckey from you. This is your last chance, and honestly you're really lucky to have it."

Blood's metallic tang seeps into Nedrah's throat as her molars sink deeper into the thin skin on the inside of her cheeks. She is determined not to fight no matter what Starla says because she knows the transitional housing facility, or even a return to prison following a parole revocation, might be her next stop if she loses her tenuous grip on a place in Starla's household. "Don't you have anything to say for yourself, Nedrah? *Anything?*"

"I'm sorry," Nedrah chokes, tears threatening to spill over in a way that she never let them in prison and does not want to start happening now. "I'm sorry that I made terrible choices." She says nothing about her family's refusal to visit her for six years, or the letter Starla sent her, during the most difficult first few months, in which she wrote that it would have been better if Nedrah had died.

Although she must be exhausted from the night shift at the hospital, Starla's white-stockinged legs are furiously pacing across the kitchen as she continues. "I still can't believe that Mom told everyone that you were in a mental hospital because she was too ashamed to tell the truth. So, when you see people from town and they feel sorry for you, it's because they don't know what really happened. Honestly, Nedrah, I don't know what would happen to you if you didn't have such a good family. You're the only screw-up our family has ever had. I know they always say that every family's got one, but you had absolutely every advantage provided to you. And I mean every advantage. Even now that you've been to prison, here I am letting you live here with my own family like nothing at all happened, when you're supposed to be in your own home, with your own husband and child, not here dependent on us like some no-account."

Starla is crying now, searching her pockets for a tissue and, finding none, pulling a new one from a paper box hidden in a cover her mother crocheted. Nedrah is determined not to give in to emotion. "Starla," she ventures in her gentlest voice, "do you want to get some sleep? My case worker helped me renew my driver's license in prison and so if you'll let me take your car I can drive myself to see my parole officer and then to work. I promise I'll be responsible. I've been real good this month, you know I have. I'm sorry."

Abraded by the grit of exhaustion, Starla sinks into the wooden kitchen chair across the table from Nedrah, hands covering her face as she nods deeply, still unaccustomed to hearing words like "case worker" and "parole officer." Their tainted ring is still distasteful to Starla, who often secretly wishes Nedrah would disappear, although in just a few months she hopes she can convince their father to let Nedrah move into one of the empty apartments in the complex their family owns. Starla drags her fingers away from her face with great effort and, voice quiet and crackling with sadness, says only "yeah" and shuffles toward her bedroom's open door, where within minutes Nedrah can see her asleep in her uniform on top of the blankets, too tired to pull them back. Poor Starla, Nedrah thinks. Poor everyone.

Still accustomed to her prison routine of getting up very early in the morning, Nedrah has been dressed for hours in preparation for a nine o'clock meeting with her parole officer in a town fifteen miles from her sister's place. So much has happened in the past month since Starla drove her home from prison that she has not had time to feel any of the emotions that she anticipated would accompany freedom. Instead, she has just felt locked down in new and different ways. On the five-hour drive from prison to the small town where they both grew up and raised their own children, Starla had talked nonstop, either to make up for six years of no communication or to get it all out before arriving home so her husband and daughters would not hear any of what she had to say. Nedrah supposed that it did not make much difference, since before she even spent her first night listening to the wind's steady roar outside her sister's small house, she knew that she had a job cleaning rooms at a family friend's motel and that her son, now seventeen and living with Nedrah's own mother, his grandmother, wanted little to do with her.

None of this has surprised Nedrah, who spent her life before Wyatt subjected to small-town gossip, perpetual fear of what neighbors and others might think, and unspoken but fiercely enforced ideas about what is and is not possible. Nedrah now knows that there are just as many different kinds of prisons as there are ways to be free, and this knowledge makes her carefully consider what to say to her parole officer as she gingerly steers her sister's old car, which Starla only uses to make the ten-mile drive to the hospital or the grocery store, onto the road's snowpack. Nedrah wants her parole officer's permission to move out of her sister's house into her own apartment on the outskirts of town, close enough to walk to her job at the motel. Starla promised Nedrah that she would try to convince their father, who still has not spoken to Nedrah, that this is a good idea, even if just because it would mean that she would not have to see her every day.

Nedrah sits in the yellow-grey office speaking earnestly and, she thinks, convincingly, to the parole officer about all the progress she has made that month by attending Narcotics Anonymous meetings every week, working daily at the motel, and reconnecting with her sister. He nods thoughtfully as he listens, noting that every one of Nedrah's mandatory urinalysis screenings have tested negative for controlled substances. "This is all still very new to you," he says as Nedrah feels her heart sink into a deeper recess that will help her to hide her anger and frustration at yet another refusal she thinks she is about to hear. "You've done really good this month, but I don't want you to lose your support system. Let's have you keep up the good work, and then maybe in another two months we can talk about this again." Their weekly visits are usually quick and mutually respectful, which makes Nedrah wonder if this is the case because the parole officer regards her family as well-respected and stable. Although this works in her favor, she cannot help but imagine how these interactions might go differently with some of the other women she served her time with and whose families also struggle with addiction and criminal justice system involvement. She thinks about Kat going home to her extended family on the Wind River Reservation and trying her best to make it, without any of the things Nedrah's family has handed to her. Somehow this only deepens Nedrah's sense of bitter failure.

Parked behind the motel where she has worked for twenty-two days, Nedrah shivers with cold and anticipation as she checks her purse for the makeup bag Starla gave her a few weeks ago when she found it while cleaning out her daughters' shared closet in a manner that reminded Nedrah of a cell search. Lowering the rear-view mirror until the narrow bar shows her eyes and the messy back seat of Starla's car, she opens the thin sliver of glittery black liquid eyeliner, closes one eye, and tries to create the kind of thick, seductive flourish that ends in a suggestive curl toward her temples. She sighs deeply as the dark liquid from the elfin brush scribbles into a jagged half-triangle, and rushes to wipe off the mess with her saliva and a tissue she finds under the seat. Nedrah is out of practice since commissary did not have nice cosmetics and, even if they had, no one from the outside ever sent her any money. Nedrah smiles at herself in the mirror as she tries again, putting the tiny rectangle of sparkling eyeshadow on the console as she waits for the eyeliner to dry. Today is Wednesday, the owner's day off, and if she finishes all her work quickly and times it right with the sleepy desk clerk's favorite television shows, she and Lance will have an entire hour alone in a room at the end of the horseshoe-shaped complex.

Nedrah hates making beds and promises herself that, once she gets her own apartment, she will leave her sheets and blankets wantonly strewn across the mattress for the rest of her life. Neatly made beds remind her of prison, and as she breaks yet another nail tucking yet another set of bleachy sheets into a motel room bed, Nedrah wonders how much longer she will have to clean rooms for a living. Although there is not much to do here and she knows that the owner probably only hired her because he feels sorry for her family, this is the only job she has ever had besides her brief stint at the prison library, from which she was soon fired for keeping all the new books to herself. Nedrah nonetheless hopes that things will get better because she thinks that all the signs are there with Lance, whom she remembers from high school and who makes good money as an electrician. What she would really like is for Lance to leave his unhappy marriage and come live with her. She could treat him right, she thinks, remembering the sight of his hard-mouthed wife and three sulking children as Nedrah watched him follow them like some trapped animal in the grocery store the week prior, avoiding her eyes.

Lance's blue pickup glides into the parking space just outside the room, and Nedrah hopes that the desk clerk will be immersed enough in the television set to forget that Lance finished rewiring the rooms three days ago, a development that Nedrah worries is going to change the dynamics of their three-week-old relationship. She lets him look at her through the window as he leans on the pickup's open door for a moment before she rushes him into the room and wraps her arms around him tightly, deftly extracting the flask of whiskey he carries in his back pocket next to his chewing tobacco. Laughing as she takes a long swig before passing it back to him, Lance leaves his boots on as he stretches out on the bed and turns on the Weather Channel, eyes narrowing slightly as he watches a wide swath of cartoon snowflakes stampede across the map of the Rocky Mountain states.

"Big storm rollin' in," Lance comments for no good reason, eyes still on the television as he settles himself on top of the bed, taking up all the space in a way that confuses Nedrah. She is trying not to show that she is annoyed when she realizes that she will have to make the bed yet again after he leaves. He closes his eyes and she looks at the bull, its back stylistically arched underneath the words "1997 Goshen County Team Roping Champion" emblazoned on his shiny belt buckle.

Nedrah tries to sound coy as she comments, also for no good reason other than to fill up the awkward minutes between now and sex, "You're a rodeo star." Half-asleep already after fighting with his wife until late, quietly as ever so as not to wake up the kids, and finishing three especially difficult electrical jobs that morning, Lance sputters back to life when he hears Nedrah say this to him.

"Wife made me quit." Lance intones. "Said it was a waste of time and money." For a moment Nedrah thinks she sees bitterness eat into his features as he gazes wistfully at his belt buckle, swaying his hips a little so it can catch the light.

Nedrah stares at Lance from across the room, his limp frame sprawled across the bed filling her with disgust. Her revulsion comes from somewhere deep down in the core of her being, where her memories of Wyatt are frozen, precious and immobile. Aloft methamphetamine's icy wave, all inhibitions, all self-consciousness, all clumsy human sensitivities that cloud the pursuit of pure pleasure in its most distilled form would evaporate. Nedrah's mind is a perpetual split-screen of the bleak, joyless world that surrounds her and the saturated gratification of immediacy with Wyatt. She wants to kick Lance to make sure he's really even still alive. Instead she whispers, as if she really means it, "That's a terrible thing to do to a person, to make them stop rodeoing," as she takes off his Stetson hat to touch his face. A few minutes of silence pass with Lance sprawled on the bed and Nedrah perched in what she hopes is a seductive way on the table while trying not to knock over the lamp, their eyes jointly fixed on the cartoon storm's slow progress across the West. "I'm getting my own place," she ventures, watching his face closely. He does not react but finally starts to smile when she leans over, hooking her forefingers into his belt loops. And, for the next thirty-five minutes until they get dressed again and he informs her from the window of his pickup that he can never see her again, both Nedrah and Lance are free.

Concluding Thoughts

Tammi, Kat, Crystal, Deb, and Nedrah, the main composite characters in this chapter, each differently experienced the complex effects stemming from the criminalization of substance abuse, addiction, and compromised mental health. The currently and formerly incarcerated rural women in our study often struggled with addiction and compromised mental health, reflecting the results of other research indicating that no significant differences exist between rural and urban areas with respect to substance abuse, addiction, and mental health problems (Herz & Murray 2003; Rhew, Hawkins & Oesterle 2011; McCall-Hosenfeld, Mukherjee & Lehman 2014). Each woman's problems with substance abuse and mental health deeply shaped her life and resulted in her incarceration, although the women's experiences differed on the basis of individual personality and the expectations for life that they and their families derived in part from their socioeconomic class and ethnic, racial, and cultural backgrounds.

Research likewise demonstrates that the dual diagnosis of addiction and mental health problems is as common in rural areas as it is in urban areas (Staton-Tindall et al. 2015; Etter, Birzer & Fields 2008; Davis et al. 2016). Like their urban peers, rural woman face barriers to addictions and mental health treatment that include stigma, affordability, and their own perceptions of whether or not they require such treatment (Afton & Shannon 2012; Logan et al. 2004). For many women from intergenerationally poor communities, prison offered the first real opportunity to receive sustained therapeutic treatment for substance abuse and mental health issues because their communities offered limited or nonexistent options for doing so in the free world. Tammi, who is from a very poor "outlaw family" in which nearly every member has been incarcerated, and her ITU "big sister" Kat, who is from the Wind River Reservation, both positively regarded ITU as a chance to make real and meaningful changes to their lives.

The intense stigma that surrounds addiction and compromised mental health limits the women's opportunities to seek help for these issues in ways that are difficult to disentangle from one another irrespective of social class, ethnicity, or race. For instance, Nedrah's decision to abandon her family for the very troubled Wyatt, along with her intense desire to form a long-term bond with Lance, an unhappily married electrician, could be interpreted in very different ways: as symptoms of bipolar disorder, as codependency, as the result of socioeconomic circumstances that discouraged her from developing an independent self, or some combination of all three. Tammi's situation could likewise be subject to various interpretations, including undiagnosed developmental disabilities, the long-term psychological impacts of childhood sexual abuse followed by adult involvement in the sex industry, cognitive damage caused by severe substance abuse, or, as with Nedrah, some combination of all three. These different interpretations have very real consequences for women's lives and self-conceptions.

Once incarcerated, women who have struggled with substance abuse and addiction must navigate the interpersonal and structural organization of the prison's addictions treatment unit and the socioconceptual underpinnings of self-help groups. Wyoming prisons resemble their counterparts nationwide in offering two primary models of addiction treatment. The first is the therapeutic community model of habilitation, which seeks to socialize people in addictions recovery into new ways of thinking they are believed not to possess; this model contrasts sharply with older models of "rehabilitation" because it presumes that such positive socialization ("habilitation") never occurred in the first place and is accordingly a necessary component of recovery (Haney 2010). The second is the twelve step model of groups such as Narcotics Anonymous, which requires admitting one's powerlessness over the compulsion to consume illicit substances and placing one's recovery in the hands of a higher power through a combination of will power and peer support.

Women in the prison's ITU program have a variety of reasons for participating in it. For some, like Tammi, participation is court-mandated as part of a sentence for a crime while for others, like Kat, the program is self-selected as a healing and welcome respite from a lifetime of struggles with drugs and alcohol. Individual women's divergent motivations for, and perspectives on, addictions treatment emphasize the challenges that correctional facilities and the women incarcerated within them face as they attempt to address addiction's deep and often intergenerational roots. Women who have experienced some amount of economic stability relative to Tammi and Kat, such as Deb and a few of the women in her financial empowerment group, tended to regard prison programming as designed to reach what they regard as a "lowest common denominator" based on the experiences of the majority of incarcerated women, whose lives have been characterized by poverty, instability, and numerous forms of interpersonal and structural violence. Before coming to prison Deb was accustomed to a fiercely independent and itinerant existence with her wife as a professional rodeo barrel racer and gambler, and ITU smacks of the very kind of power and control she is desperate to escape. Deb, as is the case among about half the women in our study, regarded ITU as ill suited to her needs and deeply resented its administration by other prisoners and yet also regarded the twelve step model of Narcotics Anonymous as little more than women telling meaningless stories about their lives.

Such different reactions among the women in our study complicate both a rosy, positive literature regarding these two prevailing addictions treatment models (Moos & Timko 2008) and a feminist criminological critique of both models as inherently rooted in the same power and control dynamic many women have struggled with throughout their lives (Sered & Norton-Hawk 2014; McCorkel 2013). Our findings suggest that rural women's experiences with addictions treatment are shaped as much by individual personality as by the cultural norms associated with particular socioeconomic and ethno-racial identities. Success in both prevailing addictions treatment models requires an interest in ceasing involvement with drugs and alcohol, sufficient confidence and extroversion to give public confessions about experiences generally regarded as private in dominant U.S. culture, including sexual abuse and other forms of trauma, a desire for self-improvement, and, for twelve step groups, an interest in organized religion or spirituality.

Women also vary dramatically in their assessments of less intensive programs designed to improve their financial management skills and assist them with developing internal and social supports to heal from addiction and manage their everyday lives once released back into community. Yet family and community can also be significant sources of stress that may make recently released women feel isolated and prone to engaging in the same kinds of behaviors or relationships that led to their incarceration in the first place. Research demonstrates that inter-generational substance abuse and addiction are especially common in communities where individuals have limited prospects for upward so-cioeconomic mobility as a result of class, race, and gender oppression (Garcia 2014; Okamoto et al. 2014; Willging, Quintero & Lilliott 2014; Park, Melander & Sanchez 2016). Rural women struggling with addic-tion and mental health issues also face intensified stigma and disadvan-tages relative to men as a result of their economic dependence on men (Wright et al. 2007; Chamberlain, Mutaner & Walrath 2004).

Our work confirms these research findings, as the incarceration of very poor and addicted rural women like Tammi and Kat is unfortu-nately the norm in their communities due to intergenerational poverty and, among Native Americans both on and off the reservation, the leg-acy of racism and genocide. These community-wide experiences with incarceration offer limited prospects to women upon their release from prison with respect to long-term addiction recovery, employment that pays a living wage given the added hurdle of a felony conviction, and general hope for the future. Yet women from working-class white fami-lies, like Nedrah, also face significant challenges upon their release from prison. Nedrah is an outlier in her family and her community, unlike Tammi and Kat, and her failure to meet family and community expecta-tions of working-class whiteness makes her an outcast relegated to her sister's basement in a town where her mother informed neighbors that Nedrah was in a mental hospital following a nervous breakdown rather than admit the truth of her incarceration.

Nedrah's sister Starla, a nurse, and her sister's husband, a manager at a mine, are hard-working people who regard themselves as success stories in their families and in their Wyoming town. Families with similar jobs on the coasts or in cities typically regard themselves as blue-collar or working-class due to a larger frame of reference that acknowledges class inequality and encourages solidarity with families in similar economic situations through union membership. As is common in Wyoming, Starla and her husband regard themselves and others who hold similar jobs as middle-class and embrace an ethos that maligns poverty, addic-tion, and related problems as the product of a poor work ethic. Nedrah is accordingly a source of great shame and stigma for her family, and while they provide her with housing and work—things that Tammi and

Kat could never hope to receive from their families—Nedrah still exists on the margins of that world, in a clandestine affair with a married man whose small-town social mores also imprison him.

It is important to remember that substance abuse, addiction, and compromised mental health do not discriminate, but the outcomes of these issues are often differentiated by race and class, as well as gender. Incarceration is a more common experience among poor people struggling with these issues only because they are unable to afford costly drug treatment, and their actions may be more subject to policing in poorer neighborhoods. Substance abuse and mental health issues are easier to conceal in wealthy subdivisions where police are rarely present, families are able to pay for drug rehabilitation, and class privilege accords a degree of privacy not granted to poorer people. This is evident in the perverse aura of glamor associated in dominant U.S. culture with substance abuse among celebrities, whose struggles with addiction are biochemically and psychologically indistinct from those of poor and working-class people whose problems with the same issues so often lead to prison.

Gender, class, ethnicity, and race all combine with individual decision making to result in particular outcomes with respect to substance abuse and compromised mental health. Prevailing approaches to these issues derive from dominant cultural understandings regarding the nature of such problems. The solutions, such as the prison's ITU program, are often steeped in normative notions of success that presume an imagined world where the realities of sexism, racism, and class distinctions do not exist. As the next chapter will discuss, currently and formerly incarcerated women have no choice but to engage with the prevailing gendered socio-institutional beliefs that inform their treatment both within and outside prison walls, sometimes in ways that deny the realities of their lives.

2

A Productive Member of Society

Dakota and Denise usually like being at the center of the cafeteria's hot, anxious hive, where they organize, store, plan, and prepare meals that feed nearly three hundred prisoners and staff throughout the day. The best part about kitchen work is how eagerly it consumes time, that most endless of prison resources, as even a lull in the endless meal preparation, serving, and cleaning presents an opportunity to listen unobtrusively as information drifts across the sea of women. Established routines allow Dakota to tell time by the orange, green, or red color of women's uniforms without even glancing at the large institutional clock mounted on the cafeteria wall. Eating in shifts at low tables bolted to the floor throughout the low-ceilinged, windowless room, where the fluorescent light is the same yellow at both noon and midnight, women parade their respective housing units' inside jokes, rumors, and troubles throughout the cafeteria. Observing and listening while pretending not to makes Denise feel exceptionally in tune with the rhythm of prison life but exhausts Dakota, who sees little more than an endless dramatic repetition of what she regards as the same basic problem: too many messed-up women living in close proximity with too much spare time.

Mealtimes punctuate prison life, even among women busy with jobs or programming, and the cafeteria is an intensely social place that reflects the facility's overall mood and the events that inform it: new rules, staff changes, contagious illness, a fight, a birth, a suicide attempt. Every day Dakota and Denise see women in the grips of every possible human emotion in response to these events, their eyes furtive, joyful, pleading, afraid, and sometimes just disconnected, with hopelessness or the initial veil of confusion brought on by some new psychiatric medication. Her vantage point from the kitchen makes her silently notice things, like how recently arrived women often clutch their thick orange trays differently from those acclimated to prison, fingers spread wide and firm as if to stave off the spinning nausea they feel with so many eyes on them, the heat of women's bodies all around, and the all-consuming fear of trusting the wrong person. At a table in the corner, a tight knot of women start singing "Happy Birthday" and a uniformed correctional officer looks cautiously in their direction, her posture unfurling to full height as her eyes focus intently on the women.

Because they have worked, lived, and spent most of their time together for more than a year, Denise knows that when Dakota suddenly remembers that she needs to check the boxes in the back of the kitchen, she really feels overwhelmed by the cafeteria's noise and constant energy. Sometimes Dakota uses that relatively quiet and solitary time in the back to prepare meals for a few women in restrictive housing units they are not allowed to leave. Although she knows that some women scream from cell to cell, terrified and angry in and at their isolation, Dakota still thinks she would like to spend a few days there just to avoid speaking to another person. Instead, she and Denise are de facto mentors to dozens of women who surface in prison after emerging from years within the drugs-men-welfare subsistence nexus with no real legal work experience. Sometimes these women also have no work ethic and, earning just pennies an hour, quickly find kitchen labor unrewarding.

Early in her career at the prison kitchen, Dakota found Carrie, a youngish woman serving a relatively short drug-related sentence, shivering in the walk-in cooler instead of moving boxes into the storage area. Dakota expected her to apologize, but instead Carrie matter-of-factly told her that she just did not want to work and had never held a paying job in her life. Back then, Dakota had never heard anyone talk like that, not even at the worst moment, right before her family's ranch was about to go into foreclosure. Dakota could understand how it would be hard to think about working in a demoralizing fast-food kitchen after the independence of making and selling methamphetamine, or not having to worry about money because a boyfriend, husband, or father handled that. Women who had managed on the outside under some very tough circumstances were almost always more circumspect about the additional challenges they would have to face after their release. Riley, who always tried so hard to meticulously organize the kitchen's stockroom, said that her most recent relapse was the result of working four different jobs trying to support her kids, which was tough with a felony record. Dakota tries not to think too much about her now-useless accounting degree when she hears women talk like this, knowing that her crime will probably forbid her from handling money in a workplace.

Denise and Dakota are part of the approximately one quarter of women at the prison who have been convicted of money crimes, a term the women use in reference to fraud, embezzlement, burglary, and, sometimes, drug trafficking without addiction. This term also encompasses those, like Dakota and Denise, who stole from their workplaces or family, or misused government funds. The monetary value of the women's money crimes rarely exceeded twenty-five thousand dollars and, in such a small prison, it is not uncommon for women to know these details about one another through the information-sharing network the women call "inmate.com." Hence Dakota is no longer surprised, after a year in prison, when a woman whose name she does not know commiserates with her in the gym about specific aspects of her case. For Dakota, such intimate knowledge about a relative stranger's life is not so different from everyday life in rural Wyoming outside of prison.

Dakota is a little more world weary than Denise, even though she is just a few years older, but otherwise the women share much in common as they move throughout their day, from their shared cell to early-morning work in the kitchen to occasional socializing with others in their housing unit's dayroom. Both come from ranching families, both went to college, and the only encounter either one of them ever had with the criminal justice system was a speeding ticket Denise got prior to being charged with using her father's Social Security number to fraudulently open up credit cards in his name. Dakota is in prison for stealing fifteen thousand dollars from the medical office where she worked over the course of six months by manipulating the statements and receipts to and from Medicare. Sometimes the two reflect on their relationships with money, especially its absence, but most of all they just feel unlucky.

When Dakota returns to the serving line after her few minutes of relative solitude in the back of the kitchen, Denise is serving with two other women and practicing everyone's name, because she read that learning to memorize people's names is a way to "get ahead," a phrase she uses to encompass everything from finding a job to leaving prison. Dakota can see Denise's eyes occasionally drift down to the name patch sewn onto a new or unfamiliar woman's uniform, but otherwise she's getting pretty good at this thanks to the latest paperbacks from the prison librarian, who is diabetic and now expects the extra portions of sugar-free food Denise gives to her. The librarian nods silently as Denise gives her an extra waxy apple and the two share a moment of meaningful eye contact. This intrigue seems a little silly to Dakota, who ignores it because she is grateful to live with Denise. So many other women Dakota meets exist in fantasy worlds to cope with quotidian prison life, kept afloat on the warm, salty waves of self-help books, idle conversations that discourage introspection, and novels with little relevance to real life.

Currently Denise has a stack of brightly covered books designed for professional women, written by a television producer. "Dakota," Denise will occasionally instruct her without taking her eyes off the page as they sit quietly in their cell before bed or during lockdown, "if you ever want a hotel to give you a room with an ocean view, the key word is *request*. That way you can make the manager think that it was his idea."

"I'll be sure to keep that in mind," Dakota says, suppressing the anger and helplessness she feels when thinking about what the future will look like for her after release. She tries not to envision what it will be like for her, an accountant, to take the mandatory household budgeting class all women must complete prior to their release. Silence covers up a lot for Dakota, just as the seductive language of self-improvement does for Denise.

Denise has been watching Itzel for a few weeks, just as she does with all new arrivals, and listening to the other women, who are also watching Itzel, talk about what they know about her. Itzel gets more than the usual amount of commentary because she is different from most of the other women: tiny, Latina, with tattooed-on eyeliner and a hard look. "She's younger than she looks," Denise tells Dakota in the kitchen between shifts, "but she had a baby eight months ago and thinks her man is going to wait for her in Denver."

"That's never gonna happen," Dakota scoffs. "No one waits for women. I heard that in here, that at the men's prisons they always get visitors and some of the women even move to be closer to those men. You know anyone in here who gets treatment like that?"

"Mm-mm," Denise says, keeping up their familiar rhythm. "We're all the same, though, those of us who aren't addicts," Denise continues. "Wrong place, wrong time, wrong decision kind of a thing. I saw her in here today with KelliAnn, you know, the one with that stupid tattoo on her neck just in case she forgets to remind us that she's from Colorado and not accustomed to our backwardness here in Wyoming?"

Dakota shakes her head as she raises her voice over the sound of the mop bucket filling with water. "I heard she smacked her baby's father upside the head with a tire iron. I never hit anybody with a tire iron. You ever hit anybody with a tire iron?"

"Well, no. But she sure did," Denise says as she starts to mop the floor. "Walked right into a trailer in Cheyenne and whacked him in the face with it. Think maybe she's got some anger issues?" Grey-white suds slosh onto the floor over the bucket's rim as Dakota forcefully places it next to Denise.

"Yeah, that's one way to put it. Not one that I would choose, though." Denise watches Dakota retreat into the storage area as the other women in the kitchen watch them both, eyes wide and searching as Denise continues to mop.

Managing Competing Realities

To explicate and analyze how women like Dakota and Denise handle their everyday lives in prison while planning for their eventual release, this chapter engages with three primary areas of the literature on women and incarceration. These three areas include the gendered components of economic crime, the process by which women become socialized into institutional norms, and coping mechanisms the women use to do their time. The first primary area, gendered components of economic crime, analyzes the factors that inform women's and men's involvement in the various activities subsumed under what the women term "money crime." Socialization into institutional norms, the second area, critically engages with gendered and racialized ideologies that predominate in prison settings, sometimes in ways that misrecognize social and economic vulnerabilities as personal pathologies. The third primary area, coping mechanisms, emphasizes the wide array of individual, interpersonal, and community strategies women use to manage the considerable constraints of everyday prison life.

Research indicates that, relative to men, few women are incarcerated for economic crimes. Yet some types of property crimes—particularly shoplifting—are almost wholly attributed to women (Caputo & King 2015). Women's economic crimes are most frequently misdemeanors and often result in fines, probation, or jail sentences rather than prison time, but when these crimes involve significant monetary value or are sustained over time, a prosecutor may choose to pursue a felony conviction and prison time. Women with few substantial assets, or who are living in poverty, are most likely to commit economic crimes that parallel their employment status, such that women's monetary gains from white-collar crimes are generally significantly less than men's due to women's lower economic status relative to men (Weisburd, Waring & Chayet 2001).

White-collar crime has a distinctly racialized component as well due to persistent racial stratification in employment, such that whites—and particularly white males—generally earn more than white women and people of color. Due to this high degree of relative privilege and decision-making authority, white-collar crime is a form of "elite deviance" that has a far greater and more widespread impact on society than street crime, which typically takes place between individuals who know one another (Michel, Cochran & Heide 2015; Michel, Cochran & Heide 2014). Gendered economic inequalities combine with individual perceptions of morality and available choices to shape the decision making of women who commit economic crimes (Davies 2003). Hence women serving prison sentences for theft, embezzlement, or related crimes often committed them in situations of economic duress that, in at least some ways, probably limited or otherwise compromised the choices open to them.

Women are arrested for the specific crime of embezzlement at higher rates than men, yet significant differences exist between the way men and women rationalize their decision to commit a money crime (Grounds 2011). Across the course of several decades, researchers have found uniquely gendered justifications for embezzlement, with men stealing money under the guise of "borrowing" to address personal problems while women often describe theft as a means to meet the needs of their children or intimate partner (Coleman 2002; Cressey 1973). Women who commit economic crime tend to situate their actions within the context of meeting a family member's or loved one's basic and immediate needs for shelter, food, or medical care, or as the result of pressure from a male intimate partner (Klenowski, Copes & Mullins 2008). Yet criminologists are hardly united in their view of why women commit economic crime. For instance, Pamela Davies (2003) takes exception to the argument that women commit such crimes because they are victims both pushed and driven to escape poverty, abuse, and hardship. Instead, she argues that women can commit crimes for very much the same reasons as men, including material gain that is not always related to poverty (Davies 2003). Following Davies, Miller and Decker (2001) find that the primary motivation for robbery among both men and women is to obtain money or material goods.

Economic crime, irrespective of the perpetrator's gender, class, ethnicity, or race, should be considered alongside the context in which it occurs and the opportunities available for legal work that pays a living wage. In 2015, the wage gap in Wyoming between men and women was forty-ninth in the country, with women primarily working in the poorly paid retail and service sectors of the economy rather than in the more lucrative mineral-extraction industries (Connolly 2016). The self-sufficiency standard, a measure that calculates how much income families of various sizes and compositions need to make ends meet at a minimally adequate level, indicates that incomes far above the federal poverty level are necessary to meet Wyoming families' basic needs (Pearce 2016). This is especially relevant to currently and formerly incarcerated women in Wyoming due to the consistency with which studies demonstrate correlations among women's offending, economic marginalization, and reduced decision-making authority in the home, with poverty found to be a strong predictor of lawbreaking in both urban and rural communities (Parker & Reckdenwald 2008). Particularly notable is that Parker and Reckdenwald also found women more likely to face arrest for property crimes in rural areas characterized by what the authors term "the traditional family index," which evaluates the presence or absence of cultural beliefs that support women's economic dependency on men and unpaid labor in the home (Parker & Reckdenwald 2008).

Dominant correctional and cultural forces regard economic crime as a personal pathology distinct both from addiction, which the prevailing mental health model regards as a mental illness, and from violent crimes, which are often (but by no means always) connected to addiction and compromised mental health. Yet irrespective of their crime and the length of their individual sentence, all women must familiarize themselves with the norms of everyday prison life as part of their socialization into the role of inmate. As is the case with nearly all forms of role enculturation, unique gender dynamics surround this socialization process. Criminologist Mary Bosworth's longitudinal study of admissions handbooks issued to U.S. federal prisoners found that such handbooks maintain a gender-neutral focus on individual prisoners' responsibility for their own conduct and efforts at reform yet emphasize the importance of more intensively policing women's sexuality and behavior (Bosworth 2007). Similarly, research conducted with incarcerated women in Canada indicates that prevailing modes of North American prison administration often reframe women's needs, including those for mental health services, as potential risks to their peers, themselves, and correctional facility staff (Hannah-Moffat 1999). The gendered meanings ascribed to risk also extend to incarcerated women's intimate relationships in ways that regard the women as dysfunctional, violent, and otherwise in need of forms of correctional intervention that may not relate to the reasons they are in prison (Pollack 2000).

Feminist criminologists have extensively critiqued the way the criminal justice system individualizes social vulnerabilities as personal pathologies in therapeutic groups designed to assist criminalized women in various ways. A five-year study conducted with formerly incarcerated women in Boston questions the utility of therapeutic programs that, following the twelve step model of addictions treatment and individual responsibility, deny that "these women have already spent too much of their lives in the hands of too many higher powers" (Sered & Norton-Hawk 2014: 119). Research conducted at two California carceral therapeutic communities for young women with children found that despite the women's consistent and pervasive struggles (and failures) to obtain steady work, safe housing, and education, both programs maintained an ethos in which "the road to recovery bypassed the social, heading instead through the women's minds, bodies, and souls" (Haney 2010:

116). In emphasizing women's individual choices, prevailing approaches to therapeutic programming in correctional facilities deemphasizes, or even ignores, the significant social, economic, and other barriers that criminalized women have faced throughout their lives.

Correctional facilities, including the people who staff and reside within them, are products of the broader cultural worlds and associated belief systems that surround them, and so it is perhaps unsurprising that societies like the United States that highly esteem independence and individualism would prioritize these values. As microcosms of the much larger cultural system of which they are a part, prisons reflect social beliefs and practices that are sometimes so entrenched within a culture as to be invisible. For instance, a U.S.-Hungary comparative study of incarcerated women's creative writing identified the presence of "institutional scripts" reflective of the dominant cultural norms at work in both facilities (Haney & Tapolcai 2010: 196). While U.S. women exclusively used the first person in their writing, their Hungarian counterparts relied on the third person to emphasize the social and relational components of their world (Haney & Tapolcai 2010).

Incarcerated women face considerable constraints as they create coping mechanisms and social worlds, however limited, that meet their needs for support, companionship, and sociality. The nuanced and inevitably complex ways in which the women do so defies easy categorization, prompting criminologist Andriani Fili, on the basis of her research with incarcerated women in Greece, to caution against work that reinforces historically persistent binaries of victim/resister and victim/criminal (Fili 2013). Criminologist Mary Bosworth, writing about her work in three English women's prisons, notes how incarcerated women cultivate identities as mothers, partners, and sisters within institutional structures that physically remove them from these relationships while rewarding passive behavior culturally constructed as feminine (Bosworth 1999). Drawing on her research at a correctional facility's drug treatment program, Jill McCorkel (2013) describes how incarcerated women strategically present themselves, and each other, in an environment designed to alter fundamental aspects of their inner selves.

Incarcerated women indisputably mobilize a vast array of complex strategies to resist or otherwise covertly disengage from the totalizing and hypersocial environment of prison, and yet they also develop equally numerous ways to mitigate its impacts. A midwestern study found a strong preference among incarcerated women for controlling unwanted emotions through individual techniques, including self-reflection, humor, and staying busy with activities whenever possible, rather than seeking help from other women or facility staff (Greer 2002). Reading, which allows for intensely private engagement with complex feelings and ideas in a setting that otherwise provides very limited privacy, has been shown to foster critical self-reflection and support in ways that make up for some prisons' limited counseling, education programs, and related resources (Sweeney 2010). These solitary forms of self-support and self-reliance may be particularly important for life-sentenced women, who face a set of especially difficult challenges as they watch other women leave prison, something they will never be able to do (Lempert 2016).

Social relationships between women in prison take as many forms as they do in the free world, including pseudo-families, close friends, acquaintances, resource-sharing or knowledge-sharing networks that help women to navigate the system, and intimate partnerships (Severance 2005). Some incarcerated women find community with other women who share spiritual beliefs that provide them with a way to cope with negative feelings by cultivating a worldview that they regard as personally meaningful (Huey Dye et al. 2014; Ferszt et al. 2009). One study of spirituality among women who were incarcerated for the murder of an abusive intimate partner or family member reported that participation in a group of women with similar experiences provided them with a sense of freedom that many had never before experienced, even prior to their incarceration (Zimmer Schneider & Feltey 2009). Other women form intimate relationships with one another, despite the fact that such relationships are universally forbidden in U.S. prisons and punishable in ways that can extend a prison sentence (Pardue, Arrigo & Murphy 2011; Severance 2004).

Studies that focus on the production and distribution of food among incarcerated women emphasize the complexities inherent to social relationships in prison, where, unlike in the free world, women generally cannot choose who they spend the majority of their time with, nor can they avoid (at least entirely) those they dislike or who have hurt them. Food is an important coping mechanism for incarcerated women as well as a means of social support. Catrin Smith (2002), on the basis of her study of three English women's prisons, emphasizes the powerful role that food plays in the power and control dynamic that characterizes all prisoners' lives, such that eating (or the refusal to do so) can potentially make a powerful statement about autonomy over one's own body. A study conducted in Canadian federal prisons likewise observes how the generally low quality of food served in prison makes the illicit trading or sharing of food items between prisoners particularly meaningful and important (de Graff & Kilty 2016). Amy Smoyer (2015), working in the United States, contends that food is absolutely central to the way that many incarcerated women build relationships with other women in prison while maintaining and sharing knowledge with one another about the outside world.

Our findings build on this literature. We argue that most currently and formerly incarcerated women find themselves juggling competing narratives as they reconcile the realities of their lives with a prevailing moral-cultural ethos that denies the structural violence of rural poverty, sexism, and felony-related discrimination. To substantiate this argument, we draw on descriptive accounts of the way women navigate socio-institutional and moral beliefs that deny the realities of their lives, focusing on the women's successes and failures at attempting to achieve their individually valued ways of working, living, and finding meaning in the world. We explore the women's economic situations prior to prison, which often involved significant debt, childcare responsibilities, and restricted or even nonexistent possibilities for earning a living. Following women through their everyday routines in prison as they work, participate in activities, and formulate plans for their futures, we analyze how women manage life after their release, when felony conviction–related stigma adds to the challenges they face as women in rural areas where male-dominated jobs in the resource-extraction fields generally exclude them and service-sector work does not pay a living wage.

On the Treadmill

Itzel hates that her body still looks five months pregnant even though eight months have passed since she gave birth. She hates the carbohydrates and starch that pile up on her orange cafeteria tray three times a day, and that she eats because she has no commissary money to buy anything else. As her small hands tightly grip the treadmill's support bars, she hopes that no one can see how exhausted she is even by this minor effort, especially when combined with her efforts to ignore KelliAnn, who has attached herself to Itzel because they both come from Colorado. Itzel tries not to listen as KelliAnn tries to engage her in conversation by using an unnecessarily loud voice and affected sense of overfamiliarity to admire Itzel's tattoos as other women begin to congregate for an aerobics class, stretching their bodies and pulling mats onto the floor. KelliAnn looks at Itzel with admiration and more than a little envy; when Itzel looks at KelliAnn, she sees a teenage girl from Boulder, an affluent northern Colorado university town where the average home price is close to a million dollars. Itzel thinks that KelliAnn's parents are probably part of the pot-smoking old white hippie contingent who moved to Boulder in the 1970s and now publicly complain about how much the city has changed since they moved there, specifically the lack of affordable housing, and then privately rejoice in how much they can sell their small houses for in order to finance their retirement. Some white people with real money do that kind of thing in smaller Colorado cities like Boulder and Fort Collins; Itzel knows because her sister, Marisol, went to college and now has a job in an office with people who know about things like that.

The gym's heavy rubber smell hangs all around them, increasingly competing with the scent of KelliAnn's $8.48 commissary shampoo and conditioner the more she bounces on the treadmill. It makes her smell rich, especially given that this amount totals more than a week's wages for women lucky enough to have jobs in prison. KelliAnn gets as close as she can without touching to see the blue ink outlining Itzel's newborn leaning his cheek against Dante's muscular arm, a serious expression on both their faces. Itzel is pumping harder and harder on the elliptical machine as KelliAnn continues her empty chatter and attempts to hold court in the prison gym before the aerobics instructor arrives and commands attention as only those who have spent twenty years in prison can among their peers.

Before Itzel came to their housing unit, KelliAnn was the resident urbanite able to intimidate the Wyoming women, who comprise the vast majority of the prison, with big-city-jail stories of fights, mental health breakdowns, and cruel correctional officers. Itzel knows KelliAnn's type well from her own stays in Denver County Jail: a white girl who, until someone tells her to shut up, tries to mirror the cadence and words she has heard while watching BET in her parents' basement. Now that she is in prison in Wyoming, Itzel knows, KelliAnn has the audience she always wanted, and tells anyone in listening distance of her profound misfortune in being arrested and prosecuted in Wyoming rather than her home state of Colorado, where she feels she would have had the opportunity to participate in more classes, programs, and other things she would like to do. Itzel, who is in the same housing unit as KelliAnn, is not interested in talking about any of these things, particularly not at one of the few times when she can exercise. She still cannot believe she is in a prison with no yard time allowed, especially in the middle of nowhere.

Itzel notices the bright orange sun that rises over blue-green mountains at the nape of KelliAnn's neck, the word "NATIVE" tattooed in deep green ink expressing her pride in being from Colorado. KelliAnn is from the Colorado that people all over the United States save up to visit during the summer months so they can see the majestic snow-capped mountains and sprawling green valleys in state parks where elk and other creatures roam confidently down town sidewalks, knowing that humans will not harm them. Itzel's Colorado is the neighborhoods surrounding Federal Boulevard that show up in bright red on the Denver Police Department maps to indicate a higher-than-city-average frequency of violent and property crimes. As with Itzel, most of her neighbors are first- or second-generation migrants from Mexico, Central America, or Southeast Asia. She is endlessly and privately entertained by the efforts young women from middle-of-nowhere towns make to describe their small-time drug dealing or fights with friends using language and mannerisms adopted from popular culture; their borrowed language and bravado, in Itzel's eyes, only emphasizes how little exposure they have had to the world.

Three women, whose names Itzel is determined not to learn, are stretching on the floor as they wait for the aerobics instructor, frustrated that yet another crafts class taught by volunteers was canceled due to a snowstorm that seemed likely to close the roads for several days. One of the women turns to Itzel and asks, hands perched on the rubber mat,

"Is it like this in Denver, or did you get to do things like all the time?" Gossip has always been Itzel's least favorite part of doing time, and she tries not to speculate on how much the women already know about her through inmate.com. Itzel pauses deliberately, predicting that KelliAnn will answer for her, and she does.

KelliAnn nods. "You're not out in the sticks there like you are here, so people come and make things with you, just so you can take your mind off being in prison, maybe send something home to your kids or parents."

"See?" the woman who asked the question says in frustration. "How can you feel like you have a future, or any chance at all, if there's no training or rehab?"

The woman standing next to her raises her eyebrows as though she is looking at small children and leans back on an unused elliptical machine, her voice deep with sarcasm. "Seriously, ladies? You won't rehabilitate yourselves because you can't make a stupid card with glitter glue?"

"It's probably a lot harsher conditions there in Denver," another woman says, "but I get that you have more to keep yourself occupied. Here we have nothing. I mean you have your hygiene, you have your writing materials, your bedding and clothes, and that's it."

"You've got me thinkin'," KelliAnn says, slowing her pace on the elliptical just a bit and now ignoring Itzel altogether. "There are a couple girls here, and it breaks my heart watching them because they don't have anything, they don't have outside support, they don't have any kind of, they don't have anything positive to do, they don't have the money to afford crafts, they can't afford schooling, there's nothing this prison's doing to keep them occupied and so they're constantly getting in trouble, and they're literally spending years in the east wing [restrictive housing]. There's girls that've spent more time there than in the regular part of housing, and they don't have anything to keep them out of trouble. And being there does something to you psychologically that you can't reverse the damage."

The three women, none of whom have ever been in restrictive housing or in a city, nod at each other. "I know this girl in here, she's from this little bitty town," one of them says, "and she's goin' crazy thinking about going home because there are three hundred people in her town. She says that when she goes back there to see her daughter play basketball, everybody will be looking at her like 'ooooh, she was in prison.'"

Itzel almost spits with annoyance as she finally joins the conversation. "That's everywhere, whatever. What are they gonna do, stand up and applaud, 'oh she done good, she really made it in prison!'"

KelliAnn shakes her head and insists, "No, it's different in Wyoming because they all know each other. Hey, Anne, you're from Rock Springs? Tell Itzel what's in Rock Springs, even though there's so many hard-up people passing through?"

Anne laughs in response. "There's nothing in Rock Springs, nothing for single moms, for addicts, no homeless shelters, no medical help, there's no housing, clothing, nothing for battered women, single moms struggling—like, low-income housing is a three-year wait. If you're homeless in some parts of Wyoming you might as well just pack your bags now."

The aerobics instructor, Lauri, strides purposefully into the room and KelliAnn tells the women to be quiet, since she knows that the Parole Board recently refused to grant Lauri parole despite her near-perfect record decades into a sentence for a crime she committed as a teenager. KelliAnn, who wants to show Itzel her command over prison social dynamics, continues. "Lauri is a perfect example of what women don't get in here. Parole told her she needs to complete more job training classes, but she can't take those classes because she's not on a short sentence. Now is that a catch-22 or what?"

Lauri has the steady, stoic gaze that Itzel always associates with her relatives and other people she knows who have served lengthy prison sentences. Instead of contradicting KelliAnn, Lauri says, "I don't want to be negative. I'm fortunate that there's a community group outside that sends me money to take classes, so I've completed four fitness certifications. I've also completed all the classes, as part of improving myself emotionally, but these are not enough to show the Parole Board job readiness. Maybe next time."

Lauri holds Itzel's gaze for a moment before clapping enthusiastically and jogging over to the small portable stereo that will play the music for this aerobics session. Once Lauri is out of earshot, Itzel turns to KelliAnn and says, "I think it's a woman thing, anywhere you go. I think women are very harshly judged, versus a man can go get a job right out the prison gate, but if you're a woman trying to—like they are so hard on women because women are supposed to be the nurturers, the care-takers, the lovers, the peacemakers. We shouldn't be out there using and being sexually active, living the criminal lifestyle because that's bad for women, but it's okay for men to do it, double standards."

"That's the thing, though, the men's prison," KelliAnn continues. "There's numerous places for a man to go in this state, y'know, you have the Honor Farm, the boot camp, you have everything, and as a woman we are stuck here, we do not get that opportunity to build fires or put out fires or cut wood or do any'a those things. We don't. I mean we do have the canine program which is an amazing program. They used to say Wyoming was a women's state; I don't think that's the case anymore."

"Are you surprised the men get better things than we do, honestly?" Itzel asks, now out of breath with exhaustion. "There's just more of them, that's all. Don't make it into something it's not."

Another woman brightly chirps, "There's welding, though! That was a good one."

"Welding?" Itzel asks, trying to wrap her mind around it.

"The welding teacher retired so we don't have it now. It was seriously hard to get into," KelliAnn says, "but the women in here want it because then you can go out and get a job in a mine or something, fixing the equipment, if they'll hire a felon."

"You have to be smart to get into welding, though, like with math and stuff," the woman continues, reconsidering her enthusiasm. "You can apply to get into welding if you're under thirty-five and if you pass these tests and get a certain score, a seven, across the board. Then you get your CRC—that's your Career Readiness Card—and you got a seven on everything, the math and the English—you need a seven, because you might be good at one or two things, but very few people get a seven."

Another woman sidles up to their conversation, frustrated that Lauri cannot seem to get the stereo to work, and offers her opinion. "You gotta be careful about all that, though. This is my second time here and the first time I got my CRC. I had it all ready to go!" She laughs as she adopts the self-deprecating and defeated tone of someone with nothing left to do but laugh at her own situation. Feigning nervous anticipation with every action, she exclaims, "So, I went around all the fast food places and kitchens and showed this card and people looked at me like I was crazy. What it's supposed to be is, you show these people your card and they're supposed to know what it's for and you have a higher chance of getting hired. I said, 'oh, I'm gonna have my card' and not one person had heard of it. Because that's what they're telling us here. That we're gonna get a good job with these cards. The point is there's a miscommunication, and it would be a good card if we could get people to recognize it out there. Now I've heard that in other states people recognize it, and it's working. Is that true in Colorado?"

Itzel shakes her head and KelliAnn shrugs. Itzel does not doubt that these rural women have a rough time of their own, but during the two years she spent at the Denver women's prison, she saw many of the same things that the Wyoming women are describing, although these problems indisputably took place on a larger scale in Colorado. She had filled out just as many questionnaires and surveys administrated by case workers and social services people designed to assess women's "readiness to change" and other vaguely worded concepts, sometimes as a condition of getting out of prison and into a particular type of halfway house or treatment facility. Itzel had noticed that the Wyoming prison seemed to offer some of the same programs as the one in Denver, classes that could be vaguely categorized as "self-help" and whose words seeped slowly, as if through osmosis, into many of the women's vocabularies. These classes were often workbook-driven and had names like "Boundaries," "Criminal Thinking," and "Thinking for a Change," and the women's evaluations of them were mixed. Some women saw them as important and life-changing, while others regarded completing such classes as necessary to appear favorably before the Parole Board. Some understood how to work the system to their advantage, both for the future and also to survive everyday life in the institution.

KelliAnn shrugs again, but she knows women who are currently in Thinking for a Change and really like it. "It depends who you are, I guess," she says. "I really tried to take the information from class to help and not to think, 'oh here's another program to get through my case plan.' I really feel it helped, there are a couple of programs like that. I think that probably, there's one class that's sixteen weeks long, we just did workbook after workbook, just a culmination of all the classes. Beyond Trauma is a great group, also, and I don't think they're gonna offer it anymore; it's the prevention-type, to communicate with your children, like about how you can't drink."

Itzel narrows her eyes, confused about why a woman would need to tell her child that. "Why do you have to tell your kids why you can't drink?"

One of the women laughs out loud. "Well, if you had a family like mine, where alcohol is a major part of everything, you wouldn't need to ask that question."

Another woman laughs. "I liked the parenting class, that was a good one. It was part of my case plan, otherwise I wouldn't have taken it. I see what she's saying, though, because parenting was part of my case plan but I took it hoping to learn something and because my case worker knows I want to go to college, so I'll get to parole out earlier. It's not like I said to myself, 'oh, I wanna be manipulative,' like that class is what I *really* wanted."

"What case plan?" Itzel asks dismissively.

KelliAnn looks concerned. "You seriously don't have a case plan? That can't be." KelliAnn guffaws a little too loudly, causing Lauri to look at her disapprovingly.

"I'm trying to get an interstate compact so I can parole back home to Colorado when my time is up," Itzel finally says out loud, after determining that the women listening to her are well-intentioned if a little naïve. "But I don't think it's gonna happen for me with the way things are going with my case worker. So even when I parole out to the halfway house I still don't know what is really going on or where am I going to start looking for a job because I am not from here, I don't know the streets. I don't know nobody, so when I get out there all I can look forward to is just whatever they have there, like 'okay, do I take a left or do I take a right?' because I don't know. 'Do I catch this bus or do I catch that bus,' like I don't know nothing about this state at all."

KelliAnn watches Lexi and Maggie, who have just a day to go until their release, walking by and says, "You could always kill your number in here, you know, do all your time so you can just walk out the door when your time is up. See those two on their way to the library? They're out tomorrow since both killed their number, unless they stir some crazy shit up."

Maggie is ever on the lookout for an opportunity to receive approval, which she learned to call "external validation" in her Boundaries class. She turns in the direction of KelliAnn's voice and smiles broadly.

"That little girl, I swear," KelliAnn says to Itzel, "she'll do anything just for someone to be nice to her." Maggie is already heading their way, barely hiding her excitement, while Lexi stalks into the library. "Hey, Maggie!" KelliAnn chirps with feigned happiness, to which Maggie is oblivious. "Did you finish pre-release? What did you do there?"

"Uh-huh," she nods. "It was pretty good. We worked on applications together, and resumes, and talked about how to get a job. Some of the girls were upset, though, that we didn't work on how to talk to landlords."

"Oh, you didn't?" KelliAnn says, hopping off the elliptical machine to show her exaggerated interest in Maggie, who Itzel now realizes is a little slow. Itzel keeps up her pace on the treadmill, not liking the way that KelliAnn is deliberately mocking Maggie without her even knowing.

"No, some of the girls said they want like a list of people who would rent to felons. I'm going to stay with my parents, so it didn't matter for me, but I felt bad for them." Maggie jumps, dramatically startled, as Lauri's stereo suddenly sputters on at high volume, and the women slink in her direction, with one calling out to Maggie to come with them as they cast a disapproving glare in KelliAnn's direction.

"You were nasty to that little girl, KelliAnn," Itzel says. "It's not her fault she's stupid."

"Hey, welcome to the real world, okay?" KelliAnn snaps, annoyed that she and Itzel might not share the kind of superior bond she thought they did. "And speaking of real world, I just wanna put something else out there for you. Promise not to get mad?" Itzel shakes her head, increasingly annoyed with KelliAnn and all the women who surround her. "There's a lot of women in here because of a man, I'm just sayin'. Connie, the one with the pretty red hair, she's in here on her second bid, this time for bringing drugs into the penitentiary to visit her boyfriend. Who does that? He made her think that she wouldn't get caught, but she shouldn't have listened to him. Lots of women do stupid things for men, like Nedrah, you didn't know her, but she just followed her man from crime to crime, all tweaked out on meth."

Itzel calmly gets off the treadmill, trying to ignore the pain shooting throughout her stiff calves and the discomfort of the loose muscles still hanging around her abdomen. "It's different with me and Dante," Itzel tells KelliAnn, shaking her head hard enough to dislodge the ideas KelliAnn has been sharing with her. They sit down by a stray exercise ball and Itzel tries hard to reign in her emotions, letting her guard down just a little for the first time in several months.

KelliAnn leans in sympathetically. "You know I work at the tilapia hatchery, right?" KelliAnn is proud to work in the prison's most coveted position although she often jokes, "Wyoming is known the world over for its tilapia" because of the state's waterless location on the high plains desert, where tumbleweeds can blow for hundreds of miles. She, like a lot of other women, is frustrated that the prison does not have available job training programs in maintenance, gardening, or other things that could readily translate to the free world because such services are always in short supply in larger towns. The situation made perfect sense to Itzel, though. Some opportunistic guy from Colorado trucked the fish away when they were ready, probably getting a neat tax credit in the process for working within a prison—and it would be hard to beat the labor prices, with the highest-paying job available at one dollar an hour.

Itzel hates the smell of fish and sometimes she catches it on KelliAnn, as if it has become permanently attached to her from all the time she spends farming the fish in large tanks in the hot, humid indoor facility where the fish are in huge blue plastic tubs. The fish follow passersby from one end of the tub to another, pressing their muscular brown-grey bodies against the hard periphery in the hope of getting food, never knowing the limit of their helpless existence destined for a freezer and a bad microwaved meal. Workers like KelliAnn facilitate the movement of fish from one tank to another as they grow, and then clean the scum left behind from the tanks. The prison describes the fish farm as "wastewater management training." It makes Itzel feel sorry for KelliAnn, despite her frustration at receiving unsolicited personal advice from her.

"A few days ago, Amanda, this girl I work with," KelliAnn begins, "she had her first baby at thirteen, she said, 'you're not a woman until you take a man's name, you're just a girl.'"

Itzel tilts her head. "A lot of women think like that, not just women in prison."

"That's not the point, though," KelliAnn says. "Like Amber, she was addicted to meth and living with this guy, who was all tweaked out. She wrote a twelve-thousand-dollar check that didn't belong to her, and bang! Anne stole eighty thousand dollars from her job to buy her old man a motorcycle and all sorts of crazy shit, and he left her the day she got arrested." Itzel glares at her. "Look" KelliAnn says, "I could go on."

"Please don't," Itzel says, holding up her hand to block the barrage of thoughts that are increasingly difficult to keep out of her head. They sit in silence until the loudspeaker calls for open movement, the ten minutes they have to get to their next destination.

Itzel feels hopeless as she shuffles back to the halls from the gym, trying to decide whether to bypass the block of phones this time because she does not want to cry in front of strangers if Dante does not answer. At least it will be quiet in her cell, where her roommate, Michelle, sleeps most of the time after getting fired from her job in the kitchen after showing up late for a couple of days. "Why are you late? You live ten minutes' walk from your job!" Michelle imitated Dakota saying. For thirty-five cents an hour, it just was not worth it for her. Most of the women Itzel has met so far, just like women in Denver, spent every penny they earned on phone calls, shampoo, and coffee, and occasionally some candy. It was so hard to be away from everyone, to not know how the baby was feeling, or what he was learning. She paid more for the lousy pay phone a few times a week in prison than she did for a monthly plan on the outside. Itzel cannot wait to get out, get some real money, get back with her man, and get their baby back. She just hopes that Dante will be there waiting to forgive her. She wouldn't be surprised if he didn't.

She watches the small cohort of women banded together around the row of shiny metal pay phones mounted to the cement block wall. One has her back to Itzel, her body curled around the phone as she disappears into the sound of the free-world phone on the other end of the line. Hair slips constantly into the face of the woman next to her, who keeps repeating herself because the person she is talking to cannot hear her tiny whisper. Finally, she gives up and raises her voice. "I'll need to get a job right away, Mom," she says. "I need to get out there and make it happen. I know I'm going to hear 'no' a lotta times, but otherwise I'm not going to be able to get out of bed, not if I don't even try." The last woman in the row sinks into the wall, her size, inertia, and grief pulling her closer to the floor as she listens to the sounds of her children, who are too young to talk. Then there's a fourth woman, twisting her fingers anxiously around the cord as she bites the inside of her cheek while listening to the phone ring, unanswered, for the fifth time.

Itzel shakes her head, frustrated by the amount of money she has spent trying to get someone on the phone who knows how Dante is doing. Through her anger she also soaks up the sound of people speaking Spanish in the background, the familiar cadence of the way people speak in her neighborhood, rather than the flat monotone of those who surround her. She sighs and keeps moving, because she is tired of waiting today. Tired of waiting. Waiting to use a phone soaked in some other woman's tears and hot breath. Waiting to eat. Waiting to shower. On a wait list for a class, a program, a case worker appointment. Waiting for sleep, knowing that the next day she will only wake up and do the same thing all over again. Waiting to leave. Waiting, alone with her thoughts. Part of her knows that KelliAnn is right in saying, even if she did not say it directly, that it is foolish to expect to go back to the same town, the same relationship, and the same whatever else expecting a different outcome. Bombarded by the sheer number of women telling so many elements of her story, she wonders if hers will really turn out so differently.

Itzel's cellmate, Michelle, turns over in her sleep and opens one eye to look at Itzel, who raises her gaze to meet Michelle's as she enters the cell. "I've got it," Michelle says, slowly opening the other eye.

"What?" Itzel says, smiling despite the day's low-simmering grief because Michelle looks like a fat crocodile lying on the muddy banks of a nature show there in her top bunk.

"Can you imagine the street value of being a phlebotomist and being able to put a flushable line when you can't find a fucking vein? Set up a PIC line in someone's leg for days. You only have to change it every fourteen days."

This is more than Itzel has heard Michelle say in two months of living with her. "What's a PIC line?" Itzel asks with genuine interest.

"Peripherally inserted catheter" glides out of Michelle's mouth. "Goes straight into the vein and doesn't have to be removed." Michelle smiles slowly and promptly drifts back into sleep.

Now that is a woman thinking ahead, Itzel says to herself. Even after so many months of her life spent in correctional facilities, Itzel never ceases to marvel at prison entrepreneurship. Without hearing her say it explicitly, Itzel guesses that Michelle will probably get out of prison and use student loans or other aid designed to help her get back on her feet in the straight-world sense to enroll in a phlebotomy course at a community college. Then she will put her PIC line plan into action, with all her profits probably reinvested in her own illicit drug use until she gets arrested again and winds up back in prison. Itzel has often wondered what some of these women, somehow always finding a means to create a throughway even after finding success blocked by so many barriers, could do with their lives if they had been born into different kinds of families. Itzel stifles a laugh as she realizes that this line of thinking does nothing to explain women like KelliAnn, who seemed to have everything handed to them only to squander it, leaving nothing but family shame and suffering in their wake. Itzel stares at the bunk above her, wondering why the fattest women always seemed to get the bunk above her in every jail and prison she ends up in, and tries to sleep.

Lockdown

After eight hours of kitchen funk and noise, the pods where Dakota and Denise share a cell are a brightly lit oasis of high ceilings and relative quiet. Both women have low security classifications because of their nonviolent crimes and record of good behavior in prison, which means that their living space is far less confined and noisy than the conditions for women with higher security classifications. Those women live in the halls, a housing unit arranged along a narrow corridor, and spend more time in their cells. Most of the kitchen workers say that the mood in the cafeteria gets louder and more aggressive when the women from the halls have their scheduled time to eat, unlike the somber tone that descends when the Intensive Treatment Unit women, who are not allowed to talk to anyone from other housing units, come in to eat.

Each of the cream-painted steel cell doors has a set of women's photographs fastened next to it, so that correctional officers can quickly identify the residents during count, when everyone is locked in her cell until officers confirm all prisoners' presence. Denise half-smiles in her cell door photograph, while Dakota blankly stares. At some point in the next hour or two, depending on how long it takes to complete count, a correctional officer's disembodied head will appear in the cell door's small window to confirm their presence. Both women feel extraordinarily fortunate that they get along with each other and share so much in common; this is not always the case in ways that run the gamut from mutual dislike to outright hostility.

It remains unspoken between them that the camaraderie Dakota and Denise share relies on their disdain for other women as much as it does on what they have in common. They regard themselves as essentially different from the women struggling with addiction, intergenerational poverty, and violent relationships, and their allegiance to one another rests on the premise that they are fundamentally unlike a significant majority of the women in the prison. Their small-town judgment of others keeps them afloat through their everyday routine, even as they know the same attitudes will follow them back to their families and communities. Both know that bored people from families just like theirs, who are just barely making it by patching together money from ranching and low-wage office work in town if they can get it, vibrantly condemn the reasons Dakota and Denise are in prison. Their money crimes—Dakota's cooking the books at a medical practice in town and Denise's using her father's Social Security number to fraudulently take out credit cards in his name—are tightly knotted up with deeply rooted cultural expectations that people should be able to care for their own families without public assistance. Dakota and Denise, like most of their white working-class peers, abhor the notion of welfare, regarding it as the last resort of the lazy who lack initiative. Yet when Dakota stole to make months-late mortgage payments on the family's overleveraged ranch and Denise committed fraud to pay the bills her teacher's aide salary could not, their actions invoked the same type of condemnation and judgment that Dakota and Denise exercise against other women in prison. To say this out loud, though, would crumble the sturdy moral wall Dakota and Denise have built between themselves and the other incarcerated women who surround them.

Dakota and Denise speak most openly together when they are alone, stretched out in the bunk beds of their small cell and unable to see the emotions on each other's faces. They lie like this during lockdown, with each woman staring into space as her mind wanders far from the painted cement block walls. Bombarded as they are by constant news of everyday prison life in the kitchen, their solitary conversations are satellites orbiting the precarious universe they have created together. "So, I'm thinkin'," Denise ponders aloud as dust motes, illuminated by the fluorescent lights that hide nothing, float through the empty space between her top bunk and the wall.

"About the letter you got from your friend back home?" Dakota asks.

"Yeah," she sighs, elongating the word with a deep sigh. "Shelley wrote and told me about how the yard sale went. Finally, I just had to accept that my little house was going to go into foreclosure since my soon-to-be ex sure wasn't gonna keep up the mortgage payments. So, I wrote to my Mom and told her to just sell everything she could, my clothes, the furniture, the washer and dryer, and whatever else was inside, and get some money to take care of my daughter. What a train wreck. What a train wreck." She pauses, envisioning the contents of her almost-foreclosed home spewed onto the front yard's rocky dirt for inspection by all her neighbors. "Anyways, Shelley's letter said that Mom pretty much gave everything away. I guess she probably felt ashamed and just took whatever money people gave her when they came."

"Like a bunch of vultures," Dakota slowly intones, silently grateful that at least her family would try to make sure that everything she had worked so hard for as an accountant would not completely evaporate while she was in prison. They might lose the ranch, but at this point Dakota just tries not to think about that, like the restitution payments and court fees that she anticipates will soak up most of the money from any job she will be able to get after her release. "Denise, it's the money thing. At least she told you. That wouldn't be a pretty thing to just walk into ten months from now." Denise is silent, spellbound by the image of all her possessions carted away by neighbors, with little money to show for the shame of it. "Hey," Dakota forces the deep-throated laugh she uses when mocking others, in the hopes that Denise will not start crying again. With each passing day Dakota is less and less able to find the energy to manage other people's emotions.

"Hey, what?" Denise's small voice barely responds.

Dakota laughs again, a sharp, derisive sound. "Remember that time we went to Debtors Anonymous? Remember? What a mixed-up group! I said we should go, because we didn't have anything to do on Thursday nights, when they meet. There was that one, she was a habitual shoplifter and the last time the judge threw her in prison after she was caught for the umpteenth time at Walmart shoving camera equipment into her bag." Dakota can hear Denise shifting on the bunk above her, gathering her limbs around her pillow. She still swims freely in her empathy for others, sometimes because it distracts her from the feelings that crowd her own heart.

"Lemme think," Denise slowly continues as if her thoughts need time to catch up before she can speak at a normal pace. "Oh, Mariah, right. The one whose mother taught her to steal? That was pretty sad. I wanted to cry when she talked about stealing from the grocery store so she could give candy to the other kids so they would like her, and then later she did the same thing for her boyfriends, or sometimes just for fun."

"I bet it helped some of those women, though. That meeting, it just wasn't for us." Dakota nods, remembering the condescension she felt subjected to at the meeting. She felt that the meeting's structure implicitly asked her to work out the reasons she stole money, especially in a context where "because I was desperate and needed it" was thought to be symptomatic of her refusal to accept responsibility for her actions.

"Yeah," Denise intones, reconstructing the scene in her mind. "There were a couple who said those meetings were helping them to get better. Like Taylor, right? We see her on the second lunch shift and she nods at us sometimes. One thing that really stood out to me was when she said that before she came here she felt like she had to have a walk-in closet full of clothes with tags still on them and a hundred dollars in her pocket."

"Because you can have a walk-in closet and a hundred dollars in your pocket in prison?" Dakota derisively laughs. "Some of these women, come on." Denise laughs out loud, thinking of the constant stream of plans they overhear from their vantage point in the kitchen, where it sometimes seems as though every other woman she hears talking about the future is poised to start her own business or therapeutic program after her release. Everything seems so easy when there are no bills due, few demands on a woman's time, and an audience of bored women eager to listen, even if just as entertainment and fuel for the listeners' derisive conversations about her later. She remembers some elements of this occurring in the group as well, only in intensified form, as women pointed out what they saw as each other's weaknesses, whether because they genuinely wanted to help or because they saw an opportunity to denigrate others.

"One thing I really didn't like about that group," Denise reflects, "was how they would kind of beat up on each other by making some of the women feel stupid or greedy for making those mistakes. Their lives were so messed up that stealing was simply the only way out of a lousy situation and, ultimately, they got caught. I don't know if they meant to do that or it just happened."

"That's just prison though, right?" Dakota falls into the hard tone she uses in these conversations when Denise is being too sympathetic to other women. "There's that survival of the fittest kinda thing going on sometimes, even though as far as prisons go things are pretty easy in here."

Denise, now sitting against the concrete wall and pushing back her cuticles to make her nails look longer, disagrees. "I don't know, sometimes I feel like it's 'damned if you do, damned if you don't.' That's how I felt listening to their stories, didn't you? Because we both had it pretty darn easy compared to some of those other women. Like, think about that girl who was so proud that she stood up to her husband who was abusing her, but then she ended up in a homeless shelter with her kids. I didn't even know there were homeless shelters in Wyoming." Dakota laughs, this time at how naïve she and Denise were before they came to prison. "No kidding," Denise goes on. "Once I was in here, at about six months I guess it was that I felt like I had lived my whole life so naïve about what goes on in Wyoming. Before I just thought, you know, 'oh, there's some bad apple families that you avoid' and, 'well, if you do drugs and party and don't go to work you get what you deserve,' but holy cow, the poverty, the abuse."

"Don't you think it's just a matter of degree, though?" Dakota asks. "My ex was a drunk; the only difference between him and some of these women's boyfriends is that he could keep a job. I feel like if you cover it up good enough, and especially if it's alcohol or maybe even prescription drugs that you get legally, it's like it's different somehow."

"That's true," Denise concedes. "Oh yeah, but then it got super weird, right, like right before we decided that we'd just sit and play cards or read instead of going back. It just wasn't our thing. There was that woman, I don't even remember which one, who said she was 'addicted to money.' She said she would do anything for money. That didn't really come together for me. I don't think money is like drugs or alcohol. You need money to survive." Dakota thinks about the women they both know whose bodies are marked by long-term addiction, like Laycee, whose face and arms are covered in deep scars from picking at her skin under the influence of methamphetamine, or Keri, whose leg has a deep purple gash from an abscess that healed badly after she injected with someone else's used syringe. Those were women who had to hustle in ways that Dakota still finds almost unfathomable, unable to get over the innate revulsion she feels at how low such women had let themselves sink, willing to have sex with anyone in exchange for money to buy some toxic substance that wrecked their bodies and lives.

"You need money to feed your kids," Denise continues. "And when your kids and family are at risk, mamas will do just about anything. Remember Cindy? She started out stealing diapers and formula that she needed for her little boy. She'd take one of those big diaper bags into a store like Target or Walmart and fill it up, and when it was empty, she would do it again. But anything that starts out righteous can end up crooked, just like us. Geez, some of those women really just don't belong in prison."

"Because we do?" Dakota retorts.

Denise sounds defeated. "I don't know."

Dakota goes on. "I think you forgot the rest of Cindy's story. She never got caught stealing the formula, so she figured she could get away with stealing steaks, the big ones, tenderloins or whatever they're called, and selling them at half-price. That took some nerve, but then she ended up with a robbery charge and her boy in foster care."

"Well, money solves a lot of problems, let's face it," Denise says, smiling with a friendly wave to the correctional officer who knocks on their window and smiles back. "We both know that."

Dakota stretches her legs in front of her, hoping that count will end soon so she can watch television before bed in the day room. "Yeah," Dakota acknowledges, "but there's also some seriously poor decision making going on in here. Look, you know like when Ashlynn explains her whole crazy-ass story and it totally makes sense when you're listening and then you think about it a little bit and it's like, 'are you kidding me?' She makes it out like her husband abandoned her and their kids and there wasn't any money so, of course, what would any woman do in that situation, according to Ashlynn? Of course! Steal a bunch of money from your perfectly good job and then be just shocked when you don't win it back at the casino! Right! Why didn't I think of that, instead of just pretending like I was going to pay it back?"

Dakota's voice rises just a little before she finishes speaking, and Denise smirks, muttering, "Meanwhile, fifteen thousand dollars later."

Everyone knows gambling is a foolish way to make money, but it does make sense when Ashlynn reenacts the story of how she came to prison, mimicking the voices of the arresting officer, the judge, and other key players with such precision that it gives the women gathered around her chills. It is easy to imagine Ashlynn holding court in any number of jails prior to her arrival at the Wyoming women's prison, even though her story does not hold together under close scrutiny. Denise knows the feeling: "I can understand why Ashlynn did that, though. Family can be so shitty. With what I did, I think my way of getting back at my dad for not being around was to steal from him. I never thought he'd call the police on me. I felt bad after I did it and wrote him an e-mail apologizing, but wouldn't you know it, he turned that e-mail in to the police and cooperated fully with the investigation, so here I am with two felonies. And it's not like he doesn't have money, you know?"

"Believe me," Dakota says, "I thought things were bad before, but I'm really stuck now, with a felony. Who's going to hire me, a felon with a college degree who worked in the kitchen at the prison? There's a stigma that comes with going to prison and it's always going to be there, especially for us women."

Denise nods emphatically as she bites off a hangnail. "It's true. But that's also because women aren't usually the ones that are the drug addicts, the drug dealers, the violent offenders, y'know, the sex offenders, or any of that. So, for people to see us as those, they look at us as a disgrace, because we are supposed to be the wife, the mother, the daughter, the provider, all of those things, the homemaker. And when we're in here, we're not. Because we've committed such a crime to put us here, that makes us a failure. I am not a failure. I am not a failure and neither is any'a these girls. And I know that there's some of them that've been here, y'know, numerous times, and there are some that were in the wrong place at the wrong time that will spend a long time here. But I also know that they're not failures. They made a mistake, just like a man did."

After lockdown ends, Dakota and Denise drift into the day room, where they can watch television and look out at the snow accumulating on either side of the chain-link fence, already half-asleep by 7:00 p.m. because of their early-morning kitchen work. Slumped in the plastic molded chairs in front of the television, they listen passively as Skylar, DeeDee, and Alaine play cards while simultaneously engaging in monologues that occasionally intersect in some semblance of conversation. They dart from substance abuse to hard luck to chaotic families, and the result sounds to Dakota and Denise like a product of noisy minds and lives that condition a woman not to expect that anyone is listening to her anyway. The two groups of women do not acknowledge each other.

Before Dakota and Denise met women like Skylar, DeeDee, and Alaine, they did not know anyone who left school in junior high or had a baby at twelve years old or grew up on a compound with many children and women living in extreme isolation, even for Wyoming. As Dakota and Denise hear it, listening half-interestedly as their attention drifts from infomercials to a disjointed reality television show, the women sometimes seem to compete with one another for rights to the most heart-wrenching circumstances. They hear variations of the same story over and over again, a parade of sadistic events: childhood sexual abuse, addicted and disinterested parents, adolescent substance abuse, and a line of men with whom the women repeated these patterns after having their own children. Dakota and Denise know that on the outside it will be hard to be seen as one kind of person, a prisoner. But it makes them more uncomfortable when they see how the same roof covers such different life stories. When women with those kinds of families speak, a jagged hopelessness seeps into the room, sharp-edged and sad.

Skylar, who is eighteen, is frustrated that a judge forbade her from communicating with her older brother because he was a codefendant in the criminal conspiracy case that landed her in prison. For her, this is another instance of the litany of injustices the system meted out to her and her siblings. Squinting a little to read the numbers on the cards, Skylar says, to no one in particular, "My brothers and sisters were partying all the time, they started getting me drunk, and getting me high and stuff when I was eight, and we didn't have any supervision, we didn't have food a lot. I didn't have clothes that fit. I would have to steal clothes out of the lost and found bin at school. The only time my brother and I got to eat any kind of regular meals was at the school where they would give you food for free. Child services were always questioning us, I remember that. We were so afraid of getting split up that every day on our way to school we would make up stories about who watched us and what we had to eat, and none of it was true but because we were so close we were just terrified about getting split up."

Not explicitly responding to Skylar but still tentatively weaving connective tissue between their stories, DeeDee announces, "I almost finished school when I was in foster care. Now I'm trying to get my GED and it is *hard*."

Alaine immediately expresses her frustration that women need to complete a GED before they may be eligible for any jobs in the prison. Even though most jobs pay much less than a dollar an hour, these are highly coveted because they allow the women to buy their own snacks, hygiene products, makeup, and other items for sale in the commissary. This is particularly important for women like Alaine, who have no financial support from the outside. Alaine, who is thirty-five years old and has given birth to six children, says, "We don't get enough of schooling and I really, I don't like it. I really struggle in school and I need help, I need that extra help. I don't think that they push you young girls enough to get GEDs, but then they don't see how the girls struggle. Like me, I don't know how to read or write, I mean I do, but not enough to really do it on my own. It's just really hard when I'm in class and we're doing therapy papers, it's hard to take notes 'cause I don't know how to spell."

DeeDee, who is earnestly pursuing the card game, echoes Alaine with her own experience: "I got really frustrated in school and I ended up dropping out because I didn't get enough help. But here they throw the

GED thing at you and they're like 'you've got to get your GED,' but there are teachers and there are so-called tutors, which means other inmates in the facility. So that right there would be a good thing because a lot of the girls do struggle in school. They have second grade reading, third grade math, and that would be a help to them, more of that one on one. For me, I've noticed I can learn so much more one on one, than a teacher helping the whole class. Then this know-it-all and that know-it-all answer and don't even explain how they got the answers. I know you got the answer, but how?"

"Uno!" Skylar exclaims triumphantly, holding her last card defiantly in the face of DeeDee, who waves her away, eyes drifting to the television.

DeeDee, whose ten years of habitual methamphetamine use consumed most of her teeth, knows that others find her hard to understand when she speaks and so often gets upset when she perceives that others ignore her. "They don't teach you anything in here anyway," she says, and fixes her gaze on the television without leaving her seat. Skylar throws her one card onto the table and declares herself the winner.

Alaine nods. "I mean we have board games and stuff like that but when your husband's drunk and fighting with you you're not gonna say, 'hey, you wanna play a board game?' Or when your drug dealer comes to you and says, 'hey, I have some pills for you, I know you just got out, I wanna celebrate,' what do you say? 'Nope, I'm in sobriety, I have to go.'"

DeeDee laughs. "Better go call my P.O. and tell 'em what you did, better hope you're not on paper too, sucka."

Skylar looks down at the blue seven she just cast on the table, a conflicted expression knitting itself across her face. "No," she says, "that stresses us out when we're put in those predicaments. But like in here we don't learn about those, we are sheltered. And I'm not sayin' that's a bad thing, because I do think that you do need ta be sheltered from the storm before you can go out and clean it up. But I also know that you need to be aware of what the storm is." None of the women are particularly interested in anything anyone is saying, and a television announcer's voice from an advertisement targeted at people deep in credit card debt fills the temporary silence in the room.

"Debt, that's the real American way," Dakota says, to no one in particular, her comment unacknowledged by anyone in the room.

"I need to figure out how to do that, how to get a loan," Skylar says brightly. "I want to open an arthouse where everyone can come. I like the ocean, I like the environment that the ocean creates. And I wanna move into a community close to an art school, and I wanna offer that art community something where they can, like, kind of a forum. Somewhere where people in culinary school can have like a kitchen and we can offer, like, weekends where they can offer their entrees, people can come in, where they could enjoy wine, enjoy cheese. Kinda like a coffee house, I wanna own something like a forum. And that's kinda like what it will be called, the Forum or something, where artists could hang their paintings on the walls or musicians can come and play, get some audience time, stage time, poetry night."

"Here we go," Dakota whispers to Denise as Skylar continues describing her plans, the stream of consciousness ideas almost palpably bouncing unheard from what women have not had to what they want but, obviously, at least to Dakota, will never be able to achieve. Dakota wants to spit.

"Who's gonna pay for this, Skylar? Your no-good brother who sexually abused you like you cried about in group? And he'll do that when? When he gets out of prison?" Dakota and Denise stay silent about their frustration with what they see as other women's delusions about the future. Some days they feel ready to choke the next woman they hear talk about starting a llama farm, running their own drug treatment program, or other plans for which they are totally unprepared. Although it remains unspoken between Dakota and Denise, they know that these fantasies are the glue that holds some very fragile women together.

"Let's just get some sleep," Dakota sighs.

Denise smirks. "Hey," she winks at Dakota, "wanna play a board game?"

Bus Ticket to Nowhere

Lexi and Maggie have been awake for hours when they hear the early morning correctional officer assigned to their pod call their last names. "Get your things and report, ladies," she announces brightly as Maggie fakes a wide smile because she thinks that is what she is supposed to do when someone is nice to her. "Gosh, on your last day I thought you'd be pounding on the door waiting to get out of here." Maggie likes this officer, who lives on a nearby ranch with her husband and numerous children and works at the prison because it provides her family with health insurance and, in twenty years when she is able to retire, will give her pension benefits. Lexi does not like anyone, least of all on a day when the future is uncertain in a way that, when she was younger, might have seemed exciting. Now she hopes to never see this friendly officer, Maggie, or the inside of a correctional facility ever again.

"Where are you ladies headed? I don't know because you don't have to report to parole," the officer explains, making polite conversation as she waits for their transportation to arrive. Both women are leaving prison after killing their number, as the women call completing all sentencing requirements, and so prison staff does not need to have any information about their destination. Their conversation with the officer consequently has an informal, chatty tone that Maggie appreciates because of its marked difference from the usually more officious communication between staff and prisoners.

"My Dad is coming to get me," Maggie smiles. "I'm really, really nervous because I have to stay with my folks for a while and they're obviously not happy with me."

The officer smiles sympathetically and nods in silence before turning her eyes to Lexi and asks, "How about you? Where are you headed?"

"Nowhere," Lexi emphasizes, closely guarding a precious piece of information about her life just because she can.

"Well," the chatty officer continues, her posture visibly more relaxed than when she is walking through the prison and constantly attuned to information transmitted via the radio she wears strapped to her belt, "I hope that big snowstorm isn't blowing through Nowhere because it's sure headed our way. I might need to stay over here in town tonight because I think the roads are gonna close."

"Oh geez," Maggie says with genuine sympathy, as if the two are friends. Lexi already has a bus ticket from the nearest small town big enough to have a bus stop and has enough in her mandatory savings account to pay for three nights in a motel on the outskirts of a place that locals call "The Oil City," if she decides to stay there. She can see anxiety start to consume Maggie, who is picking nervously at the prison-issue grey sweatsuit and tennis shoes she is wearing into the world outside and feels lucky that she is on her own, rather than waiting to face the barrage of resentment and disappointment that she guesses await Maggie in her father's pickup truck outside the prison gates. Lexi much prefers the kind of silence that she will share with law enforcement as they drive her to the bus stop.

At thirty-three, Lexi feels an anger different from what she felt when she was younger and always on the lookout for opportunities to start a fight. Back then Lexi loved the hot immediacy of an altercation more than anything else, anticipating her opponent's next move by letting her body spontaneously react with fists, teeth, nails, limbs as weapons and hair, soft flesh, anything as her target. Prison, age, and hope's foreclosure have distilled her rage into a permanent low-frequency bandwidth that has kept others at a distance, where she prefers them. Lexi does not return Maggie's wave as she watches her get into the pickup truck, its windshield pitted from dirt-covered highways and ice, clutching a plastic bag with the knitted hats and other crafts that helped the vacuum of time disappear during her sentence. Maggie's stone-faced father barely acknowledges her, as if picking his daughter up from prison is a regular occasion, and Lexi smirks as she imagines counting down—five, four, three, two—until the inevitability of Maggie convulsing with sobs, an image that fills Lexi with contempt.

Lexi is on her own today, which is how she likes it. "Well, Lexi," the correctional officer says, making one last futile attempt at conversation as she watches Maggie and her father pull away from the prison parking lot, "I hope you'll make it out there. We don't want to see you or Maggie again." Expressionless, Lexi looks at the officer and says nothing. She has spent her life dealing with authority figures who say well-intentioned things without understanding how empty and hollow they sound to someone who has moved from one foster family to another before moving out on her own, living without any attachments. When Lexi heard women in prison talk about being a productive member of society, no matter how earnest they sounded, she often took a cold inventory of everything missing from her life that would never be there: money, formal education, family, social support, stability, belonging.

"Look, to be brutally honest," Lexi had told her case worker, "I'd rather stay in here and kill my number than have a P.O. out there. Being under supervision just ain't for me."

What Lexi does not say to anyone is that she has spent most of her adult life hitchhiking throughout the West with long-haul truckers and wants to get on the road again, preferably back toward Tacoma. She spent a few months there with some people running a squat in an abandoned building, eating what they foraged from grocery store dumpsters, the eerie glow of a half-dead flashlight illuminating phrases like "consumer death culture" spray-painted on the walls. Things do not always work out the way Lexi plans, but she loves the undefined possibilities that accompany crawling up into the passenger seat and, if she trusts the driver and he feels sorry enough for her, falling asleep in the single bunk at the back of the cab as the driver continues his purposeful charge down the interstate.

The rusty blue pickup truck carrying Maggie back to her disappointed family shrinks into the distance until it finally disappears behind a hill. Lexi knows that Maggie is unlikely to come back to prison since her family will envelop her in the kind of protective huddle that will prevent her from getting tangled up in some man's mess of a life all over again. Lexi envisions Maggie telling the story of how she ended up in prison to an earnest and slightly scared audience of small-town high schoolers, warning them not to get mixed up with the wrong man, and offering her own tearful regret as an example of what might happen if they do. Later some of the students will pose for pictures with her, stretching their phone-wielding hands away from their bodies almost as awkwardly as they embrace Maggie, an exotic representative of another world they hope never to enter themselves. Lexi would rather be dead than on display like that.

Lexi does not talk to the officer who transports her to the bus stop. Instead, she watches the sky steel up, preparing to unleash the ominous swirling white wall of a mountain winter. A solitary crow's stark blackness evaporates into the grey-white distance from its perch atop a highway sign, its flashing lights the only visible color for miles in any direction. "This must be what death looks like," Lexi think to herself as she wordlessly exits the vehicle, the first snowflakes melting heavily on her face as she boards the bus. She finds a seat at the back and slouches as far down as she can, cheek pressed against the window's coolness, bony knees in grey sweatpants pressed against the seat in front of her. She aligns her bus ticket with one of the squares on the patterned fabric of the seat next to her as she feels the familiar unwanted embrace of a panic attack tighten around her. Her breath congeals into hot white clouds on the glass as she tries to will the cool into her body against anxiety's cruel heat, breathing as deeply as she can while exhaling slowly and then, finally, collapsing into sleep.

Lexi opens her eyes to the otherworldly green, yellow, and white lights of an oil refinery shining against the night sky as the bus rolls into town, her face painfully cold from leaning against the window. She unfolds her limbs and straightens her spine against the hard seat so that she can watch the town's meager lights come into focus, half-disbelieving that within an hour she will be wearing street clothes in a town where no one knows her. Grasping the two hundred dollars of twenties rolled tight as a cigarette in her fist, Lexi ignores the snow that melts with her body heat through her tennis shoes into ice water on her skin and strides purposefully into the small-town Walmart. After shaking herself out of a brief, stunned stillness at how many different kinds of bras are on display, Lexi looks back at herself in the dressing room mirror: tight jeans, cheap imitation leather boots with a thick heel, lacy black stretch cotton top. She pulls it down a little so it shows off the tattoo on her breast of a skull wearing a motorcycle helmet, the one she got when she lived with a guy in Colorado who claimed to be a member of the Sons of Silence biker gang but spent most of his time tweaked out in their trailer while she bartended to pay the bills. Lexi smiles at herself. She looks good.

In the bathroom, Lexi stuffs the dead skin of her prison greys into the plastic bags she got at the checkout line and positions herself in front of the mirror, a fresh pack of menthols and a lighter stuffed neatly into a new bra, the kind with a wire that would be considered a potential weapon in prison. She gazes seductively at herself as she leans into the bathroom mirror to paint her eyes a dark, sparkly purple, highlighting the arch just below her eyebrow with a softer violet while suffused with pleasure at buying something directly from a shelf. In prison, commissary forms were due on Fridays at seven in the morning, and there were three kinds of eye shadow and three kinds of lipstick: light, dark, and medium. Lexi is impervious to the cold as she walks a half-mile into town, a bar's nondescript neon beckoning her as she extracts a cigarette from the pack inside her bra, her breath hanging white and indistinguishable from the smoke in the winter night's bitter snap. Purple lipstick leaves a lascivious lined arc on the cigarette's filter, its ember instantly extinguished as she drops it in the snow outside.

Awash in reddish gold light, Lexi sits down at the corner of the half-empty bar and orders a whiskey from a sour woman who casts a disapproving look at Lexi's breasts before turning to the disarray of liquor bottles behind her. Lexi pretends not to notice the man walking toward her, avoiding his steady gaze even as he sits down beside her. "My name's Luke," he says, finishing his beer before asking for another. "I believe I'm supposed to say, 'what's a pretty woman like you doing in a place like this?'"

Lexi raises one eyebrow, imagining her new eye shadow sparkling dramatically in the dim light of the bar. "I'm Lexi. And I believe I'm supposed to criticize your lack of originality?"

"I think it does go something like that," he nods, half-smiling and maintaining steady eye contact. Luke deepens his voice. "So, Ms. Lexi, what's a pretty woman like you doing in a place like this?"

"Just got out of prison," Lexi says, sucking on the last ice cube of her empty whiskey glass so he will get the hint and buy her another one, which he does.

His laughter is deep as he watches her face, then leans in with his beer as she stares back. "You're serious, aren't you?"

She continues to stare into his eyes, not blinking as she sips the whiskey, its warmth almost intravenous in its spread throughout her body, and then leans in to whisper in his ear, "I was in a real bad way with money problems, so I borrowed some money that I shouldn't have while I was bartending."

Luke looks sympathetic. "And I bet you cost the state of Wyoming a whole lot more than you stole." He takes a long, deep swig of his beer and Lexi cannot see his expression as he reaches into his plaid work shirt pocket, the buttons pearly and shining. "Listen, darlin'," he says, sliding two fifty-dollar bills deep into her new bra, leaving his fingers still and warm for a minute between her breasts, "I had a real good day at the stock auction. Go get yourself a room and get out of here. You want a ride somewhere?"

Snowflakes drift in through the truck's open window as Lexi inhales deeply on her cigarette, Luke steering through the big rigs lined up and sheltering from the winter storm at the truck stop's parking lot. "You sure this is where you wanna go, honey?" he asks, leaning his head slightly to the side with concern. Lexi nods sharply, thanks him quickly, and hops onto the snowy asphalt, hurrying inside the brightly lit convenience store with a row of red booths next to the windows. She slides into one, where she can watch the truckers come and go until she chooses one to ask for a ride. Lexi never asks women truck drivers for a ride because she has found them to be much more scrupulous about following rules against picking up hitchhikers like herself and avoids younger men because they usually want sex. She'll choose an older man, probably in his early fifties, old enough to own a nicer truck with a bed in the back but not so old that he will fall asleep while driving. It takes about thirty minutes before a man who fits the profile walks into the store, uses the bathroom, and then buys some beef jerky and an energy drink.

After she watches the man exit the store, she waits two minutes and follows him into the swirling snow, climbs onto the driver's side step, and waves. He rolls the window down slightly and narrows his eyes at her until she smiles, showing her teeth beneath the new purple lipstick. "Where y'headed, honey?" she asks, leaving her destination unspecified so she can make a graceful exit if she gets a bad vibe as they talk for a few minutes.

"Portland," he says matter-of-factly, his hand already on the gear shift in ways that indicate he is not much concerned whether Lexi joins him or not. "Comin'?"

"You bet," Lexi nods, and climbs into the cab.

Concluding Thoughts

Dakota, Denise, and Itzel, the main composite characters in this chapter alongside the more minor characters of KelliAnn, Lexi, and Maggie, all juggled competing narratives as they reconciled the realities of their lives with a prevailing moral-cultural ethos that denies the structural violence of rural poverty, sexism, and felony-related discrimination. Economic need, lack of social supports, and various forms of interpersonal chaos constantly threaten to upend the rickety stage on which most currently and formerly incarcerated women enact their lives. Yet prevailing rural socio-institutional and moral beliefs deny these uniquely gendered aspects of the women's experiences, which often involve untenable socioeconomic and interpersonal situations.

The currently and formerly incarcerated women in our study often grappled with the gulf between their everyday experiences and their individual, family, community, and social expectations for ways of living, working, and finding meaning in the world. For most currently and formerly incarcerated women, their economic situations prior to prison featured significant debt, childcare responsibilities, and restricted or even nonexistent possibilities for earning a living. There are women from all socioeconomic backgrounds in prison, although the more privileged, like KelliAnn from affluent Boulder, Colorado, are a distinct minority in comparison with poor and working-class women. While Dakota, Denise, and Maggie might all regard themselves as middle-class in a Wyoming context, their families exist on the brink of the kind of poverty that shapes the lives of Lexi and Itzel. All of these ostensibly middle-class families are just one serious injury, job loss, or missed payment on a mortgage or revolving line of credit to support the ranch away from financial and social ruin. In this context, it is not surprising that Dakota and Denise could justify their economic crimes as a temporary measure to stave off this undesirable fate. It is equally unsurprising that Itzel immediately recognizes KelliAnn's class and racial privilege and accordingly dismisses her as ignorant of the challenges that Itzel faces in her own life.

Economic crimes among the women in our study were often, but by no means always, tied to the compromised decision making that accompanies substance abuse, addiction, and mental health issues. Yet other women, as exemplified by Dakota and Denise, regarded themselves as essentially distinct from other prisoners because they regarded their economic crimes as a means to support their families, or please the men in their lives, typical tropes of white middle-class women in the contemporary United States. This follows other research in which women have been found to justify economic crimes as borrowing, assisting others, or meeting the needs of children or other loved ones (Grounds 2011; Coleman 2002; Klenowski, Copes & Mullins 2008). This is particularly significant in Wyoming, which ranks next to last in U.S. wage equality, with women concentrated in the poorly paid service sector in a region where costs of living require incomes far above the poverty level (Connolly 2016; Pearce 2016).

Women's economic, violent, and other crimes are always committed in particular socioeconomic contexts that shape their decision making. For instance, Itzel's violent assault against Dante, her baby's father, may appear quite brutal in the condensed version of events contained in a police report or court adjudication documents, and yet further consideration of the circumstances that surrounded it provide context to the long-term hopelessness, mutual intimate partner violence, and alienation that resulted in an altercation that lasted minutes and will impact her for the rest of her life. Dakota, whose accounting degree facilitated her economic crime, likewise dreaded the prospect of her family losing the ranch they had owned for generations to such an extent that she was willing to risk prison in her efforts to save it. As feminist criminologist Susan Sharp (2014) observed in her research at Oklahoma women's prisons, these adverse life conditions are only compounded by the challenges posed by the stigma of incarceration.

Yet once they have committed their crimes, women enter into a world of institutional norms that reflect the social conventions that shape life in the free world, which is certainly shaped by social constructions such as gender, class, race, and ethnicity. Feminist criminologists have accordingly critiqued gender-neutral correctional policies and procedures for decades, particularly when their practice requires more intensive policing of women's behavior (Bosworth 2007; Hannah-Moffat 1999). In Wyoming, currently and formerly incarcerated women were mixed in their perspectives on this issue. KelliAnn and her peers resoundingly critiqued what they regarded as a lack of practical skills-based training available in prison relative to the training provided to male prisoners, while others positively reflected on skills gained in therapeutic groups and classes, grateful that they existed at all.

Literature that critically engages with dominant narratives at work in carceral settings, as well as women's responses to these, accordingly emphasizes the complex social worlds women create to cope with being incarcerated. The sheer number of women who reside in close proximity to one another in a prison setting encourages women to form social groups and, in so doing, they sometimes recognize patterns at work in their own, as well as other women's, past histories. Dakota and Denise stay busy by working hard in the kitchen, filling up their days as much as possible, while Itzel tries to isolate herself from other women as much as possible. KelliAnn, who is accustomed to the benefits of both class and racial privilege, seeks status among the mostly rural prisoners by making claims to urban knowledge and lived experience that make her superior.

Prison emphasizes uniformity in almost every aspect of life, from the most mundane aspects such as clothing to the more abstract, such as policies issued by the Department of Corrections that are applied and interpreted by prison staff and prisoners alike to govern everyday life for the women. Yet even within—or perhaps because of—such uniformity, the women find ways to distinguish themselves from one another, whether through isolation, through the formation of particular social bonds to the exclusion of others, or through self-perceptions. Our findings reflect literature that emphasizes how women use a variety of coping mechanisms to do their time, including strategic self-presentation (McCorkel 2013), individual techniques to control or abate unwanted emotions rather than seek support from other women (Greer 2002), social bonds and friendships (Severance 2005), spirituality (Huey Dye et al. 2014; Ferszt et al. 2009), and food sharing (Smoyer 2015; de Graf & Kilty 2016).

As we have seen, women take divergent approaches to working and living in ways they regard as meaningful before, during, and after their time in prison. Some women, like Dakota and Denise, envision themselves as essentially separate from the majority of the prison population as a result of what they regard as significant differences in life experiences, work ethics, and social class. Others, like Lexi, avoid interacting with others because they prefer independence to the truncated institutional relationships that have been their long-term frame of reference. Like their free-world peers, incarcerated women build community through their jobs, places of origin, common experiences, and, of course, affinities. Yet incarcerated women's relationships with their peers differ significantly from those of women in the free world because of their enforced coresidence, which makes it impossible to avoid each other. This constant contact creates a familiarity that, for women like Itzel, makes some of the harder truths they may be reluctant to recognize almost impossible to avoid.

Following their release from prison, women continue to contend with the competing narratives that have, in most instances, structured their lives since long before they went to prison. Following their release, felony conviction–related stigma adds to the challenges they already face as women in rural areas where male-dominated jobs in resource-extraction industries generally exclude them and service-sector work does not pay a living wage. Maggie and Lexi were released from prison at the same time but took approaches to reentry that appear at face value to be quite different: Maggie retreats to her taciturn father, while Lexi uses her sexuality to receive assistance from random men she meets, first at a small-town bar and then in a long-haul semi that will take her far from Wyoming. As is all too often the case, both women's reentry plan took a male form that offered limited possibilities for meaningful life changes.

The gendered strategies followed by so many rural women released from prison result in situations very similar to those of their urban counterparts in the level of surveillance entailed in community efforts ostensibly designed to support them that nonetheless result in increased, diversified forms of surveillance (Flores 2016; Morris 2016). Even as women like Lexi seek to physically distance themselves from the prison in a way that feels like freedom, other women, like Itzel, seek freedom in intimate relationships that they desperately hope will change for the better. Both groups of women are betting against tremendous odds in doing so.

This problem is further compounded by the fact that correctional norms, like those in the free world, esteem individualism in ways that do not reflect the structural conditions of women's lives (Sered & Norton-Hawk 2014; Haney 2010). What most women learn in prison, accordingly, is that some aspect of their inner selves or thought process is fundamentally flawed but can be fixed by following a series of steps recommended in a class, a workbook, or a particular approach to addictions treatment. The central problem with this approach, as so many feminist criminologists have argued before us, is that it individualizes what are profoundly structural problems. Yet, in all fairness, such critics rarely acknowledge the constraints facing correctional professionals, who are tasked with measuring outcomes based on very narrow parameters for success and failure, including test scores, course completion, and, of course, recidivism rates. These parameters are indisputably individual in nature, just as convictions and sentences are served by individual prisoners. Nonetheless, focusing so intently on individual outcomes obscures the reality that women in prison have much in common with respect to their struggles prior to, during, and after their incarceration. As we will see in the next chapter, interpersonal and structural violence is one of the most common of these shared themes in the lives of women who have been to prison.

3

Violence Has Flow

Earl Jr. and Janea lie motionless together in the stiff brown grass and listen, their southern eyes fixed on the western cloud ceiling gathered overhead. Here, surrounded by such vastness, the fragility and temporality of her place on earth continues to shock Janea in its absoluteness. Sky aligns with the treeless landscape, making the entirety of the prairie within her field of vision a finite stage. Sometimes Janea thinks she could keep walking until she fell off the edge, adrift in stars and velvet blackness. The slow but endless waves of cloud whiteness rippling over the late summer sky's cold blue fills them with the existential rocking of motion sickness, but still they stare, imagining themselves hidden at the bottom of a waterless ocean. Giant grasshoppers rustle and buzz around them with sounds as if they are trapped in thin paper, their movements amplified by the dryness of resolute prairie grass rising, bent and sharp, from deeply cracked brown-red soil. She wonders if there will be fires again this August.

John Ray's eight-year-old shadow spins around them in dizzy circles, grasshoppers' wiry leaping extending a wide swath from his path. He collapses next to them, his labored breathing and bony arms likely to flail out for little reason, prompting Earl Jr. to whisper harshly, "Don't get too close to Mama. You know she's hurtin' again." Framed by her boys, Janea wishes they could all disappear as she listens, still alert for the sandy cascading sound of a rattlesnake's tail that would make their eyes frantically dart across the dirt-brown that surrounds them in search of the snake to determine the best direction for their cautious, almost motionless, retreat. John Ray squirms next to her, his tiny fingers scratching at the rising red lines where the prairie grass's sharp edges have scraped his skin. Now that his big brother and father have told him dozens of times, he knows he is not supposed to touch his mother, not even to fall asleep next to her.

John Ray sighs, sitting up and itching where the grass touched him. "Is Daddy in the trailer?" he asks before trapping a sinewy grasshopper in his loose little fist.

Janea closes her eyes and Earl Jr. speaks for her, using the words she has said to them countless times. "It's not a trailer, John Ray. It's a mobile home. Only white trash live in trailers, and we're not white trash."

When Janea falls into the kind of deep, bottom-of-a-lightless-lake sadness that threatens to permanently anchor her to its peaty floor, she imagines her boys calling her from the shore and mightily struggles back to the surface, exhausted from the effort. Sometimes her thoughts pull her under again until she is gasping for the air of the present, jarred back to life by, "Mama, you listenin'?" It scares her when this clear-voiced admonition is accompanied by a tone of real fear and concern by boys who can sense their mother slipping away from them. Sometimes she hears their father's perpetual annoyance with her, as in this morning's "Mama, you listenin'? Them grits is burnin'!" from Earl Jr. At other times she hears a growing consciousness of their shared terror of Earl, a creeping maturity in the boys who have begun to observe differences between other children's parents and their own. "Mama, you listenin'?" John Ray asked her. "I don't want Daddy to hurt you no more."

Janea feels a boundless sense of helplessness when she hears these earnest statements from her sons, whose love for her is absolute. She inventories all the things they have to make the helplessness abate, to feel that staying with Earl lets her give the boys things that she never could on her own, not with no education and her only work experience confined to a cash register. Janea counts, marveling that they own everything that they have so that her boys will never feel the ominous sense of dread that she and her sister used to feel when the repo man would pull into their driveway with his empty van, leaving in his wake a sad, empty space where the television used to be. She counts the fifteen feet she can walk between the double-wide mobile home's two sides and the eighty-five feet spanning the little kitchen to the big bedroom where she sleeps with Earl. Janea knows the exact location of every object in each one of the three bedrooms and two bathrooms in their home, the bottom of which is framed by brown imitation wood latticework to cover its wheels and give the illusion of a foundation. She knows every toy strewn under her boys' bunk beds, every minor scratch in the sliding glass doors they use as a big window because there are no steps leading down to the ground below the trailer, every videocassette tape stacked neatly next to the rear-projection television they bought with cash.

"Is Daddy in the mobile home?" John Ray repeats with eight-year-old sincerity, this time using his mother's preferred choice of words.

"God damn it, John Ray, it's like he heard you," Earl Jr. hisses at his little brother, his voice full of resentment. "Here he comes."

Janea still winces when she turns her head to see Earl strutting toward them, his sinewy features a dark blur in the sun. Earl Jr. moves as close as he can to her without touching.

"Get out of the way, boy," Earl says as he nudges his older son with his heavy boots, his tone immediately losing its hard edge as he says to Janea, "I want to sit by my beautiful wife on my land."

"Mama don't like grasshoppers," John Ray chirps to his father. Accustomed to being ignored, he proudly adds anyway, "I'm catching them so they don't scare her."

"Your Mama's from Dallas, she ain't never going to get used to country life," Earl intones, "not with a redneck like me. No how. Ain't that right, sugar?"

Janea is glad she has the physician's instructions to avoid speaking as an excuse to not reply. She winces as she turns to make eye contact with him so he will not get angry because he thinks she is ignoring him. Two more weeks until the wires can come out of her broken jaw. He kisses her on the forehead and then gets up to walk away. Janea and the boys feel the slow release of pressure unbinding from their chests as they breathe together, happy to hear the sounds of his footsteps retreating and the door of their home closing behind him. They are now a year into life in Wyoming, a move Janea had hoped would calm Earl's anger. When he still worked on offshore oil rigs in the Gulf of Mexico, she would have two weeks alone with the boys followed by two weeks of tension when Earl was home again, complaining nonstop about the insults of having a boss, the inadequacy of all the other workers, and, of course, his own frustrated greatness. Now that Earl is a Wyoming drill rig supervisor, he is home every night with a new set of complaints: the weather, lazy workers, boredom, anything. Sometimes Janea wonders if anger is what keeps Earl alive.

John Ray opens his loose fist and the grasshopper springs free into the prairie grass. "Mama, you listenin'?" he repeats. "Why does Daddy get so mad at you?"

Janea knows what she would tell John Ray if it did not hurt so much to speak. She would tell him that she loves him, that his Daddy loves him, and that she will not let anything bad happen to him. Part of her is glad that she cannot talk because she thinks she would dissolve into tears, her sobs making her jaw hurt even more. She always hopes that the boys will forget their fights, but this last one, two weeks ago, was the worst ever, and now Janea is heartbroken that the time it will take her jaw to heal forced her to quit the job it took so many years for Earl to say yes to, and now only because the boys were both in school all day. Janea loved being the only cashier at one of the little stores in the town a mile down the road, close enough for her to walk or get a ride from a coworker so as not to bother Earl. Janea's job was the first time that she felt she had friends since she left Dallas, even if those friends were really only her customers: coal miners, railroad workers, and other townsfolk who liked her southern accent and effusively friendly way of interacting with them as they bought groceries, lottery tickets, and gasoline. It helped that they were really only strangers since she was by now an expert at making excuses for bruises, missed days of work, and other parts of life with Earl that were now normal for her, including the unspoken knowledge that one day he would probably kill her.

The physician on call at the small-town emergency room looked unsurprised when Earl explained that she had tripped over the laundry basket while hanging clothes outside and fallen face-first into the dirt. Earl Jr. had stayed stone-faced in the emergency room, keeping his little brother occupied with a book. They were both big enough to know not to say anything, and now Earl Jr. was mature enough to explain things to his little brother. "They'll take you away from me if you say anything," Earl Jr. still remembers his mother telling him years ago. Janea and the boys are still silently reeling from this last fight, and although they do not discuss it, they all remember its fragmented chaos, the boys screaming, smoke furiously hissing from the skillet on the kitchen stove, her lying on the kitchen floor pulsating with jagged pain. Janea remembers watching Earl walk away from her, his frame divided into the quadrilateral spaces in the latticework separating the kitchen from the living room, her eyes on a pool of hot grits congealing on the linoleum next to her. "I better clean that up," she remembers thinking to herself before she lost consciousness, "before Earl gets mad."

"Mama, you listenin'?" John Ray repeats, another sinuous grasshopper buzzing in his loose fist. "I asked you a question, Mama."

"Your Daddy and I love you," Janea says, wincing with every word.

"Well, that ol' cuss scares me," Earl Jr. says, angry enough to spit, his soft mouth twisted into a tight little knot as he stares at the cloud waves above them. "And I wish he was dead."

Janea starts awake in the fuzzy grey half-light, the bunk above her slowly coming into focus as she tries to catch her frantic breath to avoid waking her cellmate. Her boys are safe now, she reminds herself by turning to the mailed photographs of John Ray and Earl Jr. holding their own beautiful children. Twenty-eight-year-old Earl Jr. is building a sand castle on the beach in Honolulu, where he works at the Pearl Harbor–Hickam military base, and John Ray is standing in his Marine Corps uniform with his wife and their new baby. Her rapid heart rate starts to slow as she reviews the pictures taped to the cell wall, where she wakes and falls asleep to them. Once a year, when they come to visit her on leave, she can hold her grandchildren as they eat candy and soda her sons buy from the visiting room's vending machine.

For Janea, the story of how Earl Walker III from Galveston, Texas, came to be buried in a little Wyoming town's cemetery is now a seventeen-year-old blur of sounds and images: the stark burst of a single shot from the hunting rifle, a sanguine ocean soaking the double-wide's thin carpet, and the local public defender telling her that she had no police reports or other evidence to prove that she had been a victim of domestic violence. After all, the public defender told her, she could have left at any time.

Women as Victims and Perpetrators of Violence

The jagged yet daily currents of violence Janea experienced flow through the lives of many incarcerated women, often by starting with their families of origin and continuing through their relationships with intimate partners and children, some of whom the women also perpetrate violence against in various forms. To understand and critically examine the prevalence of violence in the women's lives, this chapter engages with three primary bodies of literature: incarcerated women's experiences with violent victimization, rural women and intimate partner violence, and women as violent perpetrators. The first primary area, incarcerated women's experiences with violent victimization, analyzes how sociolegal and interpersonal forms of gendered violence impact the women's lives and their experiences with incarceration. The second area, rural women and intimate partner violence, emphasizes the unique challenges facing abused women in rural areas, including lack of services, heteropatriarchal cultural norms, and the feminization of poverty. Women as violent perpetrators, the third area, critically engages with the contexts and circumstances in which women commit violence.

Research on incarcerated women's experiences with violent victimization underscores how currently and formerly incarcerated women often have extensive histories of abuse, often beginning at a young age, that can combine with substance abuse and socioeconomic marginalization to create an intergenerational cycle of criminal justice system involvement. The U.S. Department of Justice (2015a and 2015b) estimates that 85% of victims of intimate partner violence are female, with women much more likely than men to be assaulted by someone they know. Women have a higher lifetime prevalence of severe physical violence in comparison with men, are less likely than men to escape from a violent relationship, and almost always sustain greater injuries than men in violent relationships (Breiding, Chen & Black 2014). Evidence suggests that violence plays an even more significant role in the lives of incarcerated women, as a striking uniformity of experiences exists among incarcerated women worldwide with respect to violence perpetrated by family members and intimate partners, self-injury, compromised mental health, substance abuse, and fractious family dynamics, which foster a cycle of criminal justice involvement that only further penalizes the women (Malloch & McIvor 2013).

Such uniformity of experience occurs across U.S. states, with nearly all women prisoners in Georgia experiencing at least one violent traumatic life event (Cook et al. 2005), 70% and 50% of incarcerated Ohio women, respectively, experiencing rape and childhood sexual abuse (McDaniels-Wilson & Belknap 2008), half of all midwestern women prisoners reporting sexual victimization with enduring emotional effects (Walsh, DiLillo & Scalora 2011), and women prisoners in Rhode Island experiencing a significantly greater lifetime prevalence of sexual victimization than women who were not under correctional control (Raj et al. 2008). The result is that some of the women who participated in our study regard prison, as did women in a southeastern state prison, as "the safest place I've ever been," underscoring the violent experiences and other social harms that shape their lives in the world outside prison walls (Bradley & Davino 2002).

Abused young women and girls are at increased risk of substance abuse, violent or antisocial behavior, early pregnancy, and compromised mental health (Bender 2010), especially when abuse occurs frequently and takes multiple forms (Finkelhor et al. 2005). In fact, the "sheer number of victimizations was a better predictor of symptomatology than any particular type of victimization" (Finkelhor et al. qtd. in DeHart 2008: 1375). Violence appears to have a dose-response effect such that as the number and severity of violent events increase, the impact on survivors becomes markedly worse, with women raised by parents in violent or unequal relationships likely to repeat these patterns in their own adult lives (Brewer-Smyth 2004; Campbell 2002). Children whose currently or formerly incarcerated parents struggle with "packages of risk"—consisting of violent behavior, addictions, and socioeconomic marginality—suffer impacts that "appear outsized in [their] effects on child wellbeing—relative to consequences stemming from the experience of parental incarceration itself" (Giordano & Copp 2015: 258).

These realities may lead to increased social marginalization early in life, with young offenders inclined to form strong friendship bonds with other young people who have similar histories, resulting in a very limited social sphere that fosters a fatalistic, fixed worldview that inhibits personal growth (Boeck, Fleming & Kemshall 2006). Such a worldview envisions society as a hostile place in which individuals must use violence to attain self-respect, as was found in research with young Scottish women prisoners (Batchelor 2005). Involvement in the illicit drug and prostitution economy exacerbates this sense of alienation from dominant cultural norms and society more generally due to mistrust of police and reliance on extrajudicial (and often violent) modes of problem solving. For instance, a Minneapolis and Baltimore survey of 102 women offenders who had experienced 148 sexual assaults while involved in the illicit drug and prostitution economies described their decision to avoid reporting these assaults to police because they did not wish to discuss it, felt they would not receive assistance, or feared violent street repercussions from sharing information with police (Carbone-Lopez, Slocum & Kruttschnitt 2016).

Given the reality that incarceration, substance abuse, and related social problems often span generations, experiences with violent victimization dramatically impact the approximately two thirds of incarcerated women who have children, 62% of whom they lived with prior to their incarceration (U.S. Dept. of Justice 2010; Malloch & McIvor 2013). State and federal legislation, such as the federal Adoption and Safe Families Act of 1997, enables state agents to initiate termination of parental rights if a child has been in foster care for fifteen of the previous twenty-two months (U.S. Congress 1997), making permanent parental separation a reality for many children of incarcerated mothers. For rural women, these challenges can be exacerbated by cultural norms that promote a culture of silence surrounding violence against women.

Literature on rural women and intimate partner violence emphasizes how violence against women is enabled by restrictive hetero-patriarchal gender norms and small-town social-control mechanisms. It also discusses how rural women cope with intimate partner violence in conjunction with a lack of services and, where services are available, intense stigmatization associated with seeking them out. Violence against women is a serious problem in both rural and urban areas, yet research demonstrates that rural victims of intimate partner violence may be at a significant disadvantage relative to their urban counterparts. One survey comparing the perspectives of urban and rural services providers in North Carolina and Virginia found that rural services providers reported greater limitations with respect to community support, access to relevant training, staffing, and ability to meet client needs (Eastman & Bunch 2007).

Rural intimate partner violence occurs in contexts characterized by small-town social-control mechanisms that prioritize preservation of status quo community relations, including gender norms that may tacitly or even explicitly endorse violence against women (DeKeseredy & Schwartz 2009). Such norms limit women's income-earning potential, development of support networks, and abilities to be self-sufficient in ways further inhibited by a violent husband or intimate partner whose need for power and control further marginalizes the women, as researchers working with poor rural southern women have observed

(Farber & Miller-Cribbs 2014). In her study of violence in Appalachian women's lives, Patricia Gagné (1991) argued that violence against women only works as a mechanism of control within relationships if broader cultural and economic forces sanction men's domination of women.

Findings from the New York State Adirondack Mountain region indicate that rural women may isolate themselves from family and community to avoid their own or their abusive partner's involvement with a criminal justice system that may not be able to meet their needs (Roush & Kurth 2016). Women in the rural South likewise express concerns about limited police and medical responses to violence against them (Shuman et al. 2008), with one Kentucky study indicating that police and local communities actively reproduce rural women's subordinate status (Websdale 1998). Alaska Native women residing in domestic violence shelters regarded violence and responses to it as totalizing byproducts of community isolation, extreme weather, limited or poorly trained police, substance abuse, gun ownership, lack of public services such as transportation and affordable housing, dependency on public assistance due to a restricted job market, and a lack of trained mental health professionals to counsel perpetrators and victims of abuse (Shepherd 2001).

This situation appears to be worse for rural women with criminal records, who may fear police contact or mistrust the criminal justice system as a result of negative previous experiences. A Kentucky study of 709 urban and rural women who obtained protective orders against an abusive male partner found that rural women struggling with addiction, loneliness, limited social supports, illegal activities, and a history of criminal justice system involvement were more likely to be arrested within twelve months of obtaining a protection order against an abuser than their urban counterparts (Lynch & Logan 2015). Connections between intimate partner violence and male peer support emerged strongly in a rural Ohio study with women who had been sexually assaulted by a former intimate partner. Survivors of such abuse noted its widespread but tacit cultural endorsement through rural sex-segregated practices such as hunting culture, widespread gun ownership relative to urban areas, and patriarchal masculinity connected to notions of gender norms that mandate women's economic dependence on, and subservience toward, men in ways that would be regarded as impractical and outdated in most urban areas (Hall-Sanchez 2014). Yet researchers also caution that rurality is just one aspect to consider in intersectional analyses of violence against women, lest such research be misused to reinforce dominant cultural stereotypes about rural people as "backward, dumb, and violent hillbillies" (Sandberg 2013).

Rural women actively attempt to overcome these challenges with the tools and resources available to them. One study identified twenty-one separate strategies rural midwestern women used to reduce or end intimate partner violence in their lives, most of which relied on individually developed escape plans or attempts to end the relationship rather than access the legal system, a decision the researchers attributed to rural values of self-sufficiency as well as rigid gender norms (Anderson, Renner & Bloom 2014). A comparison of barriers to rural and urban Kentucky survivors of sexual assault noted that rural women were much more likely to feel that investigating cases of violence against women was a low priority for police and that only women with prominent local connections would receive proper attention (Logan, Stevenson & Jordan 2005).

Hetero-patriarchal gender norms, limited education, economic dependence on an abuser, low self-esteem, and concerns about privacy were all cited by rural Pennsylvania primary care physicians as reasons for low rates of disclosure about intimate partner violence among patients (McCall-Hosenfeld et al. 2014). Similarly, rural women in New Mexico who successfully left abusive relationships, rather than taking a short respite from them in a shelter, also had more socioeconomic resources at their disposal and fewer struggles with mental health and poverty (Krishnan et al. 2004). The relationships between intimate partner violence and decision making are complex; a survey of 548 rural Iowans found that men and women indicated a complex relationship among mutual intimate partner violence, emotional abuse, and depression, with men and women who physically abused their partner 17.5 and 11.5 times, respectively, more likely to also be victims of physical violence, and 3.0 and 2.4 times more likely to report depression (Renner et al. 2014).

Literature on women as perpetrators of violence encompasses work that critically engages with gender stereotypes about women and violence, self-injury, and the impact that women's previous experiences of violence and compromised mental health may have on their own violent actions. Researchers note that while media and other dominant cultural forces periodically draw attention to supposed increases in violent crimes committed by women, such accounts are usually sensational, as historically women have committed and now continue to commit only a small percentage of violent crimes (Pollock & Davis 2015). Moving beyond one-dimensional portrayals of women's violence as an epidemic on the rise or the actions of a small minority of unstable "bad" women requires situating women's violence in the context of the cumulative victimization that emerges from abuse, poverty, sexism, and other marginalizing social forces that considerably constrain women's choices (Wesely 2006).

Yet scholars also caution against essentialist depictions of women's violence as a direct product of victimization, as women's reasons for committing violent crimes can be as wide-ranging as men's. A Minnesota study with incarcerated women found that jealousy, self-defense, disrespect, and a desire for illicit gain were present in many of the women's explanatory accounts of their own violence, but that such violence takes place "at the intersections of disadvantage that make violence a rational act for women, as well as men" (Kruttschnitt & Carbone-Lopez 2006: 345). Throughout these wide-ranging explanations runs a pattern of some self-blame or internalization of worthlessness: incarcerated women are more likely than their male peers to engage in self-injury through cutting or other measures, with an English study reporting that women prisoners self-injure at thirty times the rate of their peers outside prison and do so in part to exercise a sense of agency over the body that otherwise feels under total control by others (Chamberlain 2015). A Canadian study similarly argued that, as a practice among women prisoners, self-injury demonstrates a complex balance of agency and their often-extensive experiences as victims (Kilty 2006).

Women arrested for domestic violence offenses differ from male batterers because women cause less harm to their partners and are often acting in what they perceive to be self-defense. In addition, women's arrest rates for intimate partner violence increased in states that require police to make an arrest when called to the scene of a domestic dispute (Miller & Meloy 2006). This policy seemingly would demonstrate the seriousness with which police take this crime as well as allow the victim to be at least momentarily away from the violator, giving her an opportunity to consult with advocates. Feminist scholars critique such mandatory arrest policies, however, on the grounds that these replicate a status quo that disproportionately disadvantages poor women by prioritizing arrest and incarceration rather than transformative interpersonal and community solutions (Bumiller 2008; Crenshaw 1991; Goodmark 2012; Miller 2005).

Women who murder abusive intimate partners are likely to do so after years of violence that exerts a cumulative, totalizing impact on their psyche, leaving them feeling hopeless, defeated, and in a permanent state of anxiety. Identified as Battered Woman Syndrome by Denver psychologist Lenore Walker in her 1979 book of the same name, this psychological illness may lead some abused women to seriously harm or even kill their abuser. While Battered Woman Syndrome is a powerful example of the negative impact of women's previous experiences with violence on their mental health, unless counterattack follows attack within hours, self-defense justifications require a skilled legal team and expert witnesses to stand in court. Most abused women lack access to such resources, and even without a history of violence or criminal justice system involvement, a majority of women who kill their abusers in self-defense receive lengthy first- or second-degree murder convictions (Leonard 2002).

Women who kill their partners appear to have three characteristics that distinguish them from the larger group of all abused women: they have been the victim of more violence at greater frequency, they have fewer educational or employment resources, and they are in longer-term relationships that often involve marriage and children (Block 2003). Similarly, a European study with late-onset female offenders whose sole vulnerability was to an abusive partner found that isolation is a common trait among such women, making it difficult for service providers or other community members to reach them because they do not have the kind of "high-risk" profiles shared by their peers with long histories of criminal justice system involvement (Nuytiens & Christaens 2015). Likewise, women who murder their children are often struggling with extreme isolation and untreated mental health issues that make them difficult to identify as "at-risk" (Meyer & Oberman 2001).

Somewhat curiously, studies of violence in women's prisons remain largely confined to sexual assault and sexual coercion, most often in response to correctional institutions' needs to comply with the federal

Prison Rape Elimination Act of 2003. Such studies emphasize the role of prison living units in regulating or curtailing violence that emerges from ongoing tensions, limited postrelease opportunities, and limited mental health treatment (Owen 2008) and the importance of addressing sexual misconduct by prison staff (Kubiac, Hanna & Balton 2005; Owen & Wells 2005). Taken together, literature on currently and formerly incarcerated women as victims and perpetrators of violence emphasizes the complex origins and manifestations of such violence.

Our findings build on this literature. We argue that rural gender and community norms, substance abuse, and limited social capital discourage women in abusive relationships from help seeking by trapping them in cycles of violent dysfunction that they can feel powerless to stop. To substantiate this argument, we draw on descriptive accounts of how women situate their understandings of these violent dynamics within the rural terrain in which they almost always lived before coming to, and to which they generally plan to return after, prison. We explore connections between women's incarceration and their experiences with social isolation, violent or neglectful family and other interpersonal relationships, and substance abuse, the latter often constituting a problem-solving strategy the women observe or learn very early in life. Following women through their everyday routines in prison as they form support groups and reflect on their relationships with others, we also document their efforts to engage in relationship-related perspectival shifts, including the symbolic weight with which some women describe mothering as a lifeline to the future.

Wanna Play a Board Game?

Icy clouds of her own exhaled breath suspended in front of her, Itzel glides across the walking path framed on either side by exposed earth and frozen sage. She walks as fast as she can, arms pumping to forcefully propel her forward, breathing deep and hard as she tries to engage every part of her body in order to free her mind from the starkness of the tiny outdoor world she is allowed to enter. The barren nothingness of the landscape she can see through the chain link fence still shocks her when she squints to bring it into focus between hexagons of wire and sees only brown winter-dormant scrub-steppe sharply conjoined on the horizon with the wide, cloudless sky's brilliant blue. Itzel remembers circling the vast green yard in vibrant conversation with other Spanish-speaking women from her neighborhood at the Denver Women's Correctional Facility while serving an eight-month sentence there right after she turned nineteen. Denver's yard felt alive, with women congregating in small groups at outdoor tables watching each other being watched by tall, handsome correctional officers who could joke in Spanish with the women, whose eyes sometimes worked a cautious glissade across the men's lean muscles.

Now everything that surrounds Itzel feels bitterly cold: the monolingual English speakers unashamed of knowing nothing of the world beyond their insular little towns, the cafeteria's reconstituted tasteless potatoes, and the harsh institutional silence punctuated only by the bare necessities of human communication: radio voices choking from correctional officers' belts, the public-address system's electronic hiss and boom, and the women chattering emptily to one another about the constrained universe of both their prison and their free-world lives. Walking the yard at the women's prison in Denver, Itzel could hear so many different English and Spanish dialects and ways of speaking among people from so many different cultures. There were white, Latina, Latino, and African American case workers with graduate degrees whose English and Spanish words seemed expensive in the weight and consideration they used to select them. There were women prisoners who also spoke this way because they had been teachers, bankers, and other types of professionals before coming to prison. Women who worked the streets of East Colfax Avenue, irrespective of their ethno-racial identities, had a culture all their own derived from the illicit drug and prostitution trade and had disarming ways of speaking that made even the shyest or most suspicious person open like a flower.

So many different people, Itzel says to herself as she tries to focus her mind elsewhere. During lockdown in the Denver women's prison, music danced from almost every one of the women's cells as Itzel lay on her bunk listening to the commingling of hip-hop, salsa, cumbia, ranchera, and country and western music at low volumes echoing through the institutional halls. In the Wyoming prison women wore headphones, as if music was a private conversation no one else should overhear. Itzel walks as quickly as she can without attracting attention from the half-dozen other women she rapidly passes as they slowly stroll on the small walking path in conversation with one another. Memories she tries to suppress flail helplessly within the sticky web of obsessive thoughts, even as she struggles to focus her thoughts on a single cohesive set of memories that do not involve her ill-fated first visit to Wyoming with Dante six months ago, the last time she saw him or anyone else she cares about.

Denver now exists in a parallel universe of expensive short phone calls, occasional letters, and constantly replayed scenes from her life: her now eight-month-old baby's birth, violent altercations with Dante about meth and money, and, most of all, the car trip two hours north of Denver to Cheyenne that changed her life forever. Itzel tries every strategy she learned in groups at the Denver women's prison to block out these intrusive memories that hungrily devour the present and leave her exhausted, her body aching from the stress of trying to contain her thoughts and avoid falling into a psychological morass from which she fears she could not escape. She tries envisioning her obsessive thoughts in hermetically sealed metal boxes hurled into a bottomless ocean, focusing on her body's movements at she circles the small walking path, and counting her heartbeats to center herself.

Nothing works. Ad infinitum, Dante's red-wheeled white Camaro hurtles north onto Interstate 25, the tall buildings of the Denver skyline erratically backlit by a Rocky Mountain summer lightning storm. Itzel hates this car, which cost more than a down payment on the house she suspects that she and Dante will never buy together. She hates the hours she spends watching through the window of their thin-walled apartment as she paces back and forth trying to calm their new baby, waiting for Dante to pull into the parking lot or to finish meticulously cleaning it to remove dirt she cannot see. As Dante retreats into the seductively high-shine, spotless realm of the red-wheeled white Camaro, Itzel is choking on creeping squalor and metaphysical dirt she senses all around her. She sees it in the eyes of people who come to her home to buy methamphetamine from her baby's father, she hears it in the shouting matches and police sirens outside her building, and she smells it in the sticky stale smell of marijuana and cigarette smoke seeping through the electrical outlets and vents as she and her baby try to sleep when Dante is gone for days at a time.

"*Merecemos una vida mejor*! We deserve a better life," she sobs in two languages for emphasis before Dante can fully open the door; he has to push to get past her and enter the apartment. A swell of emotions and hurt gathers momentum in her heart, rising over even the exhaustion of finally getting the baby to sleep as he walks past her, head lowered, muttering, "*¿Quien?*" he asks—*who*—as if he is not part of the we she shares with the baby, before catching her in a bitter, narrow-eyed stare and adding in English, "It's probably not even my baby." Itzel stares back and, caught once again in the constant current feedback loop of their shared anger and betrayals, their words start out in whispers that will not wake the baby, neither of them really listening to each other as they repeat the same accusations and list the insults they have suffered. Within a few minutes he has shoved her, or she has scratched him, or they have escalated together into the kind of fight that breaks something or leaves marks that attract sidelong glances from strangers and take time to heal. Sometimes he spits on her as the baby's piercing wail, like a high-pitched fire alarm, disentangles them because the landlord said that people are complaining about the noise.

Itzel knows that methamphetamine is not the only reason why she and Dante are living this way, although it is their only source of income and dealings with it consume most of his time. As they sit together in the red-wheeled Camaro, her eyes fixed on the lightning's erratic dance across the Denver skyline and his on the interstate heading north to Cheyenne after leaving the baby with Itzel's sister, Itzel can feel a deep tissue bruise working its way up from the swollen flesh over her cheekbone. "Now you'll stop talking," he said calmly as he got in the car after her, her hair a tight knot in his fist propelling the right side of her face into the passenger side window, which he then checked, making sure the glass was still okay. Darkness envelops them on the ground as they silently ascend into high country, crossing the state line as they begin their search for the trailer park on the outskirts of the capital city, where they will find the man with the white pickup truck.

Itzel does not speak as she and Dante survey the cluster of ramshackle trailers, their flat roofs covered with old truck tires to prevent them from blowing over in winter storms with winds that can reach speeds of seventy miles per hour or more. She imagines these tires filling with winter's ice and collapsing on their sleeping inhabitants, crushing them with the hopelessness of being flat broke in the middle of nowhere. Dante blocks the white pickup truck's exit with the red-wheeled white Camaro and stalks out of the car, Itzel following him up three splintered wooden steps through the open trailer door, an antiseptic smell like a hospital swiftly enveloping them. Itzel covers her mouth as a shirtless man fixes them in his gaze from his perch on a sunken couch, empty plastic baggies and homemade pipes made from broken light bulbs spread across the flimsy table in front of him.

"Where's my fuckin' money, *paleto*?" Dante intones as he stares back at the man, who remains seated, his eyes fixed intently on the swollen right side of Itzel's face.

"Did he do that to you?" the man asks Itzel, his head twitching slightly in Dante's direction as she looks away. "Man, you're a real dirtbag." The man shakes his head in disgust, smirking as Dante sits beside him on the sagging couch and they begin to talk. Itzel isn't listening. Instead she is staring at the homemade chemistry set of plastic jugs and bottles connected by tubes, the metaphysical squalor of the place making her hate this man whom her baby's father has just called a country bumpkin in Spanish. She suddenly realizes, there in the mountain atmosphere cold and high enough to dull her senses, that she and Dante have known each other for almost their entire lives and that nothing is ever going to change. Ever.

Neither Dante nor the twitchy white man on the couch notice as Itzel leaves the trailer through the still-open door and opens the red-wheeled white Camaro's trunk. She lifts up the trunk's floor covering to find the spare tire kit and, filled with a sudden sense of purpose, silently swings the curved edge of the tire iron through the cold night air. The heavy metal rod with its circular blunt edge makes an ominous hiss as she practices a few more times before holding it behind her back and entering the trailer, where the men are now intently absorbed with counting and dividing thin stacks of dirty twenty-dollar bills on the flimsy table in front of them. Itzel stares at the men, the sheer smallness of their activities suddenly in sharp focus. She cannot decide if they are ignoring her or are so focused on counting the money that they do not see her at all.

As she swings with all of her strength, the iron's curve makes hard contact with the bridge of Dante's nose as irises of blood and tissue stream across his face, followed by a horrible wet wail rising from deep inside him. Dante cradles his ruined face in his hands as the twitchy man grabs handfuls of now-blood-streaked dirty twenties and darts from the trailer into a neighbor's equally ramshackle home. In a haze, Itzel follows him into the dirt lot, where the red-wheeled white Camaro taunts her with its shimmering ostentation. She swings, swings, and swings again, every cell of her being concentrating on the steady collapsing of metal and window glass until the police arrive, looking frightened by her anger as their furtive glances catch her own in the squad car's rear-view mirror on the way to jail.

Ad infinitum this scene runs through her mind as she circles the small walking path, arms pumping, just as it does at most other times of her waking life. Body aching and exhaustion creeping over her, Itzel feels that she has been in prison for a very, very long time. She slows down and Johanna, whom she knows from the halls where she lives with other women who share her higher security classification, begins to walk silently beside her. Itzel lets her, too tired to protest that she wants to be left alone; after all, being alone just means more time with her intrusive memories that her mind keeps forcing her to relive. Johanna has used a black marker from the commissary to write "CONVICTS" in elaborate letters across the white rubber of her black canvas shoes, a pun that makes Itzel like her a little.

"You got Indian in you," Johanna says as they walk, falling into step with one another because Itzel is tired but determined to keep going until a corrections officer tells her to go inside. This is a statement of fact from Johanna, not a question.

"Probably," Itzel says. "My parents were from El Salvador but I was born in Denver. My name is Mayan for moon or star or rainbow. Something like that."

Johanna nods thoughtfully, her black hair wet and tightly braided against her scalp, unmoving. "You are from Denver," Johanna says. "I know girls from the Res who stay in Denver now," she tells Itzel. "They say life is easier there but I don't know." The way Johanna carefully chooses words reminds Itzel of case workers at the Denver women's prison, but she does not tell her this. Johanna, who is unafraid of silence, weighs this information carefully as they walk, and Angela and Taylar sidle up to her.

"You want to go to sweat lodge?" Johanna asks Itzel, nodding in the direction of Angela and Taylar. "White girls go there, too. Good for you. Quiet."

Angela and Taylar nod in unison and Taylar says, "We do that with Johanna. It clears your spirit." Angela points to Johanna while looking meaningfully at Itzel, getting as close as she can to her without violating the prison's strict no-touching policy. "I know Johanna from county jail. She was the only one who would talk to me in there after I killed my husband. I always tell everyone that about me right away, so that they won't change their opinion of me once they get to know my crime. So now you know, too." Itzel nods without saying anything, allowing herself to be drawn into conversation.

"Johanna has a lot of respect in here because she treats everyone the same and never gets in trouble," Taylar continues, "and she was just like that in county. She was the first one to explain to me that I was in a state of learned helplessness and so I just let everybody take control over my life, like I did when my husband abused me."

"You did not need someone to tell you that. You just needed to see it for yourself," Johanna cautions Taylar, who emphatically shakes her head in protest.

"No, when I met Johanna in county I was in shock for months, like, not comprehending what I did, so much in shock for killing my husband. It took me months to really, really realize what was goin' on and I was just trying to process it, y'know, I never really—through the whole trial I just depended on everyone else, I never really said anything, I was too scared to speak. I was the typical abused wife of a career alcoholic, just afraid of everything."

"That's because the legal system doesn't want you to speak," Angela says. "Look, a lot of women in here are like you. Mine is a drug crime and Johanna here doesn't ever talk about what landed her up in here, but I think we both relate to how some of these women are just abused and abused for years, never even have a speeding ticket, and then just snap one day."

Johanna nods, saying, "In other states many of these women who were abused wouldn't even be in prison. No one understands about Battered Woman Syndrome in Wyoming. I learned about that back when I was a drug and alcohol counselor on the Res and it really explained a lot. I didn't understand before because women in my family don't put up with that kind of thing from our men."

"We are all different," Johanna continues, "so some of us like to discuss why we are here and some of us will not. But we are all women, and this state does not like women." Itzel tilts her head quizzically, trying to assess whether Johanna is trying to tell her that she should not trust these two women for sharing so much information about their lives with a relative stranger, or if she means something else entirely. In prison Itzel always finds it hard to tell why women act in particular ways while living in such close proximity to others; some women share everything about themselves, some become strong advocates for other women, while others are secretive and stay as isolated as they can.

"Taylar didn't see a domestic violence advocate once before her sentencing," Angela tells Itzel with eyes widened for impact. "Society, including some of the women in here, sees her as a killer, not as a killer who killed her mate. That's two totally different worlds."

"It's very true, and it's *very* consistent," Taylar nods, adding, "If you see a man that does the same crime as a woman in the state of Wyoming, the man might get two years, the woman's going to get five to ten or something like that. None of us get less than any man is ever sentenced, we always get more. The judge who sentenced me told me, 'I'm going to make an example out of you. The women of this county need to know that they cannot do this sort of thing.'"

"And there's no programming for us murderers, no way for us to improve ourselves," Taylar affirms, smiling brightly in a way that seems disturbing to Itzel.

"Open movement," calls the correctional officer at the walking path, signaling the end of the women's time outside. They settle into the day room outside the halls, not wanting to return to the small cells they share with other higher-security prisoners, watching the women play board games, watch television, and talk with each other.

"Some of these girls just don't know no better," Johanna whispers to Itzel as Angela and Taylar find a deck of cards. "Their whole lives they define themselves through their families, their husbands, their boyfriends, their children, anybody but themselves as independent women. When you're poor and from the middle of nowhere, there's no one to show you another way. So, they really just don't know no better."

Johanna winks and nods at Itzel as Angela and Taylar sit down and start dealing cards. "What do you two think all the women in here have in common? Since we're talking about it anyway."

"Hmm . . ." Angela hums. "I've been here three times, all for dope, so I've seen a lot. I would say addiction, abuse, unstable homes from an early age. Some of these girls were the parent from a very young age, both for their baby sisters and brothers and for their own parents who were too high or drunk to take care of themselves. Like me, in all honesty, I definitely wouldn't be sitting here right now if I had had a different childhood or a stable foster home where I was safe."[1]

"It's true, I hear women talk about walking on eggshells all the time around a parent or husband who is physically or sexually abusive," Taylar adds, "or just really awful stuff like being a little girl and having to take care of a parent who forgets to eat or shower because they're on drugs or drunk."

As the women talk, Itzel recalls sitting in a state of shock in a Narcotics Anonymous group as she listened to a young woman recount living on a remote family compound with many other children, all of whom were home-schooled, as part of a particular religious group whose name she had never previously heard. She cautiously broached this topic with the other women, not wanting to start a conflict with women very different from herself but also genuinely curious and suspecting that Johanna would support her: "I heard one woman tell a story about growing up in a family that was almost like in a cult, and then the father died. The whole family just spiraled out of control, there were drugs and they'd been sleeping with each other, ugh. I never heard nothing like that before when I was in prison in Denver, and I thought I had heard everything."

Angela nodded. "I never heard of that kind of thing, but I had a lot of brothers and sisters going wild. My big brothers and sisters were partying all the time. They started getting me drunk and getting me high and stuff when I was eight and nine and ten and we didn't have any supervision. We didn't have food a lot. I didn't have clothes that fit. I would have to steal clothes out of the lost and found bin at school. The only time my brother and I got to eat any kind of regularly was at school for the meals they would give you for free, breakfast and lunch kind of thing. It was a little bit rough. All my brothers and sisters ended up on probation and

I ended up with a guy who was moving millions of dollars in methamphetamine, but that's another story."

Johanna watches Itzel. "See, Wyoming is a funny place. Here women do jobs that in any other state only men will do, like I known women in here who've been truck drivers, forest fire lookouts, plant managers, barrel riders," Johanna laughs, "but they also have this other side to them that even though they're doing men's jobs they're also doing all the cooking and caring for the whole damn family."

Angela looks bored, her gaze drifting toward the television. "I like your tattoo," she tells Itzel, pointing to the inside of her forearm.

"I do not," Johanna shakes her head, "because in Arapaho owls mean death."

Angela smirks playfully. "But we're not Arapaho. We don't believe that in our culture. In fact, Johanna, I'll have you know that owls are cool as shit."

"Maybe so," Johanna says, "but your prison is on Indian land."

Angela rolls her eyes, turning to Itzel. "Look, see how we get along in here, that we can say that kind of shit to each other? I know for a fact that in Denver you all group up by race and what-not. We don't do that in here. That's better, in my opinion."

"Well, see now, relationships are easy in prison," Taylar says. "That's what we all say in here anyway. It's easy because all our needs are met and we're all in the same boat. So, what that means is that you can have a conflict with someone and then say, 'Hey, wanna play a board game?' and that'll take care of it, because we learn that kind of thing in group together. In the free world, do you think that you can seriously say to your old man who's drunk and angry and ready to take a swing at you, 'Hey baby, wanna play a board game?'"

"Yeah, that's not realistic," Johanna says, her eyes settling on the tattoo reading "Dante" that snakes across Itzel's neck.

"You're Only as Strong as Your Five Closest Friends"

Janea looks around the circular metal table at the five women seated on metal stools molded to the floor in the center of the pods, where lower-security-classification prisoners like herself sleep in cells that line two stories of brightly painted white walls. After seventeen years in prison, institutionally conjoined, stacked, filed, and otherwise ordered objects are part of her world's natural order. Women sleep in slender bunks firmly bolted to walls, eat from trays taken from and returned to neatly stacked piles, wear white underwear bearing their name and institutional number, wash their hair and bodies with the same three kinds of soap and shampoo, and dress in uniforms with colors indicating their security classification. Prison order is resolute in ways that make objects and bodies appear almost magnetically compelled to return to their designated place at the appropriate time. Classroom chairs immediately restack into neat corner towers, bedsheets neatly fold into bunks, and with permission women walk along the wall to jobs, groups, meals, phone calls, case workers, and cells. Any disruption to these carefully orchestrated moving parts means chaos, a correctional officer's write-up, a trip to restrictive housing, a longer stay in prison.

Within this institutional fusion of objects and bodies, a group of six women who have gathered to talk about intimate partner violence precariously balances between an institutionally unsanctioned organization and a group conversation. This balance remains unspoken among the women, most of whom have long sentences and all of whom know that in prison accusations accrue quickly and can spark harsh consequences. Charges of inciting a riot could ensue if a correctional officer overhears them lamenting the lack of therapeutic treatment for women with post-traumatic stress disorder. Hugging or touching a crying woman wracked with loss could mean sexual misconduct charges if another prisoner observes and reports it to prison staff.

Even though the stakes are high, Janea, who still marvels at being the leader of anything, holds this group's agreed-upon weekly meetings in precious high esteem. Emma, Sadie, Grace, Alaina, and Adalynn all reside in the pods, where the intimacy of shared living almost osmotically fosters knowledge about their lives before prison. Their group came together through the same prison magnetism of objects and bodies that structures every other aspect of their lives. Janea is conscious that her sentence of life without parole accords her a particular gravitas among the women, who rely on her to structure their hour-long meetings with particular themes to guide discussion. Her job in the prison library, a rather grand name for a cramped, one-room space covered floor to ceiling with bookshelves, allows her to read all the self-help books in circulation. She memorizes as much as she can. Codependency. Cross-addiction. Defense mechanisms. Projection. These butterflies of words alight on the women, flitting between them like a secret code that helps them to interpret their lives.

Lately Janea has been reading a book about breaking cycles of poverty and violence in families. She knows that the women trust her to tell them about what she reads so they can talk about it together, since some of them learn better by engaging in groups rather than in solitary pursuits like individual reading. Janea wishes that every woman in prison had the courage to confront her past struggles, but she knows that it took her a long time to get to where she is today. When she first arrived in prison she could barely speak to the other women, let alone advise them about how they could make meaningful changes to their lives, yet after a few years of realizing that only she could make decisions about how to do her time, Janea decided that she was determined to use her time to help other women.

"Y'all know I always say that you are only as strong as your five closest friends because we all need support," she begins as the women nod. "We all need to know that we are not alone. And you are not alone. Last week we talked about the power and control cycle in unhealthy relationships, and so I thought today we could talk about how we all got into that cycle. Even better, we're gonna talk about how we're breaking out of it. What do you think?"

Alaina nods, the women silently watching her face as she speaks to avoid breaking the rule against interrupting. Janea always tells the women that people have been interrupting them their entire lives and so in group everyone should be able to speak her mind and be heard by others without judgment or interruption. "I ran away so many times starting when I was thirteen until I was old enough to be on my own because things at home were so scary," Alaina says. "I just figured it couldn't get any worse, no one could do any worse to me than what had already happened." Like Alaina, most of the women in group allude to abuse in group rather than discussing it directly, the resulting abstraction conveying violence's totalizing impact through an alchemy that transforms rape, attempted murder, and daily psychological torture into "it."

Shared experiences and mutual respect make these practices congeal into group norms, so that "it," "that," and other neutral words transform into neat containers for the depth of emotion and grief that many women find difficult to put into words when they talk about the violence that has shaped their lives. Just as Alaina "figured it couldn't get any worse," many women sometimes appear to have given up concerns for their personal safety or ability to be self-reliant. Yet Janea knows better: when she looks around the table at this small group of women, she sees resilience against terrible odds.

"I can relate to that," Grace adds after a pause, putting her hands up in the air in a surrender motion. "Well, my problem is that I just don't know how to do relationships because of all that abuse-neglect-whatnot, whatever y'all wanna call it. So many of us, we're trying to rebuild that family of origin and doin' it with all the wrong pieces and parts."

"Mmhm," Adalynn hums. "I spent my whole life since I was a teenager in a love bubble living for a man, completely dependent on him psychologically and economically. I was a modest mouse. I just wanna say, the environment that Wyoming creates, the stereotype for the woman to stay at home, take care of the man, bring him his beer—you learn early on, keep your mouth shut. If you're not seen and not heard then you're not causin' any problems."

"Same here," Emma adds. "I'm still working on how to set a boundary and how to say no."

Janea stays quiet because she likes the way the women are connecting different elements of their shared life experiences in group today, rather than individualizing or downplaying their abuse. Part of the book she is now reading deals with the social systems that create or enable conditions in which violence takes place in relationships. Janea knows that for most of these rural women, a hetero-patriarchal script of early marriage and children was a very prominent expectation, with divorce a mark of community failure for them. Although she is older than most of the women in group, she feels that she experienced far more freedom in making choices while growing up in Dallas in the 1970s than some of the young women described today. She notices that about one third of the women prisoners who have survived intimate partner violence married in their teens, with some marrying a man a decade older than themselves, beginning their marriages with a pronounced power imbalance.

Women often talk to Janea about being dependent on a man from very early in life, first through the act of early marriage and then through difficult economic circumstances or even poverty, and eventually through the desire to avoid being a single parent because of small-town stigma and the sheer hard work of raising children alone. "People get divorced all the time in big cities and start new lives for themselves. Do you feel like it's different in these little Wyoming towns, that there's pressure for women to stay with men who abuse them?"

"Oh, I don't blame those women one bit for trying to keep their marriages together." Emma's jagged burst of laughter is jarring as she speaks. "I spent most of my life in a town of five hundred people, and I was just shunned after my divorce. Like I would walk into a high school basketball game and people would literally turn away from me. He was Mr. Wonderful outside, but they don't know what he was like inside when I was married to him."

"That's a very good example of the power and control dynamic we discussed last week," Janea adds. "Abusers are often very charismatic."

"As I see it," Adalynn plainly intones, "the day I lost my freedom is the day I gained my freedom. I'm fifty-five years old. Even though I lived with the same things all of you did for twenty-five years, I've been in this facility for five years and have done more in those five years with myself than I did in that twenty-five years of marriage. Every day that I hold the TV remote in my hand in my cell and get to decide what I want to watch, I feel like a princess." The women laugh softly, not wanting to attract attention to themselves.

Sadie looks thoughtful and Janea asks her if she wants to add something. "Well," Sadie sighs, "I guess sometimes I feel left out when we talk because for me drug addiction was the main issue behind the violence in my last relationship. But like a lot of you, I think prison made me realize how stuck I was in unhealthy patterns and in unhealthy living situations, like I was asleep for so many years. I was thinking, 'Oh fuck, how do I get out of this mess?' I've done run around so much that I don't even know anybody helpful."

Adalynn, as the oldest member of the group, guffaws. "Well, I've never done drugs, I never even liked beer, but I sure understand that feeling of being asleep for years."

"Sure," Sadie continues, "but for me I feel like the pull to drugs and unhealthy men is the same. You know I don't really think I ever had much self-esteem so I found a way to get that out of *something*. Like Janea told me one time, we gauge our standards by our experiences so anything that's not as bad as the last thing is better. I knew that I'd find a bad boyfriend but then the next one was sketchy too. I wanted that acceptance, that love. It felt better than being alone."

"You know," Janea adds, "I've never been an addict but I've read a lot about addiction and learned so much from listening to other women share their stories with me. It seems like intimacy between addicts is really about intimacy with your drug of choice."

"Well, I am an addict," Alaina firmly states, "and so I can tell you that the mindset we're in when we're abusing drugs and partners are abusing us is a short-term mindset. We get into escapism, it's a coping mechanism. And sometimes that escape is just from one partner to another, even though they're practically the same guy. I was in and out of relationships, not healthy ones, abusive ones, on drugs, I gave up several children for adoption. Women really get into a mess with addiction. I really do think it's harder for us than it is for men who are addicts."

"I disagree," Sadie shakes her head, adding "respectfully" when Janea glances her way. "I see the same kind of mess with men who are addicts, too. Like my kids' dad switched from meth to heroin after we split because he married this little girl who's on heroin."

"Uh-uh," Grace hums. "Women do survival mode differently than men do, because we're more connected to other people. Maybe it's just how we're built, maybe it's how we're raised, but it's true. And for a lot of women, survival mode is the only comfort zone they have and so they're afraid to step out of it, and keep getting sucked into relationships like that again and again because they don't have boundaries."

"I agree with Grace," Adalynn nods. "No matter what happened in my marriage for years and years, I told myself I could handle the beatings. I wanted to make everyone happy because then, if they're happy I must be happy, too."

"Men lack boundaries, too, though," Sadie continues. "It takes two to tango. I think it's important to think about both sides of domestic violence because when you're violated, you become a violator. That's just the way it is. However my dad was treatin' me is how I was treatin' my mom, however my ex-husband was treatin' me was how I was treatin' my kids. And y'know what I mean, it's got flow! It's got flow, violence has more flow than peace does."

"Oh, for sure it does," Grace gushes, her rapid torrent of words making Emma and Adalynn lean back a little in their seats. "I've done a lot of bad things to my husband you know to protect myself and, um, I always want to shed the blame on him and say well he's the one that introduced me to the drug, if it wasn't for him I wouldn't do this and that, that it— well, that's not the case, like, I'm a big girl. I can make my own decisions, you know, just because he introduced me to it doesn't mean that it's his fault. For a long time I was blaming him. I need to take accountability for what I've done, you know, I'm the mean one too, you know, I'm the violent one because—and I never used to be violent, I think it was because I was a little bit angry."

"Honey, you had good reasons to be angry," Emma slowly intones. "Last time in group you told us that you remembered waking up to being raped and nearly smothered by your first husband when you were sixteen and he was twenty-five, and then he stalked you. Then you married a drug dealer—"

Janea puts a palm on the table. "We're not here to judge each other, Emma. You know that." She is gentle as she speaks since she knows that so many of the women in prison find easy targets in one another. It is much simpler, she knows after so many years of incarceration, for a woman to lash out and hurt the woman sitting next to her than it is to confront deep-rooted insecurities and other negative feelings. When Janea hears contrarian statements, she understands that these come from a place of fear and hurt. Other women sometimes recognize such statements as symptoms of oppositional defiant disorder, which Janea jokingly refers to as "mean bitch syndrome" because its symptoms include disagreement for its own sake. She knows that, deep down, none of these women really believe that men are the victims in these relationships.

Sadie quickly adds, "She's onto something, though. I was what they call a functioning addict. I still had my hair salon, but I was taking my daughter to daycare and he was just sitting at home doing nothing. We got in an abusive relationship, you know, he would hit me. I did add fuel to the fire because I did hit him, yeah, I certainly did, with a broom. I gave him sixteen stitches up there." She motions to her forehead.

"Domestic violence most definitely involves two people," Janea editorializes to the group. She rarely shares her personal experiences while facilitating these groups because her leadership among women who have shared experiences is the most precious thing in her life. "I have noticed similarities in the kinds of crimes survivors of domestic violence are in here for—it's either drug-related, child neglect because of drug abuse, or because they hurt or killed their abusive partner. Then there's the women who take the fall for an abuser's crime."

"I've seen that too," Emma adds, "because we've both been in here a long time. Some of these girls in here were in abusive situations where they don't really have much choice in the matter. They get caught up in whatever their partner is doing. I was just so shocked when I heard some of these girls, especially the ones all caught up in that whole drug world that I just can't understand, talking about feeling relieved when they got arrested because they got away from him."

Adalynn clears her throat. "I'm an old timer like the both of you, and the simple fact is that there's a final trigger. There's often multiple abusers, rather than just one partner or family member. I got married when I was barely thirteen and had four children before I was nineteen. I feel I probably shot my husband not only for what he done to me, but for everything every man had ever done to me. I was just plain ol' tired of bein' beat on."

Emma is sympathetic. "It builds, it really does, over all those years. Believe it or not, I didn't plan to kill my husband. I didn't go there to shoot him. I went there to shoot myself. I wanted to show him how bad he had hurt me, because he was cheating, and I was positive at the time that there was no way I could live without him, I was positive."

Janea notices the younger women with shorter sentences starting to fade into the background as Emma and Adalynn talk about their lives. Both women are also serving life sentences, and Janea knows that the younger women sometimes regard them with a strange mixture of respect, pity, and relief that their own situations did not end in the same unalterably life-changing way. She intervenes. "We're all here in part because of choices we made in relationships with bad boyfriends or husbands and abusive childhoods."

Grace interjects as Janea finishes her last sentence, "Most women in here have been abused really bad, most have been raped or molested growing up or they've been in abusive relationship after abusive relationship. Like, so many of us would not even be here right now if we were not following our man. I would say more than two thirds of us, maybe more."

Janea knows that Grace, the youngest of the group, lacks the other women's maturity and is still very angry at the world. She is a girl who likes to solve problems in the free world by fighting, because talking is too difficult.

"Let me finish," Janea continues. "I want to put a positive spin on all this negativity, before we spiral out. I want to acknowledge each and every one of you brave women for all the help and support you have given each other. Because one thing I see that you all have in common is that you want to use what you have endured to help others in a positive way."

Grace crosses her arms like the teenager she is and narrows her eyes at Janea, who ignores these expressions of defiance because she knows they are not personal. Grace laughs. "We need to help each other, because this place isn't doing it for us. Once you're an inmate, forget about getting any help with your trauma."

Janea stays silent although she does not like where Grace is heading, while feeling sympathetic. Grace explains, "My mental illness, my PTSD and my bipolar, is part of every aspect of my daily life. I rarely see a case worker or counselor. On paper, it says we should see a case worker once every two to three weeks, but in reality we get thirty minutes maybe once a month or even less and then if there's someone with a more urgent mental health issue my appointment gets canceled."

"She's right," Emma echoes. "They make us change counselors so much, I don't know why. I guess it's turnover. Who would want to live in this town, there's no shopping, there's no movie theater, nothing. We need regular counseling sessions to move beyond trauma and memories of what we did or did not do during abusive relationships."

"You are all feeling sorry for yourselves." Adalynn's frustrated tone slices through the air. "Especially you young girls who get to go back out into the world. You have so many resources at your disposal, you just don't use them. You have so many classes and I have taken every single one of them except prerelease: there's classes on boundaries, grief and loss, anger management—"

Grace finally breaks group rules and interrupts. "Oh, come on! I talked to a gal who did prerelease and she said it was like those L. Ron Hubbard 'Pursuit of Happiness' videos, that Scientology guy. They throw a workbook at us in all those classes, and I'm sorry but workbooks ain't gonna fix a whole lifetime of living this way. We need women's issue counselors! Women's issue counselors! Domestic violence, sexual assault, abandonment—do you know how many women have been abandoned here?"

Janea's eyes dart anxiously around the room, but no one seems to notice Grace's raised voice and gesturing. The correctional officer on duty, a local woman whose children help her raise cattle on the outskirts of town, is engrossed in conversation with a woman who seems upset. Janea concentrates on her breathing to stay fully present in her group.

"I'm not tryin' to be negative," Alaina adds, "but you all know this is not my first go-round. This is my third time here. I'm not real proud of that. When I first got out of here and went on probation and parole, I got right back into the same kind of relationship because I didn't get one domestic violence class. Not one resource to deal with violence. And domestic violence doesn't just come from a spouse. It comes from a boyfriend, it comes when you're thirteen and you're dating someone who's sixteen so you can get their drugs. Domestic violence is huge. We are in a women's prison—not one program. Not one. How does that happen?"

Emma, who tried and failed twice to get a pardon from the governor, keenly follows the progress of women as they go before the Parole Board. "I can tell you with confidence that Wyoming's Parole Board knows nothing about domestic violence. Girls in here need to learn about how to stop re-creating these patterns so they can live a law-abiding life. This place doesn't have any type of transition program for women who've been through domestic violence. One of the biggest problems of women who get caught is that they're usin' drugs because they're gettin' the shit beat outta them."

"It's common sense," Adalynn adds. "Violence should not be a taboo topic in a women's prison. Emma, remember when we tried to get staff to show that movie, *Sin by Silence*? It was made by survivors of abuse who were in prison. They told us there weren't enough counselors to debrief women after the screening. Right, that's what is going to send me around the bend after everything I've been through. I'll be a suicide risk." She laughs.

"Here's the real issue," Alaina adds. "Women have kind of been thrown into a dominant role nowadays and women don't know how to step into that role well."

Grace leans forward, nodding. "It's true. I'm the youngest one and I'm used to having a man run me around and not make any decisions on my own."

"I still miss being married, even though we had a lot of problems," Sadie says. "I know it's wrong but it rubs my heart with sadness when my sister tells me that my ex still calls my name out when he's in a drunk nap to bring him something. It always made me feel needed when he did that."

Janea watches the clock and sees that just a few minutes remain on this correctional officer's shift. "I'm going to push you a little with that, Sadie," she admonishes slightly. "It sounds like you might be basing your understanding of your own value in your partner's higher value."

Sadie looks down as Adalynn shakes her head, noting, "I think we're the exception. A lot of women in here don't want to progress. There are women who are angry, entitled, who don't want to change. They think the same way in here that they did out there. They will be back. Like I started rebelling when I was young for no reason at all. I wanted to do what I wanted to do. I didn't want my mom to tell me. I'm an all or nothing gal and that's not so good, so in here that's what I'm doing, finding my balance. I measured my marriage's success by how I could work forty, fifty, sixty hours a week and still take care of my home and cook him a hot meal every day, you know, and pack his lunch in the morning. And then I snapped and we had the fight to end all fights."

Janea, one eye on the clock, asks, "So how do we break this cycle of violence in our lives and help other women to do the same?"

"We have to recognize it," Emma adamantly states. "For me, I recognize the cycle we talked about when I see it, feelings of worthlessness, self-deception. But it's really, really hard because in here hoping that good things will happen, or expecting them to isn't optimism, sometimes it's almost like lying to yourself."

"I just want my children to have better than what I did," Alaina sighs. "There's always that fear for me with people, like maybe they won't like me, maybe it won't work out, maybe I won't be good at it, what if I break it?"

"You-know-who is comin' on," Adalynn whispers as the aging correctional officer from California marches into the pod to replace his much more sympathetic local colleague. His military bearing and cold gaze immediately generate a reverse magnetic field from which the women disperse, eyes averted. Janea sits alone for a moment at the circular table with its cold metal blur of bright silver lines swimming in perfect synchronicity beneath her hands. She looks at the wall clock and sees that she has ten minutes of free time now, which she will use to walk with a feigned sense of purpose to the other end of the carpeted town where she will spend the rest of her life.

Little Strangers

Tammi is one year, five months, and two days sober as she perches on the arm of a worn couch at the Adult Community Corrections (ACC) facility where she has paid rent while living with about two dozen other women for the last six and a half months of her prison sentence. Over one hundred men live on the other side of the facility, but facility staff remind women and men alike not to interact. When the women saunter into the cafeteria to eat, they must line up against the wall to let the men go by as that shift departs. "The last thing any of these people need is some pregnant inmate," Tammi overhears a surly staff member opine to another as she waits for a woman seated behind a high corner desk, one eye on the closed-circuit television cameras that monitor the facility, to hand her a nighttime dose of the blue hexagons that rudder her bipolar disorder. Tammi cups the pills in her hand as the staff member waves her hand. "I don't have to check you, I know you don't just cheek your pills. Good girl." The woman leans slightly over the desk to watch another exhausted staff person shuffle through a thick three-ring binder of paper, the rising crescendo of a resident's voice indicating a new potential conflict.

Tammi smiles as wide as she can at her as she swallows, proud that this staff person regards her as sufficiently trustworthy not to secretly spit out and resell her medications to other women. Being naturally slight and skinny is a distinct disadvantage for Tammi, who has never weighed more than ninety-eight pounds in her life, and she suspects that most staff members watch her more intently than other women because she has the lithe frame of a long-term addict. "I'm just built this way," she explained softly to an ACC case worker. "Maybe I didn't get enough to eat when I was a kid." Tammi's arms are neatly streaked with permanent red welts that grew from skin cells regenerating over cuts she made with blades removed from razors and the indented circles of cigarette burns, which also does not help her case. Other women complain about poorly executed tattoos that remind them of their old lives, but Tammi thinks her scars still attract repulsed stares or at best looks of concern; she was relieved when the fast-food manager said she could work in the kitchen instead of having to face customers.

Tammi still misses ITU's highly structured routine and the way it required participation even from the most unmotivated women who thought participation in drug treatment might garner them an early release from prison. Most of all, she misses the way the program required women to hold each other accountable for their treatment of others; ITU was the only time in her life that when others bullied her for being the smallest and the quietest, someone would always tell them to stop. After she graduated from ITU, Tammi was surprised at her own sense of disorientation following her move back into general population, where the women seemed so loud, so undisciplined, and so frightening after the order of ITU, where every minute was scheduled in order to keep the women focused on addiction recovery and preparation for life in the outside world. "We can tell you're from the other side," her new cellmate, a much older woman, told Tammi on her first night in the pods. "You're just too quiet and picky about things. Must be a real drag to graduate and then still be stuck in here. Just make sure you don't come back. It makes me so angry when I see you young girls from the drug world drift in and out of here like it's a goddamn hotel."

As always, Tammi just nods and stays quiet, knowing that months slide by quickly, even if not spent among women who were required to at least try to work on themselves. Tammi knows how to do time, whether with a mean-spirited foster family, in a jail sentence, or in the pods with women who have long sentences to finish. She worked as much as she could at her cleaning job throughout the last six months she spent in general population, her mop bucket trailing her as she washed already-clean floors. Other women felt resentful when they could not release right away because of denied parole plans or inadequate bed space at a transitional housing facility, but Tammi knew there was no point in complaining. It never changed anything.

Cleaning, eating, sleeping, showering, going to group in as much silence as others would tolerate from her, Tammi passed her six months as minutes on a school clock. The ACC has its own set of rules Tammi listens to other women complain about: paying rent, paying for rides in the van to and from town for work, poor-quality institutional food, and other institutional litanies. She just listens and nods, and most of the women leave her alone, as they have for most of her life in state institutions or arrangements. Last week an ACC resident, still new to the facility from prison in another state, pointed at Tammi's scarred arms as they sat together watching television from battered secondhand sofas arranged in a protective semicircle around the screen where some women seemed to spend their every waking moment at the facility. "What's wrong with her?" the woman asked everyone and no one in particular. "You're not going to get a rise out of her," her sort-of friend Alliana matter-of-factly stated from her sprawl across one of the sofas. "She's institutionalized."

Tammi does not mind because she knows that Alliana means well. She waited six months to stay at this facility, which is two miles away from where her three-year-old daughter, Ava, lives with a foster family. Although the possibility of Ava and Tammi living together in a little apartment still does not seem at all real to her, Ava's Department of Family Services case worker tells her that it could happen. The case worker sits with Tammi, listing off the things that she will need to have, do, and be before she and Ava can live together: enough cash for two months' rent money and a deposit, staying sober, participating in parenting classes, and attending Narcotics Anonymous groups. Tammi sits as still as she can, making sure to nod periodically, during these meetings so as not to show the downward-pulling vortex of emotion she feels when the case worker talks about Ava as a fully formed person with her own preferences, history, and problems.

For the first time in her life, Tammi is beginning to reflect on the minutiae of meanings that different people attach to money. A volunteer leading a class in prison puzzled Tammi when she asked the women, "What is your relationship with money like?" At first Tammi felt deeply confused by this question; never staying around very long, money came and went on whatever needed paying: rent in the motel or the trailer park, fast food, broken-down cars with balding tires. She started to really listen as the volunteer teacher began to unravel the mysteries of how other people had so much—salaried jobs, pensions, health insurance—that always seemed to belong to another universe.

Tammi is now focused on money, keeping meticulous count of every penny contained in the biweekly paper checks she hands over to facility staff from her job at the fast-food franchise. She has seventy-five dollars she earned mopping floors and cleaning bathrooms at ten cents an hour in prison. Tammi also likes working as much as she can to avoid the creeping malaise of television, endless overheard phone conversations with men, and the thick atmosphere of negativity that permeates the air around some of the other women. As she comes and goes to work, she sees them lingering in shivering circles of three-minute familiarity as their breath and tobacco smoke congeal in warm clouds just outside the door. Cigarettes are too expensive now for Tammi, whose nail-bitten fingers slide shamelessly into the coin return slot of the anachronistic pay phone forlornly mounted next to the fast-food restaurant where she works in town.

Every day is the same, which does not bother Tammi much after the structure of prison life. She wakes up early, before the other women, and waits to catch the van provided by the ACC. Each trip costs her six dollars, which means that she works nearly two hours at the fast-food place in order to pay for her transportation to and from work. She stays at work for as long as she can, taking on double shifts whenever they are available, to earn as much as she possibly can. Many of the women complain about this arduous schedule and probably regard Tammi as too beaten down by the system to care, just as she is not surprised that the town in which she is living has nothing in the way of mental health or long-term addictions-recovery support for women who have been to prison. She wishes things were different, but getting Ava back is foremost on her mind now, and so things like this quickly fade into the background, although she knows they are important. For other women, these are sources of constant complaint and frustration.

Gennessa, Lorna, and Alliana, who preceded Tammi's arrival at the ACC, were all with Tammi in prison, where they also perpetually checked the clock until the appointed time arrived for something: a visit with children, a release date, an important meeting with a case worker or future parole officer. These are women who are tired of waiting now that they are in the free world, where they want to begin living again within the indisputable constraints that surround them as mothers and as people. Tammi sits quietly with them at the picnic table near the smoking area listening to them discuss their difficulties reuniting with children, and the various struggles each one faces with caregiving arrangements. Lorna's children live with her mother, Gennessa's daughter is in foster care, and Alliana is very worried that one more relapse or arrest will prompt a judge to terminate her parental rights.

These relationships, striated along the fault lines of deep-rooted cultural expectations, are fraught with emotion. "That bitch," Gennessa narrows her eyes as she tries not to cry while discussing her daughter's foster mother, "sat with my case worker and explained, 'Well, we didn't know what to tell her and so we said, "Mommy is in heaven."'" So now she's going to figure out that's not true, and how can that not affect her for the rest of her life?"

Lorna puts her hand on Gennessa's shoulder and leaves it there, still relishing the ability to touch others. "At least she's a stranger, Gennessa," Lorna says. "Imagine if your own mother told your daughter something like that." Lorna knows, as her mother texts her constantly with reminders of how Lorna has failed in almost every human capacity and how her children, now early adolescents, seem poised to take flight on the path their mother set. "You gotta try and use all this to be a better version of you."

Gennessa covers her face. "I know. But all I can think about is walking to the playground with my kids, some little thing like that, and having everyone from town whispering, 'Oh there goes Gennessa with her kids, all fucked up on dope again.' My kids are the only thing that got me through prison and I promised myself that this time I would stay clean, no more idiots in my life, that I'd stay on track."

"The only person's behavior you can control is your own," Alliana, who never cries, firmly states. "If you start caring about shit like that there'll be no end to it. Look, unless they've walked in our shoes and seen how hard it is to get a job with a felony—at least a job that pays enough to support kids anyway—and how hard it is to stay clean when the whole world feels like it's against you, then they just have no idea. Period."

Tammi imagines the women and their children floating in space, tethered only by brittle ropes strung between them that, for some of the women, are lifelines to the future. Again and again in group she has heard women talk about losing custody of their children as synonymous with losing hope. "Losing custody of kids means taking away the obligation to be good," one woman put it when describing another woman who became too emotional to talk when she learned that her children had been adopted by another family. "Now what does she have to live for?"

"Having your kids taken away is a life sentence," Alliana adds. "That breaks my heart, not being there for my kids. Gennessa, you need to use your kids like a driving force, to never do shit like this again."

"Gennessa," Lorna cautiously adds, "I guess I just feel that you are so lucky with your daughter with a good foster family. I'm going to be fighting for full custody of my daughter when I get out of here. And with my own mother, because I know how she was when I was a kid. That would be one of my biggest triggers. If I ever lost her, I don't know if I'd have the strength to continue going."

"She's right, Gennessa," Tammi says, walking that prison line between eavesdropping for information essential to everyday life and meaningfully participating in conversation. "Your daughter is in a structured environment, with A, B, and C all lined up."

Tammi and Ava never had a life together, not when Tammi was sober, but then again Tammi never had a biological parent or caregiver like that either. To her it made sense when women deep in their addictions made a conscious choice to give up children, especially babies, for adoption. She noticed that women under twenty-five seemed especially likely to do this, while older women much more strongly identified as mothers, some even being able to proudly discuss independent grown children with college degrees and jobs. Tammi, whose quietness often prompted statements made in confidence about others, often heard these older women say that the younger women in prison frightened them as future possibilities for their own children.

Still Tammi watched in prison as women struggled mightily to stay involved in their children's lives through phone calls, a precious one dollar an hour for women who worked ten hours to earn that amount. Skype visits could only be possible if children were with a foster family; luckier women, like Gennessa, had a sympathetic DFS social worker who would facilitate one every few months, so at least her kids would not forget her face. And some women never saw children or family at all, with travel to the prison on the Nebraska border costing too much money, time, or effort.

"I had my youngest in prison," Lorna tells Gennessa, hoping her own hardships will make Gennessa see that her problems are shared, if still significant, "and my mom came to take her away from me. If they'd had that mother and child unit open that cost a million dollars to build, I could've kept her with me. And I think about that every day, how things would be different if I'da had that chance to bond with her."

"Right now, they use that mother and child center for the dogs in the dog program to shit out there, like right about where a swing set should be," Alliana reminds her. "That's about all you need to know—see how much the state cares about us or our kids? They say it's lack of staffing and the angles of the building but come on—for a tight-fisted state like Wyoming to spend a million dollars on something and never use it, not even once. Well, I call bullshit on that one."

All four women sit together in momentary silence, wanting to comfort each other, and themselves, and in so doing make things just a little bit easier for a while.

"Buck up, sister," Alliana tells Gennessa in that wry tone of familiarity. "You forget that Mommy's in heaven here?"

Concluding Thoughts

Janea, Itzel, and Tammi, the main composite characters in this chapter, each had her own experiences with intimate partners, family, and socio-economic structures that trapped her in a cycle of violent dysfunction that she felt powerless to stop. The currently and formerly incarcerated women in our study almost all had experiences as victims of and, in some instances, as perpetrators of, violence. It was common for women who participated in this project to make explicit connections between their incarceration and their experiences with substance abuse, compromised mental health, violent or neglectful family, intimate and other interpersonal relationships, and social isolation. All too often, women had these experiences very early on in life.

Violence against women is a significant social problem for many women who have never been involved with the criminal justice system. Yet feminist criminologists consistently demonstrate that physical and sexual abuse is even more prevalent in the lives of currently and formerly incarcerated women, often beginning at a very young age (McDaniels-Wilson & Belknap 2008). Numerous women in Janea's informally organized support group for survivors of intimate partner violence, like many of their incarcerated peers, describe leaving violent or otherwise abusive families only to enter into intimate partner relationships with men who treated them in the same manner. This is not surprising given that research indicates that family violence often occurs in intergenerational cycles that isolate girls by encouraging them to group together with other young people who have similar experiences, fostering a cycle of social marginalization and limited personal growth, with direct implications for the children of currently and formerly incarcerated women (Giordano & Copp 2015; Boeck, Fleming & Kemshell 2006).

As reflected in other research with marginalized and disenfranchised women, some of the women in our study spoke of their dreams for an idealized version of "normal" life, typically characterized by a "nuclear" family complete with loving husband and children (Ferraro 2006). Often, this dream is born as girls and young women try to escape abusive home environments to find a better life, which too frequently occurs via involvement in intimate relationships with men who make empty promises to them regarding social mobility or various forms of socioeconomic stability (Raphael 2000). Dissonance emerges in these relationships when there are few concrete strategies in place to achieve this dream or tools to make it a reality, and the desire for this life compels some women to remain in violent or unhealthy relationships (Wesely & Wright 2009).

Accounts of interpersonal violence are common in women's prisons; indeed, our research team was particularly struck when at least one incarcerated woman stated, "Prison is the safest place I've ever been," echoing an article titled with the same words (Bradley & Davino 2002). Variations on this particularly vivid description of prison came in many forms, with nearly all of currently and formerly incarcerated women in our study characterizing violence as a normative aspect of their lives prior to their incarceration. Notably—and in sharp contrast to many popular cultural and some academic accounts of incarceration—not a single participant in our study indicated that she felt unsafe in the prison. Women often provided examples of the violence they believed to be common in what they called "real prisons," the phrase often used to refer to larger women's facilities in other states. Just like people in the free world, women learned about these prisons through television or through stories shared by people who had been incarcerated there. According to the women, such violence typically included sexual assault by correctional officers or other prisoners, mandatory gang membership based on ethnic or racial identity, and widespread fighting.

The more we listened to prisoners, correctional professionals, and other knowledgeable individuals explain away the facility's relative safety with some version of "Wyoming is a pretty small-town place," we could not help but begin to wonder if this assessment among some of the women had a racialized component as well. The majority of U.S. prisoners are white—although people of color are overrepresented in U.S. prisons and jails relative to population size (U.S. Department of Justice 2016a and 2016b). Nevertheless, the women's prison is notable for its nearly homogenous white population, which reflects the state's overall demographic composition. Women from other states, some of whom were women of color, commented on their initial shock at Wyoming's ethnic and racial homogeneity relative to their homes. Furthermore, Wyoming white women who had received temporary transfers or who had served previous sentences in other states commented on how unnerved they felt when incarcerated with people from other ethnic and racial groups. While their assessment is problematic, many white prisoners associated the prison's lack of violence with small-town values and white racial identity.

While violence against women is a global problem, a significant body of literature demonstrates that small-town social-control mechanisms and gender norms, the cultural normalization of women's economic dependence on men, and limited or nonexistent support services all uniquely disadvantage rural women (DeKeseredy & Schwartz 2009; Farber & Miller-Cribbs 2014). Janea relocated from rural Texas with her oil worker husband and two young sons to Wyoming in the hopes that their troubled relationship would improve, but instead, rural isolation, her economic dependency on him, and the need to care for their children only made his violence against her escalate. Just as she was beginning to really enjoy the only job she ever had, as a small-town gas station cashier, her husband injured her so severely that a physician had to wire her jaw shut. The cycle of violence that framed her sons' early childhood and much of her adult life is a familiar story among incarcerated women. Unfortunately, so is the lack of community assistance that she and her children received.

Research indicates that rural women with criminal records are likely to mistrust police and accordingly be less likely to contact them for assistance (Lynch & Logan 2015), especially in rural hetero-patriarchal contexts that tacitly endorse violence against women (Hall-Sanchez 2014). Following Sandberg's (2013) suggestion to use intersectional analysis so as not to reinforce dominant cultural stereotypes of rural backwardness, our analysis remained carefully attuned to the various ways in which violence manifested in the women's lives. Itzel comes from Denver, the largest metropolitan area in the Rocky Mountain region, and committed her violent crime in Wyoming as part of a drugs-violence-gendered vulnerabilities nexus well established in the feminist criminological literature (Dewey & St. Germain 2017). Yet Itzel also experiences a form of structural violence as one of the few women of color in the prison, where her heightened anxiety at being a minority prompts her to isolate herself from the others.

This structural violence is also evident in the passivity exhibited by Tammi, the child of two incarcerated parents, one of whom sexually abused her, once she arrives at the ACC. While some of the other women virulently critique the high costs of ACC transportation and what they regard as other restrictive or even exploitative policies, Tammi's long tenure in the system has normalized such treatment for her. Yet Tammi's silence should not be construed as complacency; instead, it reflects a long, and indeed intergenerational, process of silencing that has taught her that questioning authority only results in further harms. Her worst fears seem poised to be realized given the lack of community support available to her, resulting in a situation that is familiar to many system-involved women and that causes her ACC peer Alliana to observe, "Having your kids taken away is a life sentence."

Janea, like many of the Wyoming women serving a life sentence for murdering an abuser, has come to terms with the reality that she will die in prison. She does not reflect on the reality that, as a battered woman with no criminal history prior to her offense, in many other states she would never have received such a lengthy sentence and might not have served any prison time at all. Doing so would inhibit her ability to function on a daily basis or to assist other women in recovering from the enduring psychological impacts of intimate partner violence. Women who murder abusive partners often do so after years of abuse and isolation, and while Battered Woman Syndrome's associated symptoms of hopelessness and compromised mental health have been a recognized disorder since 1979 (Walker 2000 [1979]), it can be difficult to demonstrate in court, especially for poor women with overwhelmed court-appointed public defenders to represent them. Battered Woman Syndrome, which psychologists recognize as a subcategory of posttraumatic stress disorder, emphasizes that battered women who kill their abusers are in fact acting in self-defense because they have good reason to fear for their lives due to long-term abuse and the learned helplessness, hypervigilance, and cognitive disturbances that accompany such abuse (Walker 1992). This central aspect of Battered Woman Syndrome is important from a legal standpoint because it offers "psychological knowledge concerning the dynamics of an abusive relationship and its psychological impact on the woman's state of mind to help meet the legal standard of self-defense or duress which might not be otherwise met if the history of abuse was not known" (Walker 1992: 323). Yet most abused women do not have the resources for expert witness testimony and legal defense to make this case in court, even with the complete absence of a criminal record (Leonard 2002; Nuytiens & Christaens 2015).

Throughout this chapter we have seen the toxic alchemy of structural violence transform victimized women like Tammi, Itzel, and Janea into criminals who must be contained in the name of public safety. Cognizant of these painful realities, feminist criminologists caution against popular perceptions that women are committing more violent crimes—a claim that has been made with disturbing persistence since at least the advent of second wave feminism. These criminologists observe how women's violence typically takes place in the context of considerable socioeconomic marginalization (Pollock & Davis 2015; Wesely 2006; Kruitschnitt & Carbone-Lopez 2006), as is evident among nearly all the participants in our study who committed violent crimes. Women prisoners also engage in self-injury at far greater rates than male prisoners and women who are not incarcerated, reflecting their experiences with victimization and complex relationships with their bodies and individual agencies (Chamberlain 2015; Kilty 2006). Tammi, like many of her incarcerated peers, bears scars from cuts, burns, and other self-inflicted injuries that are physical manifestations of psychological suffering too great to bear. As an intergenerationally poor rural woman, she has no more access to treatment to help her address the issues that cause her to engage in these behaviors than she does to substance abuse treatment.

As the next chapter will discuss, these various forms of violence are enduring and persist in equally complex forms following women's release from prison.

4

On the Radar

Six months into free-world life, Dakota says little from her back-row vantage point in the amphitheater classroom, still slightly awestruck every time she watches another student get up and leave without asking permission or listens to the professor encourage the students to elaborate on points that Dakota knows are plain wrong. Dakota generally suspects that the professor, who tells all her students to use her first name instead of the title she worked so hard to earn, is actually much smarter and more strong-willed than she lets on in the classroom. After all, Dakota thinks, it must not be easy for a woman to get so far in life that she publishes books and gets to talk all day for a living. As she watches the professor smile and nod at naïve observations made with the kind of confidence that can only spring from a complete and pervasive state of ignorance about the state of the world, encouraging every student who makes an observation to expand on her or his thoughts, Dakota scans her face for signs of insincerity but finds none. Then again, it is always hard to tell when big-city people are being true or just putting on a show.

At least this professor never forces her to speak, as sometimes happens in her other classes, a sunny "Dakota, we haven't heard from you today" causing all heads to turn and focus intently on what the professor thinks Dakota might want to share with everyone. Dakota is mortified when this occurs and finds it nearly impossible to speak coherently with so many youthful eyes on her, imagining every one of the students taking note of the fact that she is at least a decade older than the rest of them and hence surely a failure with little to contribute in the way of classroom brilliance. Never mind that she had a perfectly good job as an accountant before she went to prison. Never mind that she raised two boys on her own with that no-account drunk of a husband. Never mind that she planned to pay back every cent that she stole from the medical office once she got the ranch out of foreclosure. None of that matters now. In the time between now and the future she hopes to have as a registered nurse, she has to sit in classes like this one, listening to others who have little real-life experience one up each other in ways that are of little use to her.

It is October and the first frost of the season is already starting to creep across the scrubby sagebrush Dakota passes as she walks to campus from the basement apartment she rents cheaply from her cousin, who lives in the university town. Her boys still stay with her parents, who need the free labor of hard-working teenagers to help manage their ever-shrinking ranch and prefer not to come into town at all if they can avoid it. Dakota steels herself during these walks the way that she used to do before she and Denise, her one friend during her time in prison, attended workbook-based groups that encouraged them to confront the true reasons why they acted in ways that got them locked up. Dakota always wanted to speak plainly in these groups, to exclaim, "I stole because I needed the money and I fully intended to repay it!" but quickly learned to pepper explanations of her actions with the workbook language of self-improvement, all close cousins of the usual suspects lurking behind the crimes of women who, like her, do not have a drug or alcohol problem: low self-esteem, codependency, unhealthy relationships, being overwhelmed. She did not speak then, and now, on campus, she tries to keep an equally low profile, feeling lucky to be part of the nursing program even if it requires her to get a whole new degree. With her money crime, her old accounting degree is useless now.

On campus, Dakota is relieved because she can remain quiet most of the time without her grades suffering too much, yet her silence belies the ebb tide of resentment and anger that alienates her from others in the classroom when she listens to their abstract talk about what they have learned to characterize as "social problems." These problems seem to always happen somewhere else, to other people, in ways that are subject to great pity among her classmates. This kind of talk frustrates Dakota without end as she pushes her seat against the amphitheater's back wall in an attempt to retreat. The professor smiles almost constantly, reminding Dakota of a sheep-headed beauty pageant contestant who hopes her charming personality will sway the judges, nodding emphatically as she listens to the students speak. Dakota knows the professor must be hiding a sense of great frustration because she has obviously prepared so many notes and questions to discuss with a class that clearly has not thoroughly read what she assigned in the syllabus. So, again and instead, the professor patiently uses her conversational teaching style, which Dakota finds unnervingly informal, to ask questions until, like a miner searching for a coal vein, she finds a way to engage her students with the material in a way that they will find meaningful. Then, fifty minutes later, everyone can leave with a sense of self-satisfied accomplishment and, Dakota suspects, will write good teaching evaluations at the end of the semester. She has heard that helps the professors to get tenure and keep their jobs. Dakota wishes that the professor would state the simple facts she must know to be true by telling the students when they are wrong, that she knows more than they, and that their poorly formed opinions are not facts. Yet Dakota sits quietly in the back row, her anger and frustration on slow simmer for the duration of the class.

"Soooo," the professor chirps as she launches into an endless sentence, "we've been talking a lot this semester about the lies that make life possible, which we've defined as those aspects of culture, everyday interactions, and inequalities that convince individuals that the social order's status quo is natural, normal, and correct. What are some of the lies that make life possible for us in Wyoming?" A subsequent leaden pause indicates that the professor wants the students to speak, which they start to do all at once. Dakota did not care for prison any more than the next woman she did her time with, but this class makes her yearn for some measure of the order that structured every aspect of prison life. "Pull yourself up by your bootstraps," one young woman confidently half-shouts from the third row and the entire class shifts their attention to her. The smiling professor nods and asks her to elaborate by saying, "Let's unpack that."

Dakota's usual slow mental retreat from this call-and-response comes to an abrupt halt when a slight young woman looks up from her copious note taking to ask the class, "Could prison be a good example of the lies that make life possible?" The professor asks her to explain. "Well," she says, "I volunteered to teach in prison last semester and almost every single one of those women were victims of abuse and poverty. They almost seemed destined to end up in prison with the lives they'd had, being abused as children, being married to men who beat them, and then getting addicted to drugs just to cope with the pain of living." Dakota does not recognize this young woman but worries that, somehow, she knows she has been to prison. This kind of talk annoys Dakota, who wants to tell the class to stop pretending that the so-called marginalized populations they read about and discuss so often have never made choices, had jobs, raised children, given advice, or otherwise acted like normal people. She briefly pictures the slight young woman spending a night in the halls with women who lack motivation and have never worked a day in their lives. She gives up when she remembers that some people are always inclined to rationalize someone's victimization and explain away the person's bad choices.

"I spent three years in prison," Dakota imagines herself stating plainly, allowing the portent of these six words to sail forth, their weight causing them to sink rapidly over her classmates' youthful heads. Yet she remains silent since she surmises that this revelation will only render her beloved to those enamored of victimization, who will regard her with the slightly contemptuous pity people on the ranch accord an old three-legged dog no one has the heart to put down. She stays silent, fearing the angry volley that might ensue from such a public disclosure, because she has long wanted to ask others why the state of Wyoming wasted so much money on her prison time when she could have paid all the money she stole back as an accountant instead of in pathetic little restitution payments she now makes monthly from her job in the kitchen of the restaurant near the university. Dakota wants others to know that, in retrospect, her crime only staved off the inevitable as she watched her parents sell off more and more parcels of their ranch, clusters of ominous and shameful "for sale" signs circling the lonesome prairie mailboxes like hunger-lean coyotes stalking prey. Yet she also does not want them to know, because she fears that what she has to say is outside the scope of their capacity for understanding.

The professor and her students are talking, but Dakota is no longer listening. She is using every bit of her inner resolve to stay focused on the ultimate goal she hopes to achieve in just a few years and tries to think about what she will say to the Wyoming licensing board to convince them that she deserves to be a registered nurse because she only made one stupid mistake. Before she went to prison, when she was in college the first time around, Dakota was probably not so different from most of the other impressionable young people who now surround her in class. Back then administrators and other bureaucrats seemed innocuous to her, but now they all seem poised in hawk-like judgment, wielding near-absolute power over her future decisions in ways that, on bad days, make her feel furiously trapped.

On better days, she keeps up an internal dialogue with the world around her, one in which she tells her classmates and the professor that life is far, far more complicated than the neat terms, theories, and concepts they lay out like rusty bear traps in an ineffectual attempt to capture the human spirit's slippery essence. On better days, Dakota does not have to try so hard to hold back her tears, as she sits in the parole office above the bank across the street from the university, thinking about how her parole officer is the kind of handsome and earnest man she wishes she could marry. She feels a stinging sort of shame every time he characterizes her as a success story because she is going back to college in the hopes of starting a second career, keenly aware that her criminal record makes her an undesirable partner for just about any man she might want to have for herself. Her parole officer always praises her during their mandatory meetings by giving her well-intentioned compliments about how far she has come since prison. "That's all in the rear-view mirror for you now and it's up to you to choose the road ahead," he says to her nearly every time they sit together, making Dakota picture the threadbare backseat visible in her blue pickup truck's rust-specked mirror. She knows that he sincerely believes those words, but by the time they reach her ears they are pithy with the rot of false assurance.

Women, Reentry, and Recidivism

The experiences women have as they attempt to build new lives following their release from prison vary dramatically and are influenced by numerous factors, including restrictions on employment or place of residence imposed by conviction type, substance abuse or addiction histories, available support systems, and access to higher education or other training. To understand and critically engage with women's experiences of community reentry, this chapter engages with three primary bodies of literature that examine gendered aspects of reentry, social ties' impact on reentry and recidivism, and parole and community service providers' role in women's lives. The first primary area, gendered aspects of reentry, analyzes how dominant cultural expectations regarding gender norms impact the women's lives after their release from prison. The second primary area, social ties' impact on reentry and recidivism, examines how relationships with families of origin, children, intimate partners, and others influence women's likelihood of staying out of, or returning to, prison. Parole and community service providers' role in women's lives, the third primary area, critically engages with the structures and forms of support related to relationships between formerly incarcerated women and those professionally tasked with their supervision or other forms of support.

Research on gendered aspects of reentry comparatively examines how gender influences self-conceptions and perceptions of future possibilities among formerly incarcerated women and men, intersectional aspects of reentry and recidivism experiences, definitions of postrelease success, and socioeconomic and interpersonal constraints on likelihood of achieving such success. A Texas comparative study of how formerly incarcerated men and women define success found that men are more likely to judge their success at community reintegration on the basis of status-related factors, such as employment and income, whereas women emphasized their relationships with others as the primary indicator of success (Herrschaft et al. 2009). These gendered definitions of success appear to be widely accepted nationwide and influence supervision in community corrections settings where, as Wyse (2013) found in an unidentified western U.S. state, parole officers encourage men to prioritize economic responsibilities to others while discouraging women from forming intimate relationships thought to increase their likelihood of recidivism.

Studies of reentry and recidivism have emphasized how intersectional factors, including race (Richie 2012; Richie 2001) and disability (Richardson & Flower 2014), influence the type and frequency of postrelease supervision and surveillance to which women are subjected. For example, young English mothers with a history of law breaking report intense stigmatization, social marginalization, and surveillance that serve as constant reminders of their previous involvement with the criminal justice system (Sharpe 2015). These intersectional factors also influence formerly incarcerated women's definition of success, which tends to include multiple indicators rather than the singular goal of avoiding reincarceration. Perspectives on reentry success among a cohort of Los

Angeles women encompassed living what the women termed a "normal life," which involved obtaining independent housing, assisting family members and others, and completing supervision requirements in order to be free of correctional control (Heidemann, Cedarbaum & Martinez 2016). Women in a St. Louis, Missouri, study attributed reentry success to family support, supportive parole officers, postrelease services, and a positive outlook, and regarded failure as related to negative support networks, unsupportive parole officers, and competing demands (Cobbina 2010; Cobbina & Bender 2012).

Formerly incarcerated women often identify person-specific and context-specific factors as central to avoiding recidivism and meeting personal goals, as was the case among women in Canadian federal prisons who emphasized untreated addictions and unresolved trauma as primary barriers to postrelease success (Doherty et al. 2014). Intensive self-reflection and mandatory in-group sharing is a cornerstone of many cognitive behavioral and related therapeutic programs both in prison and in community corrections, yet work with residents of a northeastern women's transitional housing facility stressed the challenges women face in speaking about their life experiences, prompting researchers to suggest that silence can be a protective strategy for women as they attempt to rebuild their lives (McIntyre 2013). This echoes findings from other studies, also from the Northeast, that question the utility of mandatory self-disclosure that takes place under the guise of therapeutic treatment for formerly incarcerated women among the criminal justice and social services professionals tasked with their oversight (Sered & Norton-Hawk 2014).

Socioeconomic and interpersonal constraints on women's reentry success almost always mirror the constraints that shaped their lives prior to incarceration, with the increased social control and powerlessness that accompanies a criminal record (O'Brien 2001). Such constraints take multiple, and often much more complex, forms following release from prison. For instance, research on how Chicago women navigate the conflicting and/or competing messages they receive from social services and criminal justice professionals, family members, and others in their social circles, observes that women employ tremendous creativity in presenting themselves and their goals in particular contexts while also observing the tremendous stress doing so generates for them (Leverentz

2014). Such competing demands and expectations take gendered forms that directly impact likelihood of reentry success, especially given that many women who have been incarcerated are less likely than their peers to possess the qualifications and skills necessary to obtain sustainable, long-term employment that pays a living wage (Flowers 2010).

Felony-related employment discrimination indisputably impacts both men and women with criminal records, creating tremendous obstacles for those who lack education and other forms of support necessary to obtain work outside the poorly paid service industry, which is often the only place for individuals with criminal convictions to find work. For example, research with employers who agree to hire individuals with felony convictions in two midsized northeastern cities found that such willingness often stemmed from notions about "hiring a good worker to do a bad job" that acknowledged how limited available work alternatives are for people with felony records as well as beliefs about the importance of second chances (Bumiller 2014). Enduring and significant income inequality between men and women is exacerbated for women with felony criminal records, and interviews with women on parole in a southern state indicated the importance of economic variables, specifically the ability to find and maintain jobs that allow for self-sufficiency (Johnson 2014).

Literature on the impact of women's social ties on their experiences with reentry and recidivism explores intersectional forces at work in recidivism's timing and occurrence, the impact of social bonds and supports on recidivism, and the influence of families of origin and motherhood. In addition to their impact on women's likelihood and perceptions of reentry success, intersectional forces also appear to influence the timing of recidivism. A study conducted in an unspecified U.S. state observed significant correlations between women's recidivism and residence in neighborhoods that normalize drug dependency, limited formal education, and extensive criminal histories (Huebner, De-Jong & Cobbina 2010). While community context and relationships are important influences on the likelihood of recidivism for both men and women, researchers caution that gender-neutral approaches to recidivism fail to capture the significantly different pathways men and women follow into law breaking. For example, a gendered analysis from Minnesota and Oregon of a popular actuarial tool used by corrections professionals to determine an ex-offender's likelihood of recidivism found that the tool often resulted in a misclassification of socioeconomically vulnerable women as "higher risk," resulting in parole officers' time and resources being directed toward women in poverty (Reisig, Holtfreter & Morash 2006).

Studies that examine how social bonds and other forms of interpersonal support impact recidivism emphasize the complex role relationships play in the lives of women prior to, during, and after their incarceration in ways that can influence their reentry experiences and likelihood of recidivism. Emotional, instrumental, and informational support among family, coprisoners, and various other social actors were all identified in a southeastern study as integral to formerly incarcerated women's well-being (Clone & DeHart 2014). These varied sources and types of support were also evident in a Los Angeles cohort, in which intimate partner relationships posed risks to a woman's likelihood of reoffending, whereas supportive peers and professionals in the criminal justice and social services fields were identified by women as the strongest predictors of reentry success (Heidemann, Cedarbaum & Martinez 2014). Women who participated in research at a Chicago transitional housing facility likewise noted connections between intimate relationships and drug use as well as the potential for relationships to contribute to desistance, indicating that intimate relationships may be most accurately conceptualized as processes that can be both destructive and conventionalizing (Leverentz 2006).

Support from and responsibilities to families of origin and children directly influence reentry experiences and likelihood of recidivism. Surveys with women prisoners collected as part of a broader study in Iowa, Indiana, Ohio, Oklahoma, South Carolina, and Washington indicate that in-prison family contact and postrelease family support are protective against recidivism while in-prison nonfamily contact is a risk factor for recidivism (Barrick, Lattimore & Visher 2014). Research with women under supervision at parole offices in a midsized Virginia city found that the incarceration of women who previously coresided with children often dramatically reconfigures family structures by increasing the likelihood of divorce and decreasing the likelihood that a mother will reside with a father of at least one of her children, factors thought to increase recidivism risk (Arditti & Few 2006).

The limited research with formerly incarcerated women released to rural settings indicates unique challenges in such contexts. A study with women released from a midwestern state prison indicated that limited socioeconomic opportunities, spatial isolation, and cultural stigmatization of rural people mark the lives of rural women in ways that restrict their abilities to mother (Beichner & Rabe-Hemp 2014). Work with rural Hawaiian women found that while motherhood is a conventional identity script for women that motivates success on parole, women's abilities to fulfill dominant (and their own) cultural expectations for mothering are complicated by poverty, lack of education, unstable housing, addiction, and underemployment (Brown & Bloom 2009).

Literature on parole and community service providers' role in formerly incarcerated women's lives identifies needs expressed by the women and those tasked with their supervision or other forms of support; examines how parole stipulations restructure women's lives; and offers feminist critiques of status quo approaches to prevailing forms of supervision. To emphasize women parolees' increased needs for support with respect to employment, housing, family-related needs, mental health, interpersonal functioning, substance abuse, and social acceptance/support, a midwestern study of service providers' perceptions of paroled women followed other research suggesting that, relative to men, women on parole have greater mental health, substance abuse, and medical needs (Bergseth et al. 2011). Yet even within these considerable constraints, as found in research with formerly incarcerated Denver women, women on parole use narrative strategies to confront their stigmatized identity and recast their past/present/future selves by disassociating from their identities as drug and alcohol users and people with felony convictions and instead emphasizing their self-identification as good mothers (Opsal 2011).

For many women released from prison, parole stipulations structure many elements of everyday life by imposing particular work requirements, abstinence from alcohol and illicit drugs, restrictions on interpersonal relationships, and other forms of surveillance. The broad scope of these supervisory forms and requirements, some researchers argue, increases the likelihood that a person on parole will go to prison relative to his or her peers who have never been to prison. For instance, a cross-European study found that the rising women's prison population results from the parole revocations prompted by increased drug testing and other forms of oversight, rather than increased numbers of crimes committed by women (Carlen & Tombs 2006). A Denver study likewise argued that the totalizing forms of governance that occur as part of parole requirements both complicate and conflict with women's attempts to reintegrate into their communities and obtain freedom from correctional control (Opsal 2015).

Such acknowledgments have prompted a feminist criminological critique of prevailing approaches to community corrections and supervision; these scholars and policy experts advocate for alternatives that account for and respond to significant gender differences in both reentry experiences and predictors of recidivism. Gender-responsive probation and parole strategies that acknowledge the importance of relationships in women's lives have consistently been found to be beneficial to women who are addicted to drugs or dependent on destructive and abusive partners (Morash 2010). Some feminist researchers regard gender-responsive initiatives as meaningful and necessary yet also observe the frequency with which dominant correctional paradigms still seep into such strategies, particularly by individualizing crime as the product of choice and free will in ways that can ignore significant structural and socioeconomic constraints, such as poverty (Hackett 2013).

Our findings build on this literature. We argue that the various forms of state, community, and interpersonal surveillance rural women experience during and after incarceration create unique challenges as they transition from prison's complex social worlds into less intense, but still salient, forms of social scrutiny after their release. To substantiate this argument, we draw on descriptive accounts of the way women navigate gendered forms of rural social control and surveillance before, during, and after their time in the prison. These experiences, in some instances, present a chance for the women to critically examine or otherwise reconsider competing narratives about their lives and choices. We analyze how social expectations regarding women as caregivers, particularly to minor children, are a source of motivation for making significant life changes as well as the cause of significant financial and social stress prior to and after their incarceration. Following women through their everyday routines as they find employment, comply with parole requirements, pursue further education, and form new relationships, we also document the challenges and successes that accompany reintegration into community life following release from prison.

Welcome to Rapid City

"Are you so excited to be done today, Nedrah?" The bells hanging from the parole office's front door jingle to a tinny stop behind Nedrah, who pauses on her way out to smile back at the receptionist, whom she remembers from her tenth-grade math class. No more random drug tests, with Nedrah awkwardly hovering over the toilet to urinate in a plastic cup while Lynzi, her parole officer, averts her eyes by pretending to study the shelves of paper urinalysis testing supplies. No more surprise home visits from Lynzi at odd hours, with Nedrah hesitating to invite Lance or any of his equally married but bored counterparts to stay the night out of fear that Lynzi would sanction her with additional restrictions or, worse still, whisper the truth to one of their wives in the town's single grocery store. No more being the only woman sitting in the parole office lobby during her mandatory reporting meetings with Lynzi once a month, shifting in a plastic chair as men she recognizes from local fast-food restaurants and cleaning crews try to make awkward conversation with her.

"Nedrah," Lynzi intoned during their last meeting, with the pause and unwavering eye contact she uses to cement the importance of a point she wants to make, "now that you won't have me keeping tabs on you, I want you to remember that this is really the first time in your life that you've ever been alone." Nedrah had nodded, only because she wanted to leave the office as soon as she could. "Promise me you'll think about that, I mean, really think about it?" Lynzi asked, and Nedrah silently nodded again as she answered the last round of questions and signed the final pieces of paper that officially rendered her off parole. Her three women friends from the Narcotics Anonymous meetings she still attends weekly—Jenna, Leanne, and Randi—have all done time and, like their peers, refer to this momentous occasion as "being off paper," a phrase Nedrah still associates with existing outside the system in free-floating, almost nebulous ways. It always makes her think of a television news story she saw about disaffected war veterans squatting on Nevada desert land, their water tanks, solar panels, and rickety, weather-beaten trailers the sad manifestations of their alienation from society. "Living off the grid," Nedrah thinks she remembers them calling it.

Steely snow clouds roll in over the mountains as Nedrah makes the short walk back to the apartment complex her family owns and where, out of the miasma of shame, avoidance, and pity that suffuses their dealings with her, they let her live in an unoccupied rental for free. There in the building on the edge of town, she smokes a single cigarette on evenings when she is alone, eyes drifting over the sea of scrub-brown grass outside her living room window. The prairie comes to life if she waits long enough for something to happen: a courageous little prairie dog alerts her clan to the presence of a rattlesnake, a hawk descends with deadly grace to pluck a newly awakened prairie vole from its nest, or, once in a while, a herd of startled pronghorn dart in unison away from town. "Good for you," Nedrah tells them as if they can hear, not sympathizing with any particular aspect of the food chain. "Lay low and stick together while you can."

Loneliness eats into Nedrah at a deep psychic level that she cannot fully articulate to herself, although she knows how she loves the primal, fire-building warmth that accompanies relationships of a singular nature, the kind that involve the clandestine sharing of keys and text messages quickly deleted. She likes that she owns a part of Lance, who tells her every three weeks that he has to stop coming over, that he and his wife are really going to work things out this time. She knows that the men she meets when she is cleaning rooms at the motel where she works, and the ones from high school she encounters at the post office, are all looking for some precious, unnamed thing they momentarily believe she possesses. People in this small town always say there are no secrets, and everyone knows Nedrah was in prison, but she still has plenty others do not know.

Friendship fills up the hours between these life-sustaining secret encounters with the town Lances: Jenna, Leanne, and Randi come over after NA to eat pizza at her place sometimes, and her son, Blaine, brings in her mail once a week before spending an hour talking with her in a way that always feels like an obligation he must meet with equanimity. Nedrah imagines that Blaine approaches shoveling snow with the same attitude. Her sister Starla stopped speaking to her shortly after she moved out of her basement and into the apartment, and her parents barely acknowledge her beyond cursory occasional visits in which her mother brings her a casserole baked from dried noodles, ground beef, and canned soup. None of this bothers Nedrah, whose world revolves around the intensity of the relationships she shares with the people who come and go through her apartment door.

When Blaine rings the apartment's doorbell with a polite briefness unique to him, Nedrah knows he will be outside holding the usual thin pile of bills and "Dear Resident" letters offering high-interest credit cards. He sits on the secondhand couch and tells her about a movie he watched the night before about Australia. "The whole country started as a prison colony," he says, "only the prisoners wore normal clothes, had jobs, got married and had babies, and just tried to be happy. I bet it was hard, though, being shipped out there to the middle of nowhere."

"Sounds like this town," Nedrah tells him from the kitchen, where she is reheating some of her mother's casserole in the microwave.

"You know what, Mom? That's really negative. There are a lot of nice people here."

"Hmm," Nedrah hums, handing Blaine a bowl of the casserole that reminds her too much of prison cuisine to eat. "I guess I just haven't met them yet." Blaine eats eagerly, his head lowered over the bowl.

"You still headed to Rapid City next weekend?" Nedrah asks, thinking about how excited Blaine seemed the last time they talked about visiting the South Dakota School of Mines, where he hopes to go to college.

"I don't know, Mom." He shakes his head. "Seventy thousand people is an awful lot of folks cooped up together in one place. I'm used to being here where everyone knows each other." Nedrah has long since reconciled herself to having no influence over her son's life, which seems hermetically sealed in the same small-town package of religion, artificial politeness, and constant gossip that suffocated her in the years before Wyatt freed her from all that. For Blaine and everyone he knows, the prospect of living among the strangers of Rapid City opens up all manner of possibilities, most of them frightening.

"Well, I think it sounds exciting," she tells him, preparing for a barbed retort that probably is just a repetition of what he heard his grandparents say about her while they raised him during her prison sentence.

"That's your problem, Mom. All you think about is what's exciting. That's not reality." Nedrah gives him a perfunctory hug as he leaves; parole is so far removed from his everyday realities that she does not even mention that today is a momentous occasion for her.

Free-world relationships still strike Nedrah as a more amorphous version of the prison social ties that emerge from so many people living within close collision range to one another. Yet women at the prison almost always formed intense bonds with one another of the kind that free people seemed to keep secret. When Leanne, Randi, and Jenna come over after they finish at NA, knowing that Nedrah is skipping a meeting tonight just because she can, part of Nedrah feels a little like she is back in prison, yet there is also freedom in their shared familiarity with a system that incarcerated all of them at different times in their lives. Tonight they have brought the pizza.

"Off paper," Leanne smiles widely at Nedrah before slipping into her wry sense of humor. "Now we just have to wait for you to screw up." The women settle onto the secondhand couch and around the coffee table, starving after the emotional outpourings at their meeting.

"You missed a good one tonight, Nedrah," Jenna adds with seriousness. "Please don't stop going just because you don't have to. You need to keep up your support system."

"It's funny," Randi says, folding her parka into a seat on the floor as she eats. "There's so much camaraderie between women in prison. I don't know about the rest of you, but I never had that before. Sometimes I miss just being around a bunch of women."

"It's true," Leanne says. "It's kinda like a sisterhood in there. Most of us have kids, the same problems with abuse, which led to us doin' things we didn't really wanna do. If a certain somebody had been at her NA meeting tonight she would've heard one of the guys talk about being afraid to ask anybody for anything, and the road that sets you on."

"One of the guys, really?" Nedrah says, eating her pizza. She tries to avoid picking up men at NA because her friends would judge her. As with addictions treatment groups in any small town where everyone knows each other, complex social dynamics extended from the group to social situations and other encounters. Some people avoided them for precisely this reason.

"I don't know." Jenna lights a cigarette. "My attitude in there was always, 'don't mess with me unless you wanna be my friend.' I still write to some of those girls, the ones that were like family to me. There's a few I really took home with me. I even put money on their books."

Randi is laughing. "Someone is thinking of you thanks to their commissary."

"Hey," Leanne says seriously, and then pauses to take a drag from Jenna's cigarette. Lately Nedrah wonders if Leanne and Jenna are a couple keeping their relationship a secret. She can relate to that, because keeping anything a secret in prison, or in this small town, is no small feat.

"If not for prison," Leanne continues, "I never would've learned to set boundaries. I'll never forget one day at the tilapia hatchery, because I was lucky enough to have one of the best jobs making the big bucks, a dollar and forty cents an hour, I really got to put that shit into practice. I told this girl who kept getting too close to me waiting for the fish baskets, 'Look, you, you're in my bubble. Just let me do my job. I will get the basket to you.'"

Jenna nods, taking the cigarette back from her. Nedrah notices how closely they sit together on the couch and tries to hide her smile. "It was the same for me," Jenna says. "When I started doing things like that, setting boundaries with friends in there, I would cry and just lose it like, 'Oh, they hate me!' Now I know it's just my own insecurities. Those groups on boundaries, and being able to practice what I learned while I was in prison, really helped me in all of my relationships back in the free world. I really didn't know how to express myself; it was very uncomfortable for me."

"The simple fact is," Randi says, "if it's uncomfortable you need to be doing it."

"Being Native," Leanne adds, "I was a minority in there and so being judged, I really didn't judge people even on their crimes like a lot of girls did. I would always say hi to them because it's lonely in there, not having nobody say hi to you, you know. I never minded it, I thought, 'Let people go ahead and judge, I don't care.' Those little things make a big difference to women in there who are struggling and feeling like the whole world forgot about them."

"I'd watch the long-termers and do what they did," Randi says. "Some of those women just amazed me, knowing that they were gonna die in prison, just by the simple fact that they could get up in the morning and manage to smile. I knew a couple of those ladies and

I'd just look at them and go, 'Now there is a woman who is strong and doesn't care who sees it.' Those ones doing ten, fifteen, twenty years, they're all in a different department. I always envied the bonds they had with each other."

"I think other women had genuine love for each other," Jenna adds. "I knew a lot of women that met in there and genuinely cared about each other. Remember Laurie and Kay? Laurie got out and she stayed by Kay's side, waiting for her, getting involved with her family and her kids. But really for most—and I've been a lesbian all day long for my whole entire life so I can say this—it's a game and it's just horrible."

"Yeah," Leanne shakes her head, "but remember all those bullshit rules we had to follow and the only real reason for them was to keep women from getting together that way? Like I just don't see hair braiding as sexual. I don't see how passing and receiving hygiene, all the little soap and toothpaste, is foreplay, or sharing commissary food with someone who doesn't have any. If I saw somebody struggling, I would share, because some of those girls only live off of state pay in there and that's not very much, not enough to buy all their hygiene."

"Oh, I hate working in a motel for that reason," Nedrah laughs. "Every damn time I see one of those little bars of soap it just takes me back to prison, like the smallness of everything, you know? And it's funny because you know normal people would never think of it that way."

"I do get it, though," Randi adds. "Some of these women definitely do that gay for the stay. I was in the fish tank with this little eighteen-year-old girl who kept going on and on about her boyfriend and she wanted to get married to him and have kids. But sure enough when we got up to housing in general population, she was going around like, 'I'm not sure I know my sexuality' because I guess she thought she was going to be lesbian or bisexual now. Then she got sent to the hole after she got caught with this thirty-some-year-old woman in the shower. I was like, 'Are you freakin' kidding me?' It's pathetic, the 'I love you, I love you' that gets thrown around in there. Look, the fundamental problem is that some women just don't know how to be alone."

"You gotta remember, though," Leanne insists, "for anybody who has suffered from depending on drugs or trauma earlier in life, the emotional range just doesn't develop as well as for other people. Plus, if you add to that how women gossip because it's the only way they are allowed to have any kind of power at all, for most of them anyway, prison is like one of these small towns, where everybody knows everybody's business."

Jenna emphatically nods. "And that's usually women's role in relationships, we're codependent, the followers. A lot of women come into prison broken, and that's the biggest common denominator in there. So it's no surprise that they look for that attention in there, although in my opinion it's like looking for a Cadillac in a junkyard. I mean, you don't want two broken vehicles hooking up, like what are you going to have, a Yugo?"

Leanne laughs and puts her head on Jenna's shoulder. "But homophobia runs so deep in there. Staff got so fearful by the time I left because of DOC regulations and PREA stuff, never mind there's never been a single rape case, that if you had short hair and didn't bat your eyes like a typical idiot female, you'd get housed somewhere they could really watch you. There were only really like seven of us in there, out of three hundred–some."

"Oh," Randi sighs, "I just remembered when Annie lost it after they shipped Carrie out of state after they both got a write-up for being sexual together. She kept asking the guards, 'Can you at least prove to me that she's still alive?' That just about broke my heart."

"That's prison, though," Nedrah says matter-of-factly. "If you think about it, group really isn't that different, only there it's other inmates keeping an eye on you. I remember this one girl tried to complete ITU three different times and would always drop out because the other girls didn't like her. Everybody talks about everything in prison, like in the 'Beyond Trauma' group you do sign papers saying it's private, but it's a prison. It's a prison where everybody talks about everything."

"Nothing's private in prison," Leanne states. "So somebody finds out something about you and it goes through the whole prison. You get somebody with sexual abuse issues talking about them in group and some little bitch will tell everyone, 'Oh, well, I knew that dude and he would never do something like that' and then the story goes all the way around. Or somebody reveals that they have Hep C and no one wants to touch their trays."

"But they're required to talk," Randi intones. "That always kinda confused me, maybe bothered me a little bit, too, because it seemed so inconsistent. Like they would say, just like in the twelve steps in the free world, 'secrets keep you sick.' Well, okay, I get it. So I would tell my counselor things, but I wouldn't clean myself out with everybody else that way. I've been settin' boundaries my whole life, I just didn't know there was a word for that. I never would tell those women in there everything. You have to be very careful."

"There's a lotta drama in prison," Nedrah says.

"Holy cow, yes," Jenna adds. "I always felt bad for those women with money crimes or other charges that had nothing to do with the drug world, because they had just absolutely no idea how to cope in there. I remember right before I was gettin' ready to leave, there was this girl planning to escape and I think this woman, she was a money crime, new to general pop, thought she was trying to be a good person, hold herself to a higher standard by telling one of the guards. She was thinking that was the right thing to do—it's not. A lot of girls have been snitched on outside and if they label you a snitch, that's it, you're enemies. And someone finally just had to explain to her, this is the drug world in here, because a majority of people are caught up in that before they come to prison. They think differently, do differently, feel differently. That's stabbing them in the back, but she really thought she was doing the right thing."

"You associate with nasty little snitches," Leanne nudges Jenna. "I didn't know that about you."

Jenna shrugs, her face bearing traces of hurt. "She told the guard. Not me."

Randi laughs. "See, this is why I'd just stay out of relationships altogether in there. I'd just sleep or read, mostly at night though. During the day there's literally nothing to do if you're not working or in groups, so I'd just sleep. It wasn't really worth my time, or the heartaches, so I just stuck to myself unless someone truly wanted to be my friend."

"I found that I created a really rich inner world in prison," Leanna shares, "much more so than here in the free world where there are so many distractions. But really the key to staying out of any kind of trouble in there is keeping busy. Randi, sounds like you were lucky not to have a bunch of write-ups, because if you're sitting there with nothing to do there's a tendency to get caught up in the drama. It's very easy to get bored and just stir-crazy and start getting really edgy. I worked constantly, I studied, I made crafts for my family."

"Same here," Jenna nods. "I was go-go-go all the time, and it kept me oblivious to all the drama going on in the pod. I always tried to be there for people to talk to, and people came to my door all the time to confide in me about stuff or ask for advice and how to put things, because I would try to advocate a lot for the other girls."

"See, that's so good, because it doesn't happen a lot like that at a women's prison," Leanne slowly laments. "The thing is that, at least when I was there, there were less than three hundred women and most of them wouldn't stand up to fight for their rights. They'd just cower down and say 'okay' and we'd get run over. That's just what happens. You know the men don't stand for it, they stick together and they all fight against it. They might not like each other, but they all fight for the common good. Not in the women's prison, uh-uh."

"Too busy back-biting each other," Randi sighs. "I guess I'm old and I've just seen this so many times that I just didn't even care anymore when I was in there. I would just go to my room, just let them do whatever they were going to do, you know? But it's not right."

"The free world's not so different in some respects," Jenna says thoughtfully. "I see a lotta women here who organize their whole lives around some man and his wants and desires, and their kids if they have any. I get the impression sometimes that some women just have no earthly idea who they are as individual people. So, when you get the prison version of that, of course it's going to just be pathetic."

Randi checks her phone and exclaims, "Shit, I gotta open the gas station tomorrow at four-thirty in the morning and we're comin' up on ten p.m. I better go." She gathers her things as Jenna and Leanne fold up the empty pizza box.

"What's that?" Leanne starts as the women turn toward the clicking sound right outside the apartment door. "Does someone have a key to your place, Nedrah?"

When Nedrah is in the company of her three friends from NA, she feels like a different kind of woman, like someone who has strong opinions she can vociferously defend with confidence and who has interests and goals all her own. She likes listening to them speak this way when they come over, and gets the feeling that Leanne would defend her against an intruder out to cause harm.

"Yeah," Nedrah says, not sure how to continue. These women all seem to have whole and intact selves in a way that confuses Nedrah, even scaring her with their impermeability. To Nedrah, they seem to move through the world surrounded by an aura of self-confidence that deflects any attempt to disrespect or undermine them. "Lance from school. Remember him?"

Randi bursts out laughing, zipping up her parka and shaking her head as Jenna and Leanne exchange looks with a meaning Nedrah cannot discern. When he enters the room, the panic in Lance's eyes quickly subsides when he sees that there is no one present who is friends with his wife or his sisters or is the parent of one of his children's friends. He feels naked in the worst possible way, here on the edge of town with these adult women he still thinks of as "the bad girls" from their time in high school together. "Don't worry, Lance," Randi sings in an artificially high-pitched voice. "We won't tell." She playfully presses her palm against his chest on her way out the door, and he shrinks against the door frame as the three women file out into the night.

"Yeah," Leanne smirks, her contemptuous stare making him look helplessly toward Nedrah. "We're nobody. Wouldn't wanna be, not in this shithole town full'a people like you."

The End of the Line

Sheree makes it a point to stay silent as she lets her male colleagues angrily vent their frustration during their morning meeting about yet another set of new documentation and assessment requirements for parolees under their supervision issued from the Department of Corrections' Central Office in Cheyenne. When she first started her job as a parole officer seven years ago, visible manifestations of anger in any form thrust Sheree's entire being into the near-obsessive routines of hypervigilance: checking the distance to the always-open office door, calculating the time it would take to reach the can of pepper spray she wears in a holster on her belt, listening closely to determine if her colleagues are still present in the parole office and able to come to her aid. Now Sheree regards angry people as juvenile at best and imagines their brains missing some key cluster of cells that impart impulse control and rationality.

Mostly, Sheree now finds anger boring and knows that the angry people under her supervision are furious with a system that has wielded near-total control over their lives. Their anger only feels personal because, to them, Sheree represents that system. She could understand how that would make a person feel hemmed in, but she also knows it was their own choices that got them there in about 99% of cases.

In her first year as a parole officer, Sheree often wished that she was allowed to carry a gun, especially during the mandatory home visits she made to check on parolees with histories of violence. She used to dread pulling up to a banged-up trailer surrounded by dogs to do a routine check for alcohol, firearms, controlled substances, or the presence of people her parolees are forbidden to contact. It used to be hard to hold back tears when prying herself loose from the arms of small children who, she suspects, saw her as the only stable adult in their lives who keeps a regular schedule. Her work cell phone used to buzz nonstop with text messages and calls from people under supervision, and back then she always felt obligated to help them, sometimes in ways that made her own family life suffer. Sheree's dreams, when she was rested enough to have them, featured a cacophony of needy, sometimes tearful voices all clamoring for her attention: "Sheree, I can't mail this back to the court, can you come over and pick it up?" "Sheree, my boss hates me and I want to quit because that horse's ass told everyone in the kitchen I'm a felon," "Sheree, this is too hard. I just want to go back to prison. I know how to do time." And then from her supervisor, "Sheree, where's the presentence investigation on this new parolee? How many home visits can you squeeze in this week? Why did so-and-so relapse on your watch?" Then she would wake up and hear some versions of those same things the next morning.

Sheree used to watch the men under her supervision for signs that they were looking at her a little too closely, trying to ascertain if a slight reddening of her face, rise in vocal pitch, or other nonverbal cues betrayed fear, insecurities, or other tell-tale signs that a person might be easily manipulated. She really cannot fault the ones who do this for honing their powers of observation, since she knows how small and powerless most people feel in prison and how things that seem so absolutely trivial in the free world take on momentous importance inside, like how many candy bars a person can have at one time. People have to watch each other in prison, no matter what kind of uniform they wear and regardless of their gender, although it still strikes Sheree as deeply unfair that the kinds of things most men fear in prison, like rape, seem to be almost normal experiences among many women in the free world.

Now she just tells them all the same thing right from the beginning and knows that, for the vast majority of parolees under her supervision, she is just another state agent with the power to tell them what to do. She tries to treat everyone equally and explain things simply without insulting their intelligence, a challenging balance when so many of the people who report to her office have limited formal education, cognitive deficits from years of substance abuse, undiagnosed disabilities, or all three, and feel too ashamed to ask her to repeat or more fully explain a point they do not understand. Sheree knows that the implications of not fully understanding a parole requirement could land a person in jail for a temporary sanction or send the person back to prison, so she takes her time in explaining the court-mandated conditions that each person must abide by, which typically include maintaining a job, attending recovery support groups such as Narcotics or Alcoholics Anonymous, and paying child support, restitution, or other court-imposed costs on a predetermined schedule.

"Look," Sheree says, sometimes pointing straight at the men for emphasis on the first meeting so they know she means business, "when you get a loan to buy a car, what happens if you don't repay the loan?" They all know, and tell her, the car gets repossessed by the bank. "Right," Sheree continues. "I'm the bank here. If you don't do everything you promised the Parole Board that you would, I'm gonna repossess your freedom." She felt a sly sense of pride when, on her way to fill up her coffee mug in the break room one morning, she overheard the senior-most agent in the office using her trademark phrase in a meeting with a man just released from prison.

Now that same agent is angrily complaining about the new reporting and assessment requirements from Central Office as Sheree stares at the black poster directly above his head, its bright white letters reading "Felon + Gun = Prison. It's That Simple." "When I started as an agent twenty years ago," he is shouting at no one in particular, "we had one sheet of paper, and the rest of the time we were out in the field making a real difference in offenders' lives. Now I spend so much time on the damn computer writing about the who, what, where, how, and why of their lives that I can't get out there to actually know what's going on with them." Sheree knows fighting Central Office instructions is useless because in their little town, they may as well be in another solar system from the capital in Cheyenne. She lets him finish, knowing that he is venting frustrations they all share, and allows a meaningful silence to hang in their midst for a minute or two.

"Look, we've all got a job to do here," Sheree finally intones in a voice deeper than the one she normally uses at home with her husband and two children. "We all know all about dealing with the consequences of bad decisions, and I include the state's decisions in that category, too. We don't have to like it, but we got to do it all the same."

Everyone present lets out a collective sigh, with one agent mumbling resentfully, "I hate feelin' like some goddamn bean counter."

Sheree hates feeling like a small-time accountant, too, but she regards words spoken in her office as weighty and meaningful commodities not easily taken back. "Have a good day, everybody," she says as they file out of the room and back into their offices for another seven hours of meetings, report writing, and a thousand other attempts at problem solving. Sheree's own desk in the office across the hall from the conference room is as orderly as she can make it despite groaning under the weight of printed reports. She tries not to imagine the voluminous physical manifestations of the information stored in her computer in the multiple computerized databases that she and her agents must use to track and monitor offenders' progress through, out of, and, for approximately 24% of them across Wyoming, back into, prison.

Sheree is not looking forward to her next meeting because she knows that she needs to enforce some difficult terms with this parolee's relationship with her toddler, the kind that might lead to relapse among substance abusers like her. Sheree put her own kids to bed early the night before so that she could come back into the office while her husband watched television in case the girls woke up. "Promise me you won't have more than two beers?" she asked on the way out, not waiting for a response. Sometimes Sheree jokes with her friends that she has three children, two she gave birth to and one she married, but lately this assessment seems less and less funny to her. Poised over her paper files with two secure databases open on the computer screen in front of her that track Tammi's participation in drug treatment and other groups in prison as well as her predicted risk of reoffending, Sheree felt the kind of creeping intuitive sense that amid the scores on a ten-point scale, case worker notes on progress, mood, and medications, and detailed descriptions of Tammi's family and criminal history, she was dealing with someone swept into a furious current and struggling mightily not to drown.

Sheree has access to a version of Tammi's life history, replete with information that Sheree does not know about even her closest friends. The report from Tammi's presentence investigation alone, which the court uses to determine sentencing structure that impacts parole requirements, is the result of a laborious process led by parole officers. Sheree and her colleagues usually spend about sixty hours, more than a full week's work in between multiple other tasks that need completion, collecting the wide scope of information required in a presentence investigation (PSI): conducting criminal background checks from all state police departments, interviewing a family member to include information on how the parolee grew up and whether he or she was abused, determining employment history, assessing relationships with children and significant others, gathering substance abuse histories, and collecting a statement from the crime victim, if one exists.

Sheree often tells new agents that PSIs are really "home studies" that presents a holistic portrait of the context in which a person committed a crime. Words that try to capture the totality of Tammi's life circumstances strike Sheree as woefully inadequate summaries of the full situation confronting her as she tries to obtain custody of her three-year-old daughter, Ava, who has recently been diagnosed as being on the autism spectrum and is living with a foster family while in the state custody of the Department of Family Services. Sheree is so tired that she has to read out loud, the ugliness of the words like vicious little knives piercing the solitude of the office at night: "unstable lifestyle since birth," "mother incarcerated, parental rights relinquished," "traumatic brain injury caused by abuse," "diagnosis of bipolar disorder not otherwise specified," "severe and long-term emotional and sexual abuse by multiple perpetrators," "age thirteen at birth of first child," "second child born addicted to opiates," "first child's father unknown, lethal Fentanyl overdose second child's father's cause of death." Every single one of Tammi's family members has been under probation or parole supervision by an agent in Sheree's office.

Sheree knows that Tammi is one of those women who left prison wearing the clothes she wore when booked into county jail, no matter the season of her release. She pictures her leaving the back gate to be transferred to the ACC facility, jeans and synthetic top a little too tight from the starchy carbohydrates served in prison. Yet Sheree also knows that Tammi worked extraordinarily hard in the ACC to save up as much money as she could from her meager food-service income to get an apartment in town in the hopes of reuniting with Ava, whose DFS case worker is a member of the same tightly knit church that Ava's foster mother attends. The week prior, Sheree had struggled not to make waves before ending a phone call with this case worker, who told her, "This little girl is truly blessed to have this family. They've done a double international adoption from China and five other adoptions. Mom stays home full-time. They'll give her a good, wholesome life. We all have to think about the best interests of that little girl. For goodness sake, Sheree, she was born a heroin addict." When she heard that, Sheree finally had had enough and told the case worker that she had another appointment; after all, she would have to see this woman at the grocery store and PTA events for a long time after Tammi was off her case load.

"Tammi," Sheree sighed in the night quiet of the office before turning off the light to get some sleep before a difficult day, "I feel like you just never had a chance."

Tammi always arrives early at the parole office, hoping as always that no one will notice how long it takes her to write answers onto the two-page form she must complete at every visit. It asks her to write down information about experiences she has had since her last visit with her job, court or child support payments, law enforcement, vehicle information, current medications and prescribing physician, and treatment classes. Tammi knows all of this information, but the words blur together sometimes in confusing ways when she feels rushed. She also knows that sometimes letting others have information about her problems with reading and writing comprehension creates the same kinds of vulnerabilities that come from taking a big bag of candy from a stranger on the playground. Now that the form is filled in, her blue-inked handwriting as neat as she could make it, she fills the time waiting for Sheree rehearsing the information she knows about Ava from her last three supervised visits with her at the Department of Family Services office, which is located two doors down from the same nondescript building that houses the parole office and a chiropractor.

Ava is three years old and her favorite color is red. She lives with a nice family that buys her pretty clothes and keeps her clean and happy. Tammi's own foster families always seemed to take her in for the little bit of money they would receive from the state, then something would always manage to go wrong with another sibling, or at school, and she would have a new family with different faces and habits. It occurs to Tammi that no one has ever hit Ava, although she cannot be sure, and she is happy that Ava has been in the same place for most of her little life. In ITU Tammi spent weeks writing a mandatory paper, which the other women called "a parenting paper," about the impact that her addiction had on Ava's life. The other women said she failed to hold herself accountable because while she wrote about how sorry she was that Ava suffered because she was born addicted to heroin, she wrote from her heart in the paper about how glad she is that Ava was with nice, loving people.

Tammi thinks that in ITU the other women expected her to write that Ava should be back with her own biological mother, but Tammi was not in mothering shape when Ava was born. Tammi remembers how relieved she felt when her own mother, still locked up in a Nebraska prison, relinquished her parental rights when Tammi was six years old, because it meant that Tammi might be adopted by a nice family like the one that hoped they could have Ava forever. "I'm probably going to be in here for a long time," her mother had written to her, the small piece of stationery from the prison commissary oddly crumpled when the DFS worker shared it with her. Other women had a frame of reference for parents and families, but Tammi has always absorbed those ideas by listening to other people talk about their own. Now she is hoping that things can be a little bit different, that maybe she and Ava can be together.

"How's it going, Tammi?" Sheree says with genuine concern as she swings the door wide open enough for Tammi to pass. She immediately goes in front of Sheree, knowing that Sheree has to keep her in full view at all times while she is in the office.

They sit across from each other, Sheree with her computer screen to her right and Tammi moving her chair slightly to avoid the harsh sunlight streaming in between the blinds.

Sheree starts. "How have things been going for you, Tammi?"

"Okay," Tammi says slowly and then stops. Sheree seems pretty good as far as parole officers, case workers, and other state agents go, but Tammi still tries to disclose as little information as she possibly can in her dealings with her. She can tell that Sheree does not like this, so she continues. "I am proud of the boundary that I set with Cody," she says slowly.

Sheree brightens. "That's great! Tell me about how you went about that."

"Well, I just told him I can't see him while he's not healthy."

"That's really good. How did Cody respond to that? Did he understand?"

Tammi sees that Sheree is happy with her now, so she tries her best to use the words she learned in ITU, to show that she really means to stay sober this time, even knowing that relapse had sprouted like a bloody perennial each time one of her family members had announced they were done with drugs for good.

"I told Cody about how addicts know how to heal pain through drugs and that he needs to find another way to deal with his pain. He pulled over and tried to talk to me when I was walking home from work, but I told him I couldn't talk to him. My recovery is too important to me."

Sheree nods and waits, hoping that Tammi will say more. Tammi's sense of the pain she describes is visceral rather than intellectual, and words collapse and dissolve whenever she tries to capture how dope dulls the sharp edges of hopelessness and ugliness that otherwise threaten to cut her and her relatives.

They could pass an entire afternoon this way, Sheree thinks with frustration, and decides just to confront Tammi with the stakes facing her and Ava.

"Tammi, you're toeing the end of the line here. Do you want to be a mother?"

"What kinda question is that?"

Tammi's eyes widen in genuine shock, making Sheree realize that Tammi's DFS case worker may not have fully explained that one more relapse, one more slipup, will likely prompt the judge to terminate her parental rights and award custody of Ava to her foster parents. Sheree tries not to consider that the case worker's omission may have been intentional, and instead decides to push Tammi to think about the consequences of interacting with her family members or others she generally terms "old associates."

"The kind I just asked, Tammi. You heard me."

Tammi starts to pull into herself. She is so thin that in the beginning Sheree probably forced her to take more drug tests than was necessary. Sheree understands why Tammi tries to disappear in this way but also needs her to understand that she can lose her daughter forever this time.

"Tammi, you're one week out of the ACC and you got your own place now. I know you want Ava in your life but right now this is all brand new for you. When I came by on a home visit you barely had food in the fridge and the whole place smelled like cigarette smoke. You know that DFS can't support bringing a three-year-old into that kind of environment. And you can't have contact with Cody or anyone else in that lifestyle, period. None."

Tammi pulls at a piece of skin by her thumbnail until a drop of blood appears and she quickly tucks it back into the sleeve of her torn sweater, her eyes on the ground.

Sheree feels like she is looking at a sick little girl who feels powerless to make any kind of real changes. Getting into a government-subsidized apartment, keeping a job at a fast-food place, and going to twelve step meetings was a major challenge for her, and Sheree is struggling to envision her ever being able to care for an autistic toddler without a community support system.

"But I love Ava," Tammi mumbles, barely audible, and in those words Sheree hears the panic and inadequacy that any unprepared amateur feels under observation. Sheree realizes that Tammi has nothing left to say, so she reminds her of the continuing responsibilities she has: keep going to meetings, keep going to parenting classes, and keep paying bills on time. A sinking feeling lowers into Sheree as Tammi silently nods. "I love Ava. I really do."

"I know you do, Tammi. That's why it's really important that you keep doing what you're doing. I can't promise anything. I don't know what

DFS is going to decide. I just need you to remember there are more people involved here than just you, okay?"

"I know that. I want Ava to have a good life."

They continue in this pithy vein for several minutes before Tammi slinks, shoulders folded in on her thin frame, out the door and back to her little apartment a few minutes' walk across town. She is confused by the meeting and knows that something is happening to Ava, but she fears that asking too many questions will just upset Sheree and make things worse, so that maybe she could not see Ava at all. Tammi wants to hide in the darkest part of her small closet, where no can find her, and cry. She really had hoped that getting her own apartment, a safe place for Ava, would mean big changes for both of them, and yet here she was, walking back home by herself.

She tentatively pushes the door, which is open and slightly ajar. She can see Cody's wiry figure bent over his cell phone, fingers rapidly text messaging someone. He looks up, slightly surprised to see her as she makes what she hopes is a serious and angry face at him. "There ain't nothin' in the back of the closet," he winks on his way out the door, "so don't go in there and look. I'll be back for it later."

Tammi feels hopelessly devoid of the energy to be angry at her brother because this is his way in the world, and yet still the sucking sense of isolation and futility pulls her, shaky with dread, toward the back of the closet. There she crouches among meager piles of her dirty clothes, her hands moving almost involuntarily across the old carpet until she finds the plastic grocery bag wrapped tightly around something she knows is inside. Time suspended in a sticky opioid web, Tammi will not be able to recall in court the trajectory of events that ended with snowflakes melting on her face in bright blotches of cold on her dope-stunned flesh. She will not recognize Officer Scheck, who has arrested her on four prior occasions, when he pulls over and tells her, with the weary voice of someone weeks from retirement, "Tammi, we're gonna have to go down to the jail again. S'pose you know that first I need to read you your rights." The Miranda warning will come through the air, as Tammi sits in the back of the patrol car watching the heavy wet snowflakes fall as the world slowly rolls past her, now as ever.

Officer Scheck still has not gotten used to arresting women, which he almost never did at the beginning of his police career, back when police work was among men, mostly bar brawlers and cattle rustlers. He never felt bad about locking them up, but now he has this little girl from a family of dirt-bag men sobbing in his holding cell, incoherent with grief because she is going to lose her baby forever. "This world," he sighs as he looks hopefully up at the paper calendar and mouths "fourteen days" before he picks up the phone to call Sheree, who is married to one of his younger deputies. It is only common courtesy, he thinks. "Sheree," he tells her, "you ain't gonna like this, but I want you to hear it straight from me"—and already Sheree intuitively knows the reason he is calling. Whenever Sheree feels tears welling up in her eyes despite her most strenuous efforts to avoid them, she opens the top drawer of her desk to look at the framed picture of her girls on a Florida Gulf Coast beach, their smiling faces framing the ebb tide's wet sand as they chased crabs, screaming with happiness. Yet this time her emotional containment strategy fails to work and instead she sees Tammi pulled under, wordlessly, into the inky wet deep.

No Excuse for What I Did

Marisol is in constant motion as she cuts the plantains, chops the red-dark *pasilla* chile after soaking it in water, husks the tomatillos, and grates part of the neat circle of cinnamon-infused chocolate from the grocery store across the street from their home near Denver's Federal Boulevard. Itzel bought it yesterday as she wandered through the aisles listening to music and conversation completely devoid of English's hard edges. Every brightly painted advertisement in Spanish she read at least three times, feeling as though her prison case worker achieved a miracle in facilitating her interstate compact home to Colorado. Itzel knows that Marisol, her sister because they share the same father, probably does not normally prepare such involved dishes from El Salvador, the country of her birth. *Plantanos en mole*, the one she is making on this Saturday afternoon, takes up far more time than her busy schedule allows her as a full-time social worker, caregiver to Itzel's daughter Isela, and constant source of advice for family members about how to navigate the complex world of low-wage work and stay off the police radar that is their life in the United States.

Marisol is the only person Itzel knows who has graduated from college, has no criminal record, and works at a professional job where she earns the same amount of money every week, even if she has to take a day off because she is sick. Marisol is always moving as she rushes from one task to another, trying not to become embittered by the similar nature of the tasks she performs for her social work clients and her own family members, the only difference being that the mental case notes she makes on her family members eat away at her spirit in ways she finds difficult to replenish. She spends a lot of time thinking about this as she travels between jail, prison, and the various Denver County government and nonprofit offices tasked with providing forms of social and financial benefits to what sometimes seems to Marisol to be a permanent underclass of people struggling with poverty, addiction, precarious housing, homelessness, and the lifelong consequences of criminal convictions.

When she is at work, Marisol listens to inmates at the Denver County Jail talk about aspects of their lives that relate to her role as a social work advocate for them, sometimes lowering their voices in Spanish to remind her of what they think they have in common with her. Marisol does not like this when it happens. "*Mira, es lo mismo para ti*," a man in county jail whispered to Marisol after he saw a white correctional officer curtly inform her that she needed to leave the facility prior to shift change.

"No, it's not the same for me," Marisol had answered in English, her voice slightly raised because she did not like the self-satisfied look in the orange-clad man's eyes. "I didn't make a choice to break the law. You did. That officer is just doing his job. It has nothing to do with racism. Plenty of deputies in here and every other county jail treat me just the same and they are Black and Latino, just like me." The man gave her a nasty look and shrugged, as if Marisol was the one who did not understand the true nature of the criminal justice system's operations.

Now Marisol is in the apartment listening to Itzel talk about prison, speaking in English only because Marisol wants Spanish to be a second language for Isela. "Prison in Colorado is like 'no inmate left behind' compared to Wyoming," Itzel is saying. "There was so little for those women to do compared with the women's prison here in Denver, or even out in La Vista," she says, but Marisol tries to focus on cooking the *mole*, keeping her hands and body in motion to shut out the ugly sounds of her sister talking just like anyone else in a correctional facility who feels entitled to therapeutic treatment and support groups that Marisol and her colleagues cannot afford in the free world. Marisol hopes Itzel will construe her silence as empathy since Marisol desperately needs someone to help out at home. The ad hoc caregiving arrangements that Marisol has developed over the years as Isela grew from a baby to a preschooler have necessarily relied on a circulating network of equally exhausted and overburdened female relatives.

Now that Itzel is out of prison and living in Marisol's spare bedroom, Marisol wants a life of her own so that she can focus on getting a better-paid job that will allow her to move to a neighborhood where incarceration and low-level drug-economy involvement are not the norm. Listening to Itzel complain about how no one in the family could visit her in prison because of the distance or because their own criminal records prohibited them from being on the approved visitors' list, Marisol restrains herself from reminding Itzel that she could not come visit because she was too busy holding the family together. Caring for Isela made it impossible to drive the five hours from Denver to the Wyoming women's prison on icy country roads for an hour-long visit. Years of having to depend only on herself while so many other people depended on her to sort out their lives have taught Marisol that sometimes in relationships it is better to focus on her longer-term goals than on the short-term satisfaction of expressing her true feelings.

"Marisol?" Itzel asks when she sees that the contents of all the bowls and saucepans are now simmering in the tall, wide stockpot she bought on sale in Little Saigon, a few streets over from their apartment building. Only the plate of plantains, which will go in right before they eat, remains on the counter next to the stove. Marisol utters a noncommittal sound to indicate that she is still listening as she stands with her back to Itzel, stirring the satiny brown sauce in the stockpot. "I couldn't imagine," Itzel says. "I couldn't imagine, Marisol. My heart goes out to all those women I knew in prison who lost their children. I ask God about it often. I really do. I ask God, 'Why am I so blessed with Marisol caring for Isela, compared to these women who have no one to help them?' Because of you, I am truly blessed. There is no excuse for what I did, and the suffering it caused you."

Marisol sits down at the kitchen table and looks into her sister's eyes. She does not share with her how humiliated she felt when Itzel's parole officer searched her home to make sure that she had no alcohol, drugs, or guns. She does not say how Isela calls her Mami because she knows her every need and that Itzel is misreading this as an intuitive biological link, rather than as the product of necessity. She does not complain that their other sister, Raquel, has been staying with her for the past two weeks while continuing to flail lazily in a vortex of the same neighborhood associates that Itzel's parole officer instructed Itzel to avoid. Instead, she simply says, "I'm so tired." The sisters sit without speaking, the traffic on Federal Boulevard, the simmering pot of *mole*, and their breathing the only sounds in the room.

"I am tired, too," Itzel eventually says, still uncomfortable with silence after the constant buzz of prison sociality. In prison, a woman could say nothing all day and still silently participate in dozens of conversations within earshot; even in restrictive housing women would shout from cell to cell just to hear the sounds of each other's voices and know that they were not truly alone. Itzel fills up the free-world silence with chatter, vocalizing what she learned by unobtrusively listening to the day room conversations among old timers like Janea and her group. Itzel always secretly envied the easy, albeit resigned, camaraderie of women doing life sentences and the wisdom they seemed so readily able to impart. "Women have a tendency to live by default," Itzel repeats from memory, "with preprogrammed ways of thinking that aren't always healthy for us." Marisol just nods, weary of what she thinks of as women's jail-speak, as she half-rises out of her chair as soon as she hears the sounds of movement emerge from her bedroom. Raquel and Isela are waking up from their Saturday afternoon nap together.

Raquel looks far too thin as she stretches her arms over her head, pulling sleeping Isela behind her toward the kitchen table, where Raquel puts her in her lap like a baby. Marisol serves her and Itzel a bowl of *mole*, carefully pouring the sauce over rice and the cooked plantains and adding some chopped cilantro. Isela opens her mouth like a little bird as Raquel feeds her spoonful after spoonful from the bowl while deliberately speaking in Spanish that Isela cannot understand. "You're talking in El Salvador," Isela whines, but Raquel and Itzel ignore her, knowing Marisol does not allow talk about prison, jail, or related matters in front of the little girl. Marisol starts to wash the dishes, turning the tap on full force to drown out the sounds of her sisters talking about Dante's newest set of criminal charges. She coughs loudly when English words burst like firecrackers into their Spanish, piquing Isela's interest as she tries to follow the conversation. "*En español, por favor,* this is not a conversation for good little girls to hear," Marisol says as evenly as she can.

"What?" Raquel shouts in English as she throws her spoon on the table, brown spots of sauce spreading across Marisol's carefully ironed tablecloth, "*Mira,* I don't know how to say 'co-conspirator' in Spanish! I don't know all those fancy words that you do. Maybe you want to translate for us so Isela won't understand, like how you do for people like us in jail?"

Isela stops chewing her plantains, not quite sure what is happening, her little face starting to crumple in ways that only Marisol notices and understands. Marisol dries her hands, leaving the dishes in the sink, and says to Isela, as if her own sisters are not there, "Let's go for a walk and get some ice cream." Raquel sighs dramatically, rolling her eyes at what she regards as Marisol's misguided aspirations to a different kind of life, and Itzel looks at the ground, as unsure as Isela about how to react, a sick, sinking feeling spreading throughout her body as she reflects on the news that this latest investigation Dante is under may or may not result in criminal charges against her.

Isela struggles into the pink jacket that Marisol paid full price for at a department store and Marisol puts on the old black flats she got secondhand from a coworker, the worn spots covered with black magic marker to save money. "Can you please turn off the stove when you're done?" Marisol asks Raquel and Itzel, as if nothing has happened, and they nod, eager to continue their conversation without her there. As she walks down the apartment building's stairs, Isela's warm hand in her own, Marisol has the familiar sensation of personal defeat that accompanies particularly final and totalizing events in her clients' lives. She knows this feeling from sitting in jail visiting rooms with women wailing because their parental rights are being terminated by a judge, from being in court with men about to be sentenced to years of incarceration followed by immediate deportation to Mexico or Central America, and from countless other scenarios that changed people's lives forever. Marisol, who is always a bystander rather than a decision maker in these life-changing events, sits stoically as they occur while heightening her powers of observation the way that she imagines shipwrecked sailors do as they survey the wreckage on the beach around them. Then she asks herself, wherever she is and whomever she is with: what can I do right now, with the tools that I have available to me, to help those around me to survive and flourish?

Marisol knows that Raquel is now sitting at her kitchen table speaking in urgent Spanish to their sister, giving her all kinds of bad advice about what to do now that Itzel is probably, again, involved in another drug case that will lead to another prison sentence. Raquel is probably telling Itzel that she knows someone in Mexico who can take her in for a while, but that doing so will mean that she might never be able to return to the United States. Thinking about the ever-increasing intricacies of the plans Raquel will formulate, and the choices that Itzel will make from the options available to her, forces Marisol to go into social worker mode as she takes stock of the wreckage that surrounds the lives of her sisters and so many other people she loves.

"'*Helado*' means ice cream in El Salvador," Isela proudly beams as she raises her face toward Marisol, her pink-clad arm extending to point at a sign bearing the word on a storefront window. One of her baby teeth looks like it might be coming loose in the front of her mouth. Marisol nods and smiles at her as they continue down Federal Boulevard, with Isela thinking about ice cream and Marisol wishing, more than anything she has ever wished for before, that she and Isela could keep on walking until they reached a place where none of this would be their normal.

Concluding Thoughts

Dakota, Nedrah, and Tammi, the main composite characters in this chapter, all differently experienced the way socioeconomic forces combine with individual choices to shape the circumstances and conditions women face on their release from prison. All three women, like many of the women who participated in our study who had been released from prison or reflected on their expectations for reentry, navigate gendered forms of rural social control and surveillance before, during, and after their time in prison. For other women, like Itzel, reentry meant relocating far from Wyoming to their homes in other states, whereas others returned to the small rural communities where they had spent the vast majority, or even all, of their lives. Irrespective of where they relocated to postrelease, the experiences women had following their release often prompted them to critically examine or otherwise reflect on competing narratives about their lives and choices.

Research indicates that most formerly incarcerated women aspire to live a "normal life" characterized by independent living arrangements, no obligations to the criminal justice system, and the ability to care for family (Heidemann, Cedarbaum & Martinez 2016). Yet this "normal life" often involves a loving husband, children, and forms of socioeconomic stability difficult to achieve. Formerly incarcerated women may feel compelled to remain in abusive or unhealthy relationships with men in the hopes of someday fulfilling the dream of a life that is off-limits to them as a result of their marginalization. Women aspire to achieve this goal amid a web of social relationships and obligations that require them to present themselves and their aspirations in different ways to criminal justice and social services professionals, family members, and others in their social circles (Leverentz 2014). These significant life changes, as well as the need to discuss them with loved ones and parole officers alike, occur at a time when at least some women might prefer to remain silent about their experiences with incarceration as a means of distancing themselves from it (McIntyre 2013). We accordingly remained incredibly inspired and humbled by all of the currently and formerly incarcerated women who chose to speak with us at length about their experiences.

The notion of success took different forms among the women who participated in our study and largely depended on what they regarded as a "normal life." Dakota had some measure of professional success as a result of her college degree in accounting, which is rendered useless following her incarceration for stealing money from the medical office where she worked. Like many of her peers, she views education as the pathway to upward socioeconomic mobility and accordingly enrolls in a nursing program that she hopes will result in a second career. Dakota bristles at the numerous indignities she feels she faces as a restaurant worker attending college in her thirties and tries unsuccessfully to manage her bitterness at the social ostracism that she feels accompanies both of these age-inappropriate roles. For Nedrah and Tammi, success takes the form of relationships that fulfill traditional gender role expectations for women.

The respective definitions of success used by Dakota, Nedrah, and Tammi are the products of their past experiences and the degree of family support they received, as was the case for the vast majority of women in our study. Both Dakota and Nedrah were fortunate to have parents who took on the caregiving responsibilities for their children, whereas Tammi's daughter was placed in foster care, just as she was at a young age. Each woman's expectations are shaped, in significant part, by their understandings of what their socioeconomic and individual circumstances, including their status as women with felony convictions, might make possible for them. Dakota, who grew up doing the hard work of trying to keep a ranch afloat with her family, envisions herself as a self-sufficient person able to meet her goals through hard work, and while she feels bitterly frustrated by her inability to work in accounting, she attempts to move past her shame at having been incarcerated to make a new life for herself. Nedrah comes from a deeply religious family where only one woman, her sister Starla, works outside the home, and relationships to children, husbands, and family members are the most central aspects by which women define themselves; her foremost struggles are with intimate partners whom she uses to help define her own sense of personhood. Tammi, from an "outlaw family" well known to Wyoming law enforcement, grew up in foster care prior to her first incarceration as a juvenile; with no role models or community support, the best she can imagine for herself is reunification with her daughter despite the indisputable challenges raising a child will pose to her.

Yet family and associated socialization processes are not, by any means, the only influence on the women's lives. Parole officers, social services agents, and other authorities also have prominent roles in the lives of most women who have served prison sentences. For most women under parole supervision, the stakes are high given that being on parole increases the likelihood that a woman will return to prison due to the possibility for parole revocation (Carlen & Tombs 2006). This reality takes on additional dynamics in rural areas, where small-town life means that parole officers are likely to encounter those under their supervision in a variety of social contexts, from the grocery store to the bar, the latter of which is likely to result in a revocation. Small towns have few secrets due to smaller population sizes and the number of people who know not only each other but also their respective family histories in ways that have direct implications for women on parole. Dakota and Nedrah both come from families with no history of criminal justice system involvement, and none of their relatives have struggled with state agents in the same way as women from intergenerationally poor families have. The situation facing Tammi, who comes from an "outlaw family," prompts Sheree, her genuinely concerned parole officer, to observe that Tammi almost never had a chance at living a life free of substance abuse, poverty, and other negative social forces that have plagued her brother, Cody, her parents, and so many others in her family. Like nearly half of women in both rural and urban jails (Lynch et al. 2016), Tammi struggles with mental health issues and cognitive impairments that are difficult to disentangle from her family's socioeconomic circumstances and associated instability.

Yet it is important to note that parole officers, however professional and sympathetic to the life circumstances of those under their supervision, may not always attend as carefully to the structural challenges facing formerly incarcerated women. Overwhelming caseloads, reduced budgets, concerns about personal safety, and significant stress indisputably make being a parole officer a very difficult job. In their study comparing incarcerated people and probation or parole officers working in rural areas, Ward and Merlo (2015) found that incarcerated people regarded the most pressing issues in their lives to be structural concerns, such as employment, housing, and the ability to pay fines, whereas the officers regarded personal issues, particularly limited motivation to change and associated likelihood of reoffending, as the most problematic. Urban studies with parole agents and the formerly incarcerated women under their supervision have also found differences between priorities regarded as most important, with relationships playing a much greater role in the women's definitions of success, while parole officers tended to regard relationships as potentially destabilizing to women's success (Herrschaft et al. 2009; Wyse 2013).

Parole supervision takes on particularly complex forms in rural areas, where people know one another and strangers are the exception rather than the rule in most towns. When Susan traveled to every Wyoming county to conduct interviews at probation and parole offices, within hours of her arrival in each new town she was almost always asked about her motivations for visiting the town by well-intentioned local people and provided with advice on the area in a way that would never occur in larger towns or cities. Such expressions of genuine concern speak to a level of interconnectedness that, while very much appreciated by Susan, may take on a different tone for formerly incarcerated women who, in almost all instances, have failed to adhere to dominant sociocultural and gender norms. Accordingly, our study's consideration of rural social dynamics offers a unique contribution to existing feminist criminological research that critiques the prevailing correctional focus on individualization of crime as the product of choice and free will (Hackett 2013).

This prevailing focus on individual choice and free will is complex and extends to aspects of the women's lives that are less directly connected to parole supervision, particularly substance abuse treatment and long-term addiction-recovery groups. While participation in such treatment or groups may be one of the conditions of parole, many women in our study emphasize their importance in their lives. For instance, Nedrah's friends from Narcotics Anonymous, all of whom have served prison time and who visit her apartment to celebrate her being off-paper, encourage her to remain active in the twelve step program even though she is no longer required to attend. Yet they also offered mixed assessments of their experiences of release into the small town where they had lived before going to prison; as did many women in the study, they draw parallels between life in a relatively small prison of approximately 250 women, where everyone knows everything about each other, and life in a small town where the same is true and where individuals can feel limited in their abilities to progress in their self-development or to make real and meaningful changes to their lives.

Social ties have a profound impact on reentry and recidivism for both men and women, and all addictions treatment models accordingly emphasize the importance of avoiding what twelve step groups, for instance, concisely characterize as "people, places, and things" that make those in recovery want to abuse substances. Women's pathways into lawbreaking are almost always connected to relationships, and researchers have found that relationships dramatically impact women's experiences with reentry and recidivism (Clone & DeHart 2014; Heidemann, Cedarbaum & Martinez 2014; Leverentz 2006). Relationships with children are among the most significant of these social ties, making social expectations regarding women as caregivers—particularly to minor children—a source of motivation for making significant life changes. Yet children can also be the cause of equally significant financial and social stress prior to and after women's incarceration.

Like many rural women released from prison, Tammi faced significant barriers to reentry success due to her inability to meet dominant cultural expectations as a result of her poverty, lack of education, unstable housing, addiction, and underemployment (Beichner & Rabe-Hemp 2014; Brown & Bloom 2009). Confirming other research on women who enter the system as girls or very young women, numerous forms of structural and interpersonal forces limit the opportunities and supports available to Tammi and her peers (Gaarder & Belknap 2006). Yet children are just one of many concerns facing currently and formerly incarcerated women, as is particularly evident when Itzel learns that she may be arrested and subsequently prosecuted on new criminal charges shortly after reuniting with her daughter and sisters. This example, like so many others throughout this book, emphasizes the sheer number of U.S. people who are touched in some way by the criminal justice system, irrespective of whether or not they have been incarcerated themselves.

These problems are far reaching and impact nearly everyone in U.S. society, whether through tax payments that subsidize the prison system, exposure to mass media representations of the criminal justice system, or first-hand knowledge of incarceration. Therefore, the next chapter—our conclusion—offers evidence-based alternatives to the architecture of gendered violence, which involve building the kind of community and systems of mutual support that many rural people pride themselves on fostering.

Conclusion

Near the end of this project, Susan found herself sitting at an adult community corrections facility with "Kylee," who was serving the rest of her prison sentence while working and living in the free world. Kylee and Susan had just spent the past few hours in the facility's common room talking about the significant challenges facing formerly incarcerated women as they attempt to reunite with loved ones and save enough money to eventually live independently while working at poorly paid service-sectors jobs, the only work open to them as Wyoming women with limited education and skills. The few available mental health and addictions recovery services and the particularly gendered aspects of felony-related stigma in rural areas only exacerbated these problems by reducing the women's abilities to form supportive relationships in the community.

Despite these considerable challenges, Kylee's perspective on her situation resembled what so many of her rural peers expressed to our research team throughout this study. She blamed herself and her individual choices, which she made in contexts heavily constrained by addiction, intimate partner violence, and poverty, for her situation. If anyone was to blame for her situation, Kylee expressed with great conviction, it was she. Kylee's worldview, which she shares with most of her rural peers, did not readily facilitate clear distinctions between her own life situation and those of women with more socioeconomic stability, peer support, and opportunities for self-development. This worldview also positioned larger towns or cities, which might offer greater potential for work and freedom from rural social control mechanisms, as dangerous and threatening. Hence, even if she had the means to relocate, her small town remained comforting in its familiarity even though its residents subjected her to gossip and socioeconomic exclusion as a result of her long-term struggles with addiction, incarceration, and associated poor reputation.

Kylee paused thoughtfully after describing her regrets about the past and her hope for a better future. Then she said something that, in so very many ways, encapsulated the rural/urban divide that has unfortunately come to characterize so much of U.S. politics, resource allocation, and identity. "Whenever things get really bad," Kylee stated resolutely, "I remind myself that I could be living someplace really awful. Like New York City, where no one knows their neighbors or helps each other. I can't even imagine how hard it must be living in a place like that." Kylee and Susan, both country and western music aficionados, almost immediately burst into laughter as they recognized the unintended similarity of Kylee's statement to a song by renowned musician Hank Williams, who used the wry wit for which this rural music is best known to capture many people's desire to remain in areas that urbanites dismissively regard as provincial and otherwise backward. "You can send me to hell or New York City," Williams sings about his desire never to leave his rural home. "It'd be about the same to me." This sentiment reflects both the rural/urban divide and rural people's pride in their small-town communities, which mass media and academic discourse alike often dismiss using a long list of pejorative assessments that depict them as uncultured, racist, xenophobic, and otherwise inferior in comparison with those who live in urban areas.

The vast majority of Wyoming residents are registered Republicans, and many voted for Donald Trump in 2016 in the hopes that his administration would somehow return lost jobs to the coal and other resource-extractive industries that are Wyoming's economic mainstay. Their poor and working-class white counterparts in rural Pennsylvania, West Virginia, and other states did the same because they felt helpless as they watched their communities' economic stability further decline in ways that have prompted a rural brain drain among skilled young people and higher rates of addiction and chronic underemployment among those who remain. Across the United States, these social problems are eroding the small-town ethos of community support that defines many rural people's conceptualizations of their lives, selves, and neighbors. Yet rural people's concerns about their socioeconomic marginalization exercised major political influence in the 2016 presidential election—much to the shock of major metropolitan centers of influence. This suggests that politicians, academics, and others concerned with contemporary issues, including mass incarceration, would do well to listen to what rural people have to say.

Assessments offered by Kylee and her numerous rural peers who have been to prison provide powerful insights into national conversations about criminal justice reform that are currently lacking due to their focus on urban populations. The untold stories of currently and formerly incarcerated rural women, whose lives we have attempted to represent in all their complexity, feature a different set of dynamics than those of their urban counterparts. These differences raise a central question that we will attempt to answer in this conclusion: what does Wyoming, the most rural U.S. state and a frontier place in every sense of the word, have to offer to ongoing debates about mass incarceration? The short answer, as we will see, is something that rural Americans have rightly taken pride in for generations: community.

The New Frontier of Mass Incarceration

As we have seen, the idea of the frontier has remained a salient—albeit highly problematic—concept in the dominant U.S. cultural consciousness since at least the mid-nineteenth century, when the central tenets of Manifest Destiny required widespread acceptance of the belief that the U.S. West was an uninhabited space free for the taking by tough, independent-minded settlers. The term "frontier" continues to capture the notion that self-reliant, courageous individuals' willingness to make forays into previously unknown areas enables the possibility for great success and new possibilities. Individualism, that key aspect of the frontier ethos, has been mobilized for generations to inspire people in the United States to tackle everything from space exploration to entrepreneurship.

Individualism—rather than community—likewise remains a central tenet of prevailing approaches to addictions treatment and other therapeutic programming offered to women in prison. This is unsurprising given that the criminal justice system is designed to detain, prosecute, and incarcerate individuals who have committed crimes, rather than address the social and interpersonal forces that inform the decision making of those who break the law. The individualistic nature of U.S. society is particularly apparent in the dominant cultures of Wyoming and many other western and predominantly rural states, where the idea of the self-reliant person is highly valued. These are deeply rooted values that do not acknowledge the inherent interconnectedness of all social problems and of all individuals in society. The term "individualism" itself was coined by French political scientist and historian Alexis de Tocqueville in his famous *Democracy in America*, in which he argued that residents of the United States, which was still a very young country at the time the book appeared in 1835, were at risk of creating a socially disconnected nation of isolated individuals. De Tocqueville characterized individualism as follows:

> Individualism is a reflective and peaceable sentiment that disposes each citizen to isolate himself from the masses of those like him and withdraw to one side with his family and friends, so that after having thus created a little society for his own use, he willingly abandons society at large to itself. . . . Selfishness withers the seed of all the virtues; individualism at first dries up the only source of public virtues; but in the long term it attacks and destroys all the others and will be absorbed in selfishness. (de Tocqueville 2000 [1835]: 482–83)

Written around the same time that the romanticized notion of the frontier and its associated ethos was developing in the United States, de Tocqueville's book remains one of the most influential texts on U.S. democracy. Its enduring popularity has prompted critical engagement with the continued relevance of de Tocqueville's observations to contemporary U.S. society. Scholars have noted that the kind of individualism first observed and articulated by de Tocqueville has dramatically expanded to a majority of U.S. residents as a result of declining community traditions, increasing privatization of services for the needy in lieu of state support, and the valorization of self-centered consumerism in mass media accessed by a majority of people (Elliott & Lemert 2006: 7). These cultural shifts help to explain why the white settler upper class descended from Europe's feudal social systems supported the individualist ethos in the United States of de Tocqueville's era, whereas today even poor and working-class people do so. The result, as we have seen, is ever-rising incidences of widespread social alienation's symptoms—addiction, fear, and a host of other problems—as individuals abandon their communities, with some perhaps feeling that their communities have abandoned them in the process.

While this extreme form of individualism has its roots in the frontier ethos, the frontier is also a geographic category used by federal, state, and municipal government agencies. Such agencies use the term "frontier" to describe regions of the western United States that cannot be accurately characterized as "rural" because of their population densities, which are sometimes as low as six people per square mile, and associated lack of services.[1] This dynamic directly shaped our research team's decision making, as there are so few people in Wyoming that we would have compromised our participants' confidentiality if we had not used our data to carefully construct the composite characters whose stories have shaped this book. Although we chose not to do so, some of the women insisted that we use their real names in order to demonstrate the great conviction and earnestness with which they shared their experiences with us.

Wyoming is both a literal geographic frontier and a place where the dominant cultural ethos of the frontier continues to reign. The findings shared in this study offer direct implications for the U.S. prison system, which has itself reached the horizons of a new frontier in terms of the sheer number of people who are incarcerated, on probation or parole, or experiencing the lifelong consequences of a felony conviction. Very much like the frontier myth that continues to exercise powerful influence in U.S. politics and dominant culture alike, mass incarceration is the result of widespread popular acceptance of assumptions that undergird the existence of the criminal justice system in its present form. The U.S. voting public endorses addressing deeply rooted social problems, particularly addiction, through criminal justice solutions designed by the politicians they elect. There is no great conspiracy by the criminal justice system to promote mass incarceration, which occurs as a result of the majority of the general public's expression of political will, which in turn reflects fear-based responses to widespread substance abuse, addiction, and social inequalities. Such is the nature of democracy in a society characterized by ever-widening inequalities between rich and poor, those with stable jobs and contingent workers, where the criminal justice system is fodder for countless films, series, and other forms of entertainment, and where individuals rely far more on electronic communication than on meaningful social interaction.

Social isolation and inequality breed fear. Mass incarceration accordingly has widespread popular support as the result of three fear-based beliefs that recast community problems as individual dysfunction best left to the domain of the criminal justice system. Poised on the new frontier of mass incarceration, everyone in the United States has a responsibility to critically engage with these three beliefs, and the assumptions in which they are rooted, as the only alternative is an ineffective system with high rates of recidivism and high costs for all concerned. These three fear-based beliefs, which we unpack in detail below, are as follows: drug-abusing women are a threat to public safety, law-breaking is an individual choice rather than a community problem, and women released from prison pose a long-term risk to society.

Drug-Abusing Women Are a Threat to Public Safety

According to the first fear-based belief, women who are addicted to drugs pose a danger to others because their need to obtain illegal substances prompts them to commit other crimes, such as stealing, harming others, or selling drugs. People abuse drugs and alcohol for many different reasons, including to feel better, to forget, and to abate the symptoms of undiagnosed mental health conditions, including depression and anxiety. The United States continues to be a world leader in terms of the sheer number of people who take legally prescribed mood-enhancing and pain-killing drugs developed by multi-billion-dollar pharmaceutical companies, and the associated opioid crisis raging across the rural and suburban United States is evidence of how the boundary between licit and illicit drug use is rarely clear in practice. It is true that the compromised decision making that accompanies substance abuse and addiction can lead to impaired driving, interpersonal violence, and other acts that indisputably harm communities. Yet the accounts of rural Wyoming women in our study reveal that the greatest threat that drug-abusing women pose is to themselves and their loved ones rather than to the community at large.

As is the case among women incarcerated throughout the United States, a significant majority of women who participated in our study struggled with substance abuse and addiction. Their criminal convictions resulted from a number of different charges that may or may not have reflected their involvement in the use, possession, distribution, or sale of controlled substances. Many women reported that they used drugs to cope with the pervasive structural and interpersonal violence that shaped their lives, and a majority of women were familiar with the illicit drug economy, whether as a user, small-scale seller, or intimate partner to a man involved in using or selling drugs. Tammi struggled throughout her life with substance abuse and addiction, which she and her family experienced as part of their struggles with intergenerational poverty, limited or nonexistent community support, and entrenchment in both the criminal justice and social services systems. This was not the case for all women. Itzel, for instance, committed a violent crime during an illicit drug exchange involving her intimate partner and another man; while hers was not a drug crime per se, a cycle of intimate partner violence, economic instability, and limited support in raising a child all directly contributed to the assault she committed. Other women, like Nedrah, became drug users later in life through an intimate relationship, with a combination of addiction and a dysfunctional relationship working in tandem with their choices to destroy their lives as they knew them. All too often, the women harm themselves and their loved ones far more than they pose a risk to public safety.

Law Breaking Is an Individual Choice, Not a Community Problem

The second fear-based belief holds that women who commit crimes have made personal choices free of context and are social deviants who must accordingly be separated from society. As is the case nationally, the Wyoming women in our study committed their crimes in contexts that were typically characterized by severe socioeconomic constraints, fraught interpersonal relationships, substance abuse, and compromised mental health. Their individual choices reflect a host of community problems, including limited support and associated reduced ability to ask for help, lack of opportunities for work that pays a living wage to women, and caregiving responsibilities for children or other loved ones. All too often, the women's view of their own lives was one in which their crimes resulted from choices they made while trying to navigate these community problems.

Violence, addiction, compromised mental health, and poverty are ever-present themes in the lives of currently and formerly incarcerated women. As was the case among a number of women who participated in our study while serving long sentences for murder, Janea killed her husband after he subjected her to years of violent physical and psychological abuse, only to be informed by her court-appointed public defender that she was culpable for his death because she could have left the marriage at any time. Yet, with two children, no real work experience, and a limited education, the option to leave her husband simply did not exist from her perspective. Dakota stole from her employer because she envisioned doing so as her only available option to save her family's ranch from foreclosure. Like Janea and Dakota, Tammi, Itzel, and Nedrah all ended up in prison as a result of relationships with family members or intimate partners that, for the latter three, mired them in the illicit drug economy. In almost all instances among the women who participated in our study, the events that appear on court adjudication and related documents appear as individual actions that do not reflect the community and social factors that often equally contributed to the women's crimes.

Women Released from Prison Pose a Long-Term Risk to Society

The third fear-based belief is rooted in the assumption that women who have been to prison require long-term monitoring that extends far beyond parole requirements because employers, educators, and other members of society have the right to know that they have committed a crime. High rates of recidivism nationwide are often offered as evidence of the long-term risks that formerly incarcerated women pose to society. A majority of the women who participated in our study expressed concern that leaving prison meant returning to the same family and community situations in which they made decisions that resulted in their incarceration in the first place. In their view, such situations often tested women's abilities to practice the prison-based addictions treatment and other therapeutic treatment designed to offer women a sense of agency and control over their lives. Once they were released, pervasive felony-related discrimination further limited women's options to find work outside the poorly paid service sector, locate housing, access substance abuse and other mental health treatment they regard as meaningful, and conform to parole stipulations that determine whether women can remain in the free world.

A woman's risk of reoffending is directly tied to the amount of support she receives once she returns to the community, and women who served multiple prison sentences and participated in our study were often those who struggled the most with substance abuse and had the least postrelease support. Tammi, for instance, had literally been raised by the system in foster care before being incarcerated as a result of multiple drug-related convictions; once she was released, the lack of support in the community, combined with the limited options available to her, virtually guaranteed relapse and rearrest. Itzel, due to her intimate partner's enmeshment in the illicit drug economy, spends her time after release frantic with worry that she will be prosecuted in another drug case and weighing the potential risks and benefits of going on the run. Nedrah, conversely, who sought to escape her tightly knit family in a small-town community through a relationship that revolved around substance abuse, does not experience the same hardships once she is released from prison. Her family, while humiliated by her incarceration, feels obligated to house and care for her—albeit in a basement or an apartment on the outskirts of town. Dakota, who also relies on family members to find housing she can afford on her low-wage service-sector earnings, is subjected to scrutiny by university administrators as she attempts to obtain a new professional qualification since she can no longer work in accounting as a result of her crime. She does so with the knowledge that the realities of felony-related employment discrimination make her future as a nurse uncertain at best. As was all too often the case, these women faced release from prison bearing greater burdens than they had prior to their incarceration.

A Blueprint for Dismantling the Architecture of Gendered Violence

We have argued in this book that an architecture of gendered violence—the primary pathway to incarceration among the Wyoming women in this study—reflects the way the suite of concerns facing currently and formerly incarcerated women throughout the United States manifests in a rural context far from the coastal metropolises that dominate the production of criminal justice discourse and scholarship. Each chapter articulated one of the four components of the architecture of gendered violence, which can be broadly characterized as addictions, individual-ization, and stigmatization.

We have used the term "architecture" to convey how socioeconomic forces combine with individual choices to create life situations for a ma-jority of currently and formerly incarcerated women in our study. Like a house built to withstand the hostile prairie winter, the architecture of gendered violence is sturdy, enduring, and, above all, hardly noted as exceptional among most of the people who live within and around the rural western landscape. Yet, just as it was constructed, it can also be dismantled. Doing so requires recognition of the reality that the prob-lems leading to incarceration are community issues manifesting in the lives of individuals. Our blueprint for dismantling the architecture of gendered violence operative in the women's lives accordingly requires community—rather than individual—solutions.

Addictions

Women who struggle with addictions must have opportunities to receive treatment prior to their involvement with the prison system. Since the 1980s, jails and prisons have been the most populous addic-tions and mental health treatment facilities in the United States and often house people too poor to access costly drug treatment. Drug court, a time-intensive but cost-effective alternative to incarceration for those who agree to abide by its terms, should be offered to all Wyoming women struggling with addiction as a means to keep them in community and facilitate their reunification with loved ones and integration into the workforce. For many women, the stress generated by their inability to be meaningfully involved in their children's and other loved ones' lives made it difficult to focus on substance abuse and other therapeutic treatment while incarcerated. It was also diffi-cult, as we have seen, to translate communication, coping, and related skills learned in a correctional context back into free-world life follow-ing release. The opportunity to acquire these skills while remaining in community under supervision that does not mandate the lifelong consequences of a felony conviction—as is a benefit of participation in many problem-solving courts nationwide—would offer meaningful assistance to women who want help in their journey toward addiction recovery.

Prison is an expensive but necessary social institution. Not all women want or think they need treatment for substance abuse or mental health issues, and the criminalization of illicit drugs creates a situation in which incarceration is a last resort for those stuck in cycles of self-harm. Given the extremely high prevalence of substance abuse and addiction histories among incarcerated women, prisons require adequate resources for substance abuse treatment, including trained, well-paid staff with opportunities for professional development and advancement. Women who participated in our study frequently recognized that correctional case workers, counselors, and other staff, while well intentioned, were exhausted and overwhelmed by the demands of their jobs. Supporting staff in meaningful ways is particularly important given that many front-line criminal justice professionals have extremely stressful jobs that can lead them to abuse alcohol and other substances as a means to cope, particularly in an environment that encourages stoicism to the exclusion of self-care.

In Wyoming as in many other states, ongoing budget cuts result in reduced substance abuse, therapeutic, and educational programming in ways that will eventually confront communities with the need to find innovative ways of addressing the widespread social problems that result in incarceration. One way to do this involves expanding existing centers that support women who have been victimized by intimate partner violence or sexual assault and to offer residential services, job training, and other forms of support for formerly incarcerated women. Such centers exist in most rural areas' larger towns and, given their sensitivity to the violence that informs so many formerly incarcerated women's lives, offer great potential to expand their services if properly funded. Another example of the potential for rural innovation is Wyoming Pathways from Prison, a national award–winning college-in-prison program provided by volunteer University of Wyoming faculty, staff, and students and their Wyoming Department of Corrections colleagues at no cost to prisoners, the university, or the state of Wyoming.[2] Yet being innovative does not mean delegating essential services such as addictions or other therapeutic treatment to the untrained or unsupervised; for example, women expressed concerns that ITU is largely administered by prisoners rather than trained staff.

Individualization

Individualism, as we have seen, is a dominant cultural value at least as old as the United States. Yet, for women who have been to prison, the reality is that individual independence is predicated on the opportunity to earn an income, which relates to education, experience, and willingness of employers to hire ex-offenders. Women need to receive relevant job training that systematically considers the constrained socio-economic realities of their rural communities, ideally in the form of a community-based strategic plan that considers local employers' needs across the state and provides incentives for employers to hire women who have been to prison.

Community is a central aspect of reentry success, as are mentors who can provide the necessary emotional and social support to formerly incarcerated women as they transition from prison to community life. Community groups, twelve step and other free addictions recovery programs, churches, and other existing organizations in many rural areas' larger towns are all places where formerly incarcerated women find support upon their release. Extending mentoring support to women through these groups could potentially offer great benefits. These benefits are practical as well as psycho-social, and could include mutually agreeable offers of transportation, work, and other forms of support for which rural community members routinely rely on one another. Such community-building efforts present great potential to help formerly incarcerated women move from the hypersocial and highly structured environment of prison to the free world, a process that presents indisputable challenges in an individualistic society.

As has been observed by so many feminist criminologists before us, relationships play a central role in women's lives, guiding the agency they express at the intersection of highly formative events and forces that are nearly entirely out of their control. Prevailing therapeutic models in corrections tend to minimize the importance of relationships and the conflicted role they play in women's lives. Currently and formerly incarcerated women who participated in our study strongly suggested that correctional administrators and the staff they supervise provide more classes and other focused support to help them foster relationships free of violence and power-and-control dynamics. Women often described relationships fraught with examples of intimate partner violence, codependency, and other problems, and then characterized those relationships as the most important thing in their lives at the time that they committed their crimes.

None of this is surprising given that the women's constrained agency often came from grabbing hold of shelter in a storm, not only in response to their own desires and goals but also as a defiant rejection of prevailing social and gender norms. Yet classes, programming, and other efforts both within and outside prison continue to address women's crimes as the product of individual decision making. Our findings suggest that such efforts should also include consideration of how the structural violence of poverty considerably limits women's abilities to leave an abusive relationship, especially for women with significant caregiving responsibilities who are facing the isolation from community that often occurs as part of the power and control dynamic at work in many abusive relationships.

Stigmatization

In addition to considerable challenges related to addictions, poverty, caregiving obligations, and a host of other constraints, women face significant stigmatization as a result of having been to prison. Changing legislation that currently requires women to disclose their criminal record to prospective employers would lift some of this burden, as would restoring voting rights to all former prisoners so that they can advocate for themselves like all other citizens. Stigma is internalized as well as imposed by social forces, a point made painfully obvious to the research team each time a woman described those who had not been to prison as "normal people," as if the women themselves were abnormal and inherently dysfunctional. The fact that they felt this way, though, indicates that women need opportunities to feel what they regard as "normal" while incarcerated, including through regular access to exercise and the outdoors as well as through opportunities for work release.

For a number of women, being "normal" means the opportunity to be in regular communication with their children, an option that was not available to women as often as they would like it to be due to the state-determined high cost of phone calls and the high price of travel and lodging for cash-strapped families. The considerable stigma of nonresidential mothering could be tackled by offering more ways to keep women in contact with their children, such as overnight visits to help make the costs of travel lead to more than an hour-long visit. The Mother-Child Building, originally built to house female prisoners with their infant children, has remained closed because the prison struggles with near-constant understaffing due to a combination of the prison's extremely rural location, which leads to high staff turnover, and the state legislature's choice not to provide a budget to facilitate sufficiently desirable salary and benefits packages to attract people to positions to staff it.

Women would also welcome more opportunities to earn money while they are in prison, such as by crafting items for sale through the Department of Corrections, as a means to have an income for commissary, phone calls, reentry planning, or to send home to help support their families. Once released, women need assistance in connecting with opportunities and activities in their communities, to volunteer, join groups, or learn new skills that make them feel connected to others. All of this work will require social-change education among those in rural communities, with the goal of people becoming more compassionate, welcoming, and supportive to women once they are released from prison. Such social-change work must be supported and aligned with the criminal justice system, but it is unrealistic to expect prison administrators to solve deeply rooted social-change problems while also managing the indisputably difficult task of keeping order in multiple correctional facilities. Placing the blame for the women's enduring problems squarely on the prison system entirely misses the central point of mass incarceration as a community problem, given that prisons typically house individuals convicted of a crime after a host of other negative life experiences. Community members also need to understand how many missed possibilities for intervention generally occur before a woman is sentenced to prison; as an earnest Wyoming high school teacher said to Susan about the college-in-prison program Wyoming Pathways from Prison, "You work with the ones we fail."

After Oregon, another western state, Wyoming, has the second-lowest rate of recidivism in the entire United States. This fact is quite impressive until we consider that this second-lowest recidivism rate in the nation is as high as 25%, meaning that one in four people incarcerated in Wyoming eventually returns to prison. Despite that fact, it is tempting to conclude with a grand assessment that touts Wyoming as a model for reducing recidivism, if only because reducing recidivism is the central-most measure used in corrections nationwide to support particular programs, models, and approaches to the exclusion of others. If former prisoners do not return to prison, this argument holds, prison must have taught those ex-offenders new skills and thought processes that ensured they would not break the law again. Yet, this argument does not entirely align with our central conclusion, that community building is the antidote both to mass incarceration and to reducing recidivism. We accordingly argue that the central question asked in corrections should not be "how many women return to prison?" but rather "can women sustain themselves in the long term after being released as felons?"

As we have seen, rural communities' greatest strengths and most profound weaknesses are interconnected with respect to the experiences of rural women before, during, and after their time in prison. Many rural women recently released from prison frequently answered interview questions regarding their struggles and supports in the reentry process with some version of the same point: everybody in this town knows each other. We do not want to conclude by painting too rosy a portrait of the indisputable challenges facing formerly incarcerated women when they return to their communities, or even to new ones, as residents in a state with a population of half a million people quickly learn about newcomers through existing social networks, particularly when those newcomers have been recently released from prison. Instead we want to suggest something that U.S. social scientists all too often ignore in their focus on urban areas: rural communities offer powerful possibilities with respect to how they might better utilize and promote their strengths to reduce the number of women who go to prison in the first place and increase support during and after a prison sentence for those who do.

The pathway to realizing these possibilities, however, will require far more community support and investment than currently exists, in addition to greater academic attention to the vast swaths of the United States that are variously classified as rural, remote, or, as in Wyoming's case, frontier. Otherwise, currently and formerly incarcerated women will remain at the margins of rural society and ignored by scholarship and policy that disproportionately focuses on, and derives from, urban experiences that do not represent the realities of rural people's lives.

NOTES

INTRODUCTION

1 For more on women's reentry experiences pertaining to employment and perceptions of success, see Heidemann et al. 2016; Herrschaft et al. 2009; Johnson 2014;
Wyse 2013.

2 Specifically, Daly identified five distinct pathways that led the women in her study
to a New Haven, Connecticut, felony court: "harmed-and-harming" women
with histories of childhood abuse or neglect who commit violent acts, "battered
women," "street women" involved in illicit drug and sexual economies as a means
to support an addiction while homeless, "drug-connected women" with de facto
involvement in the sale or manufacture of illicit substances, and "other" women
motivated by a desire for material items or money (Daly 1992: 36–39).

3 Creative nonfiction genres, including autobiography, written by currently and formerly incarcerated women also acknowledge the socio-structural and relational
factors that inform women's pathways into crime; see, for instance George 2010;
McConnell 1989; Scheffler 1984; Solinger et al. 2010; Waldman and Levi 2011;
Wozencraft 1993; Sweeney 2010.

4 Contemporary scholars refer to this approach by using the term "treatment industrial complex," which derives from the phrase "prison industrial complex," as
shorthand reference to the punitive-therapeutic confederation that aligns carceral
and social services apparatuses that regard prostitution as a mental health, rather
than an economic, issue (cf. Dewey and St. Germain 2017).

5 For feminist critiques of widespread androcentrism in the field of criminology,
see Carlen 1990; Comack 1999; Naffine 1996.

6 Historical research likewise emphasizes that women's criminal justice system
treatment reflects gendered moral norms; see, for instance: Bosworth 2000;
Dodge 2002; Faith 2011; Freedman 1981; Freedman 1996; Knepper and Schicluna
2010; Kunzel 2008; Linders and van Gundy-Yoder 2008; Shteir 2011; Turner 2015.

7 An extensive body of literature engages with the role of public perceptions,
particularly fear of crime, and the feedback loop created by media and dominant
cultural demonization of criminalized individuals and subsequent justification for
their carceral management; see, for instance, Cheliotis 2010; Chesney-Lind and
Pasko 1997; Chesney-Lind and Eliason 2006; Fiddler 2011.

8 For more on the historical rise of mass incarceration, its collateral consequences,
and critiques of it, see Alexander 2012; Clear 2007; Dagan and Teles 2016; Davis

2003; Davis 2005; Gilmore 2007; Gottschalk 2014; Murakawa 2014; Perkinson 2010; Wacquant 2009.

9 Notably, this incorporation of feminist work into state policy and practice also occurred in similar ways, and with similarly mixed and sometimes troubling results, in the movements against intimate partner violence (Bumiller 2008). For critiques of the implementation of gender-responsive policy and programming in Canadian correctional settings, see Hannah-Moffat 1995; Hannah-Moffat 2004; Hannah-Moffat 2010.

10 For theoretical and analytical reflections on feminist criminology's future, see Heidensohn 2012; Henne and Troshynski 2013; LeBaron and Roberts 2010; Jacobsen and Lempert 2013.

11 More specifically, Standing refers to the precariat, which he defines by the seven forms of labor-related security its members lack:

[1] labor market security: adequate income-opportunities . . . [2] employment security: protection against arbitrary dismissal, regulations on hiring and firing . . . [3] job security: ability and opportunity to retain a niche in employment, plus barriers to skill dilution and opportunities for "upward" mobility in terms of status and income; [4] work security: protection against accidents and illness at work, through, for example, safety and health regulations, limits on working time . . . [5] skill reproduction security: opportunity to gain skills, through apprenticeships, employment training and so on, as well as opportunity to make use of competencies; [6] income security: assurance of an adequate stable income, protected through, for example, minimum wage machinery . . . [7] representation security: possessing a collective voice in the labor market. (Standing 2011: 10)

12 See chapter 1, "Hitting Rock Bottom," for an extensive review of the literature related to rural illicit drug use and addiction.

13 To our knowledge, no central body keeps track of the number and demographic characteristics of state prisons for women, making it necessary for Susan to determine this number herself by conducting an extensive review of all the websites maintained by the respective state agencies tasked with prison administration and oversight. For a complete list of all twenty-seven U.S. federal prisons for women, see Female Offenders, Federal Bureau of Prisons, www.bop.gov.

14 These states are Arkansas, Arizona, California, Colorado, Florida, Georgia, Illinois, Indiana, Louisiana, Michigan, Mississippi, Missouri, New York, Ohio, Oklahoma, Oregon, Pennsylvania, North Carolina, South Carolina, Texas, Utah, and Virginia.

15 Arkansas, California, Colorado, Idaho, Indiana, New York, North Carolina, Virginia, Georgia (which has three), and Texas (which has six)

16 Alabama, California (1), Colorado (1), Delaware, Indiana, Kansas, Kentucky, Louisiana, Maine, Maryland, Minnesota, Mississippi, Nebraska, New Hampshire, North Carolina (1), Oklahoma, Oregon, Rhode Island, South Carolina, South Dakota, Tennessee, Texas (1), Utah, Vermont, Virginia, Washington.

17 Alabama, Alaska, California, Colorado, Connecticut, Delaware, Florida, Georgia, Indiana, Iowa, Kansas, Kentucky, Louisiana, Maine, Maryland, Massachusetts, Michigan, Minnesota, Mississippi, Montana, Nebraska, Nevada, New Hampshire, New Jersey, New York, North Carolina, Ohio, Oklahoma, Oregon, Pennsylvania, Rhode Island, South Carolina, Tennessee, Texas, Utah, Vermont, Washington, Wisconsin. The United States Office of Management and Budget, which establishes U.S. government statistical practices, defines a "city" as a populated area of more than fifty thousand.

18 According to the U.S. Department of Justice's Bureau of Justice Statistics, there were "more than twice as many white females (48,900 prisoners) as black (20,300) or Hispanic (19,300) females in state and federal prison in 2016. However, the imprisonment rate for black females (96 per 100,000 black female residents) was almost double the rate for white females, at 49 per 100,000 white female residents" (U.S. Department of Justice 2016a). Native Americans, the smallest ethnic minority group in the United States, are the most overrepresented of all groups relative to population size (Janisch 2014).

19 For examples of participatory and other types of especially innovative feminist work with incarcerated women, see Fine and Torre 2006; Lawston 2009; Lempert, Bergeron, and Linker 2005; Walsh 2015.

20 For more on the work of Wyoming Pathways from Prison, please see www.uwyo.edu/gwst/wpfp.

21 Sociologist Cynthia Duncan's *Worlds Apart: Poverty and Politics in Rural America* does a masterful job describing the everyday dynamics of life in three rural communities in Appalachia, New England, and the Mississippi Delta.

22 The Bureau of Land Management (BLM), the federal agency tasked with the oversight of public land primarily in the western states, manages fifty-eight million acres of public land in Wyoming (U.S. Bureau of Land Management 2018).

23 We explore issues related to rural political visibility at length in the conclusion.

CHAPTER 3. VIOLENCE HAS FLOW

1 Angela's observation on her family life resembles what sociologist Laurie Schaffner identifies in her research as the concept of the "parentified child," a relatively common phenomenon among incarcerated girls and women in which minor children (sometimes from a very young age) must care for addicted, incapacitated, or otherwise neglectful adults by fulfilling a parental caregiving role, or must provide significant care for younger siblings or other relatives in ways that far exceed their cognitive development and maturity level (Schaffner 2006: 94).

CONCLUSION

1 For examples of this definition, see maps and definitions available on the websites of the National Center for Frontier Communities (2018a and 2018b) and the Wyoming Department of Health (2018).

2 For more information on the program model, see Wyoming Pathways from Prison, University of Wyoming, www.uwyo.edu.

WORKS CITED

Adler, Frieda. 1975. *Sisters in Crime: The Rise of the New Female Criminal.* New York: McGraw Hill.

Afton, Jackson, and Lisa Shannon. 2012. Barriers to Receiving Substance Abuse Treatment among Rural Pregnant Women in Kentucky. *Maternal & Child Health Journal* 16(9): 1762–70.

Agustín, Laura. 2007. *Sex at the Margins: Migration, Labour Markets, and the Sex Industry.* London: Zed.

Ajzenstadt, Mimi. 2009. The Relative Autonomy of Women Offenders' Decision-Making. *Theoretical Criminology* 13(2): 201–25.

Alexander, Michelle. 2012. *The New Jim Crow: Mass Incarceration in the Age of Color-blindness.* New York: New Press.

Amundson, Michael. 1995. Home on the Range No More: The Boom and Bust of a Wyoming Uranium Mining Town. *Western Historical Quarterly* 26(4): 483–505.

Anderson, Jeffrey. 2001a. Northern Arapaho Conversion of a Christian Text. *Ethnohistory* 48(4): 689–712.

———. 2001b. *The Four Hills of Life: Northern Arapaho Knowledge and Life Movement.* Lincoln: University of Nebraska Press.

Anderson, Kim, Lynette Renner, and Tina Bloom. 2014. Rural Women's Strategic Responses to Intimate Partner Violence. *Health Care for Women International* 35: 423–41.

Anderson, Tammy. 2005. Dimensions of Women's Power in the Illicit Drug Economy. *Theoretical Criminology* 9(4): 371–400.

———, ed. 2008. *Neither Victim nor Villain: Empowerment and Agency among Women Substance Abusers.* New Brunswick, NJ: Rutgers University Press.

Arditti, Joyce, and April Few. 2006. Mothers' Reentry into Family Life Following Incarceration. *Criminal Justice Policy Review* 17: 103–23.

Barbaret, Rosemary. 2014. *Women, Crime, and Criminal Justice: A Global Enquiry.* Abingdon, UK: Routledge.

Barlow, Aaron. 2013. *The Cult of Individualism: An Enduring American Myth.* Oxford: Praeger.

Barrick, Kelle, Pamela Lattimore, and Christy Visher. 2014. Reentering Women: The Impact of Social Ties on Long-Term Recidivism. *Prison Journal* 94(3): 279–304.

Batchelor, Susan. 2005. "Prove Me the Bam!": Victimization and Agency in the Lives of Young Women Who Commit Violent Offenses. *Journal of Community & Criminal Justice* 52(4): 358–75.

Baunach, Phyllis Jo. 1985. *Mothers in Prison*. New Brunswick, NJ: Transaction.

Beck, Ulrich, and Elisabeth Beck-Gernsheim. 2002. *Individualization: Institutionalized Individualism and Its Social and Political Consequences*. London: Sage.

Beichner, Dawn, and Cara Rabe-Hemp. 2014. "I Don't Want to Go Back to That Town": Incarcerated Mothers and Their Return Home to Rural Communities. *Critical Criminology* 22: 527–43.

Belknap, Joanne. 2014. *The Invisible Woman: Gender, Crime, and Justice* (fourth edition). Belmont, CA: Wadsworth.

Bell, Shannon. 2009. "There Ain't No Bond in Town Like There Used to Be": The Destruction of Social Capital in the West Virginia Coalfields. *Sociological Forum* 24(3): 631–57.

Bender, Kimberley. 2010. Why Do Some Maltreated Youth Become Juvenile Offenders? A Call for Further Investigation and Adaption of Youth Services. *Children & Youth Services Review* 32: 466–73.

Bergseth, Kathleen, Katie Jens, Lindsey Bergeron-Vigesaa, and Thomas McDonald. 2011. Assessing the Needs of Women Recently Released from Prison. *Women & Criminal Justice* 21: 100–122.

Bernard, Mark. 2011. Cannibalism, Class, and Power: A Foodways Analysis of the Texas Chainsaw Massacre Series. *Food, Culture & Society* 14(3): 413–32.

Berry, Kate, Nancy Markee, Nanci Fowler, and Gary Giewat. 2000. Interpreting What Is Rural and Urban for Western U.S. Counties. *Professional Geographer* 52(1): 93–105.

Bishop, Michael, and Mark Plew. 2016. Fuel Exploitation as a Factor in Shoshone Winter Mobility. *North American Archaeologist* 37(1): 3–19.

Bletzer, Keith. 2009. Modulation of Drug Use in Southern Farming Communities: Social Origins of Poly-Use. *Human Organization* 68(3): 340–49.

Block, Carolyn. 2003. How Can Practitioners Help an Abused Woman Lower Her Risk of Death? *National Institute of Justice Journal* 250: 1–7. www.ncjrs.gov.

Bloom, Barbara, Barbara Owen, and Stephanie Covington. 2004. Women Offenders and the Gendered Effects of Public Policy. *Review of Policy Research* 21: 31–48.

Boeck, Thilo, Jennie Fleming, and Hazel Kemshall. 2006. The Context of Risk Decisions: Does Social Capital Make a Difference? *Forum: Qualitative Social Research* 7(1), Article 17 (unpaginated).

Bonner, Robert. 2002. Buffalo Bill Cody and Wyoming Water Politics. *Western Historical Quarterly* 33(4): 432–51.

Bosworth, Mary. 2007. Creating the Responsible Prisoner: Federal Admission and Orientation Packs. *Punishment and Society* 9: 67–85.

———. 2000. *Engendering Resistance: Agency and Power in Women's Prisons*. London: Routledge.

Bowen, Anne, John Moring, Mark Williams, Glenna Hopper, and Candice Daniel. 2012. An Investigation of Bioecological Influences Associated with First Use of Methamphetamine in a Rural State. *Journal of Rural Health* 28(3): 286–95.

Bradley, Rebekah, and Katrina Davino. 2002. Women's Perceptions of the Prison Environment: When Prison Is "The Safest Place I've Ever Been." *Psychology of Women Quarterly* 26(4): 351–59.

Breiding, M. J., J. Chen, and M. Black. 2014. *Intimate Partner Violence in the United States*. Atlanta, GA: National Center for Injury Prevention and Control, Centers for Disease Control and Prevention.

Brennan, Tim, Markus Breitenbach, William Dieterich, Emily Salisbury, and Patricia van Voorhis. 2012. Women's Pathways to Serious and Habitual Crime: A Person-Centered Analysis Incorporating Gender Response Factors. *Criminal Justice & Behavior* 39(11): 1481–1508.

Brewer-Smith, Kathleen. 2004. Women behind Bars: Could Neurobiological Correlates of Past Physical and Sexual Assault Contribute to Criminal Behavior? *Health Care for Women International* 25: 835–52.

Britton, Dana. 2003. *At Work in the Iron Cage: The Prison as Gendered Organization*. New York: NYU Press.

———. 1997. Gendered Organizational Logic: Policy and Practice in Men's and Women's Prisons. *Gender & Society* 11(6): 796–818.

Brookman, Fiona, Heith Copes, and Andy Hochstetler. 2011. Street Codes as Formula Stories: How Inmates Recount Violence. *Journal of Contemporary Ethnography* 40(4): 397–424.

Brown, Emma, and Frances Smith. 2006. Place and Space: The Where and Why of Drug-Use Location among Rural African American Women. *Journal of Family Nursing* 12(2): 185–200.

Brown, Marilyn, and Barbara Bloom. 2009. Reentry and Renegotiating Motherhood: Maternal Identity and Success on Parole. *Crime & Delinquency* 55: 313–36.

Brown, Ralph, Shawn Dorins, and Richard Krannich. 2005. The Boom-Bust-Recovery Cycle: Dynamics of Change in Community Satisfaction and Social Integration in Delta, Utah. *Rural Sociology* 70(1): 28–49.

Bryne, Bridget. 2003. Reciting the Self: Narrative Representations of the Self in Qualitative Interviews. *Feminist Theory* 4(1): 29–49.

Bumiller, Kristin. 2014. Bad Jobs and Good Workers: The Hiring of Ex-Prisoners in a Segmented Economy. *Theoretical Criminology* 19(3): 336–54.

———. 2008. *In an Abusive State: How Neoliberalism Appropriated the Feminist Movement against Sexual Violence*. Durham, NC: Duke University Press.

Butler, Anne. 1997. *Gendered Justice in the American West: Women Prisoners in Men's Penitentiaries*. Urbana-Champaign: University of Illinois Press.

Campbell, Jacquelyn. 2002. Health Consequences of Intimate Partner Violence. *Lancet* 359(9314): 1331–36.

Caputo, Gail. 2014. *A Halfway House for Women: Oppression and Resistance*. Boston: Northeastern University Press.

Caputo, Gail, and Anna King. 2015. Shoplifting by Male and Female Drug Users: Gender, Agency, and Work. *Criminal Justice Review* 40(1): 47–66.

Carbone-Lopez, Kristin, Jennifer Owens, and Jody Miller. 2012. Women's "Storylines" of Methamphetamine Initiation in the Midwest. *Journal of Drug Issues* 42(3): 226–46.

Carbone-Lopez, Kristin, Lee Ann Slocum, and Candace Kruttschnitt. 2016. "Police Wouldn't Give You No Help": Female Offenders on Reporting Sexual Assault to Police. *Violence against Women* 22(3): 366–96.

Carlen, Pat. 1990. Women, Crime, Feminism and Realism. *Social Justice* 17(4): 106–23.

Carlen, Pat, and Jacqueline Tombs. 2006. Reconfigurations of Penality: The Ongoing Case of the Women's Imprisonment and (Re)integration Industries. *Theoretical Criminology* 10(3): 337–60.

Carlson, Robert, Merrill Singer, Richard Stephens, and Claire Sterk. 2009. Reflections on 40 Years of Ethnographic Drug Abuse Research: Implications for the Future. *Journal of Drug Issues* 39(1): 57–70.

Carr, Patrick, and Maria Kefalas. 2010. *Hollowing Out the Middle: The Rural Brain Drain and What It Means for America.* New York: Beacon.

Carrabine, Eamonn. 2005. Prison Riots, Social Order, and the Problem of Legitimacy. *British Journal of Criminology* 45(6): 896–913.

Carrington, Kerry, J. F. Donnemeyer, and W. DeKeseredy. 2014. Intersectionality, Rural Criminology, and Re-imagining the Boundaries of Critical Criminology. *Critical Criminology* 22(4): 463–77.

Carrington, Kerry, Russell Hogg, and Alison McIntosh. 2011. The Resource Boom's Underbelly: The Criminological Impact of Mining Development. *Australia & New Zealand Journal of Criminology* 44(3): 335–54.

Carrington, Kerry, Alison McIntosh, Russell Hogg, and John Scott. 2013. Rural Masculinities and the Internalization of Violence in Agricultural Communities. *International Journal of Rural Criminology* 2: 3–24.

Carrington, Kerry, Alison McIntosh, and John Scott. 2010. Globalization, Frontier Masculinities, and Violence: Booze, Blokes, and Brawls. *British Journal of Criminology* 50(3): 393–413.

Carrington, Kerry, and Margaret Pereira. 2011. Assessing the Social Impacts of the Resources Boom on Rural Communities. *Rural Society* 21(1): 2–20.

Cassity, Michael. 2011. *Wyoming Will Be Your New Home: Ranching, Farming, and Homesteading in Wyoming, 1860–1960.* Cheyenne: Wyoming State Historic Preservation Office, Wyoming State Parks and Cultural Resources.

Chamberlain, Anastasia. 2015. Embodying Prison Pain: Women's Experiences of Self-Injury in Prison and the Emotions of Punishment. *Theoretical Criminology* 20(2): 205–19.

Chamberlain, Diala, Carles Muntaner, and Christine Walrath. 2004. Gender, Occupational, and Socioeconomic Correlates of Alcohol and Drug Abuse among U.S. Rural, Metropolitan, and Urban Residents. *American Journal of Drug & Alcohol Abuse* 30(2): 409–28.

Chapple, Simon. 2008. Writing Law into "New Western History": Law and Order in Wyoming and New Mexico. *Australasian Journal of American Studies* 27(2): 44–65.

Cheliotis, Leonidas. 2010. The Ambivalent Consequences of Visibility: Crime and Prisons in the Mass Media. *Crime, Media, Culture* 6(2): 169–84.

Chesney-Lind, Meda. 1986. Women and Crime: The Female Offender. *Signs: Journal of Women in Culture & Society* 12(1): 78–96.

Chesney-Lind, Meda, and Michele Eliason. 2006. From Invisible to Incorrigible: The Demonization of Marginalized Women and Girls. *Crime, Media, Culture* 2(1): 29–47.

Chesney-Lind, Meda, and Katherine Irwin. 2008. *Beyond Bad Girls: Gender, Violence, and Hype.* New York: Routledge.

Chesney-Lind, Meda, and Lisa Pasko. 1997. *The Female Offender: Girls, Women, and Crime.* Thousand Oaks, CA: Sage.

Chesney-Lind, Meda, and Noelie Rodriguez. 1983. Women under Lock and Key: A View from the Inside. *Prison Journal* 63: 47–65.

Cicero, Theodore, Matthew Ellis, Hilary Surratt, and Steven Kurtz. 2014. The Changing Face of Heroin Use in the United States: A Retrospective Analysis. *JAMA Psychiatry* 71(7): 821–26.

Clear, Todd. 2007. *Imprisoning Communities: How Mass Incarceration Makes Disadvantaged Neighborhoods Worse.* New York: Oxford University Press.

Clone, Stephanie, and Dana DeHart. 2014. Social Support Networks of Incarcerated Women: Types of Support, Sources of Support, and Implications for Reentry. *Journal of Offender Rehabilitation* 53(7): 503–21.

Cobbina, Jennifer. 2010. Reintegration Success and Failure: Factors Impacting Reintegration among Incarcerated and Formerly Incarcerated Women. *Journal of Offender Rehabilitation* 49: 210–32.

Cobbina, Jennifer, and Kimberly Bender. 2012. Predicting the Future: Incarcerated Women's Views of Reentry Success. *Journal of Offender Rehabilitation* 51: 275–94.

Coleman, James. 2002. *The Criminal Elite: Understanding White Collar Crime.* New York: Worth.

Comack, Elizabeth. 1999. Producing Feminist Knowledge: Lessons from Women in Trouble. *Theoretical Criminology* 3(3): 287–306.

Comfort, Megan. 2008. *Doing Time Together: Love and Family in the Shadow of Prison.* Chicago: University of Chicago Press.

Connolly, Catherine. 2016. *The Wage Gap between Wyoming's Men and Women.* Report prepared for the Wyoming Women's Foundation. Can be accessed at: http://wywf.org.

Contreras, Randol. 2012. *Stickup Kids: Race, Drugs, Violence, and the American Dream.* Berkeley: University of California Press.

Cook, Sarah, Shannon Smith, Chantal Tusher, and Jerris Railford. 2005. Self-Reports of Traumatic Events in a Random Sample of Incarcerated Women. *Women & Criminal Justice* 16: 107–26.

Corner, John. 2006. Archive Aesthetics and the Historical Imaginary: *Wisconsin Death Trip. Screen* 47(3): 291–306.

Covington, Stephanie, and Barbara Bloom. 2006. Gender-Responsive Treatment and Services in Correctional Settings. *Women & Therapy* 29(3/4): 9–33.

Craig, Susan. 2009. A Historical Review of Mother and Child Programs for Incarcerated Women. *Prison Journal* 89(suppl.): 35S–52S.

Creadick, Anna. 2017. Banjo Boy: Masculinity, Disability, and Difference in *Deliverance*. *Southern Cultures* 23(1): 63–78.

Crenshaw, Kimberlé. 1991. Mapping the Margins: Intersectionality, Identity Politics, and Violence against Women of Color. *Stanford Law Review* 43(6): 1241–99.

Cressey, Donald. 1973. *Other People's Money: A Study in the Social Psychology of Embezzlement*. Belmont, CA: Wadsworth.

Currell, Sue. 2017. You Haven't Seen Their Faces: Eugenic National Housekeeping and Documentary Photography in 1930s America. *Journal of American Studies* 51(2): 481–511.

Dagan, David, and Steven Teles. 2016. *Prison Break: Why Conservatives Turned against Mass Incarceration*. Oxford: Oxford University Press.

Dahle, Thorvald, and Carol Archbold. 2015. "Just Do What You Can [. . .] Make It Work!" Exploring the Impact of Rapid Population Growth on Police Organizations in Western North Dakota. *Policing: An International Journal of Police Strategies & Management* 38(4): 805–19.

Daly, Kathleen. 1992. Women's Pathways to Felony Court: Feminist Theories of Lawbreaking and Problems of Representation. *Southern California Review of Law and Women's Studies* 2(1): 11–52.

Daly, Kathleen, and Meda Chesney-Lind. 1988. Feminism and Criminology. *Justice Quarterly* 5: 438–97.

Davies, Pamela. 2003. Is Economic Crime a Man's Game? *Feminist Theory* 4(3): 283–303.

Davis, Angela Y. 2005. *Abolition Democracy: Beyond Prison, Torture, and Empire*. New York: Seven Stories Press.

———. 2003. *Are Prisons Obsolete?* New York: Seven Stories Press.

Davis, Melinda, Margaret Spurlock, Kristen Dulacki, Thomas Meath, Hsin-Fang Li, Dennis McCarty, Donald Warne, Bill Wright, and K. John McConnell. 2016. Disparities in Alcohol, Drug Use, and Mental Health Condition Prevalence and Access to Health Care in Rural, Isolated, and Reservation Areas. *Journal of Rural Health* 32(3): 287–302.

de Graff, Kaitlyn, and Jennifer Kilty. 2016. You Are What You Eat: Exploring the Relationship between Women, Food, and Incarceration. *Punishment & Society* 18(1): 27–46.

DeHart, Dana. 2008. Pathways to Prison: Impact of Victimization in the Lives of Incarcerated Women. *Violence against Women* 14(12): 1362–81.

DeKeseredy, Walter, Joseph Donnermeyer, Martin Schwartz, Kenneth Tunnell, and Mandy Hall. 2007. Thinking Critically about Rural Gender Relations: Toward a Rural Masculinity/Male Peer Support Model of Separation/Divorce Sexual Assault. *Critical Criminology* 15: 295–311.

DeKeseredy, Walter, Stephen Muzzatti, and Joseph Donnemeyer. 2014. Mad Men in Bib Overalls: Media's Horrification and Pornification of Rural Culture. *Critical Criminology* 22(2): 179–97.

DeKeseredy, Walter, and Martin Schwartz. 2009. *Dangerous Exits: Escaping Abusive Relationships in Rural America*. New Brunswick, NJ: Rutgers University Press.

Deller, Steven, and Melissa Deller. 2011. Structural Shifts in Select Determinants of Crime with a Focus on Rural and Urban Differences. *Western Criminology Review* 12(3): 120–38.

Deloria, Phillip. 2004. *Indians in Unexpected Places*. Lawrence: University Press of Kansas.

———. 1999. *Playing Indian*. New Haven, CT: Yale University Press.

Deloria Jr., Vine. 1992. *American Indian Policy in the Twentieth Century*. Norman: University of Oklahoma Press.

De Tocqueville, Alexis. 2000 [1835]. *Democracy in America*. Chicago: University of Chicago Press.

Dewey, Susan, and Tonia St. Germain. 2017. *Women of the Street: How the Criminal Justice–Social Services Alliance Fails Women in Prostitution*. New York: NYU Press.

Dobash, Rebecca, and Russell Dobash. 1986. *The Imprisonment of Women*. London: Blackwell.

Dodge, L. Mara. 2002. *"Whores and Thieves of the Worst Kind": A Study of Women, Crime, and Prisons, 1835–2000*. DeKalb: Northern Illinois University Press.

Doherty, Sherri, Pamela Forrester, Amanda Brazil, and Flora Matheson. 2014. Finding Their Way: Conditions for Successful Reintegration among Women Offenders. *Journal of Offender Rehabilitation* 53: 562–86.

Donnemeyer, Joseph. 2016. Without Place, Is It Real? *International Journal for Crime, Justice & Social Democracy* 5(3): 27–40.

Donnemeyer, Joseph, and Walter DeKeseredy. 2008. Toward a Rural Critical Criminology. *Southern Rural Sociology*, suppl. Special Issue: Rural Crime 23(2): 4–28.

Donnemeyer, Joseph, John Scott, and Elaine Barclay. 2013. How Rural Criminology Informs Critical Thinking in Criminology. *International Journal for Crime, Justice & Social Democracy* 2(3): 69–91.

Draus, Paul, and Robert Carlson. 2009. Down on Main Street: Drugs and the Small-Town Vortex. *Health & Place* 15(1): 247–54.

Draus, Paul, Harvey Seigal, Robert Carlson, Russell Falck, and Jichuan Wang. 2006. Perspectives on Health among Adult Users of Illicit Stimulant Drugs in Rural Ohio. *Journal of Rural Health* 22(2): 169–73.

———. 2005. Cracking the Cornfields: Recruiting Illicit Stimulant Drug Users in Rural Ohio. *Sociological Quarterly* 46(1): 165–89.

Dudley, Kathryn Marie. 2002. *Debt and Dispossession: Farm Loss in America's Heartland*. Chicago: University of Chicago Press.

Duncan, Cynthia. 2015. *Worlds Apart: Poverty and Politics in Rural America*. New Haven, CT: Yale University Press.

Dyck, Erika. 2014. History of Eugenics Revisited. *Canadian Bulletin of Medical History* 31(1): 1–7.

Eastman, Brenda, and Sheila Bunch. 2007. Providing Services to Survivors of Domestic Violence: A Comparison of Rural and Urban Service Provider Perceptions. *Journal of Interpersonal Violence* 22(4): 465–73.

Elliott, Anthony, and Charles Lemert. 2006. *The New Individualism: The Emotional Costs of Globalization.* New York: Routledge.

Etter, Gregg, Michael Birzer, and Judy Fields. 2008. The Jail as Dumping Ground: The Incidental Incarceration of Mentally Ill Individuals. *Criminal Justice Studies* 21(1): 79–89.

Faith, Karlene. 2011. *Unruly Women: The Politics of Confinement and Resistance.* New York: Seven Stories Press.

Farber, Naomi, and Julie Miller-Cribbs. 2014. Violence in the Lives of Rural, Southern, and Poor White Women. *Violence against Women* 20(5): 517–38.

Faul, Mark, Michael Dailey, David Sugerman, Scott Sasser, Benjamin Levy, and Len Paulozzi. 2015. Disparity in Naloxone Administration by Emergency Medical Service Providers and the Burden of Drug Overdose in US Rural Communities. *American Journal of Public Health,* suppl. 105.S3 (July): e26–e32.

Ferraro, Kathleen. 2006. *Neither Angels nor Demons: Women, Crime, and Victimization.* Boston: Northeastern University Press.

Ferszt, Ginette, Dawn Salgado, Susanne DeFedele, and Mary Leveillee. 2009. Housing of Healing: A Group Intervention for Grieving Women in Prison. *Prison Journal* 89(1): 46–64.

Fiddler, Michael. 2011. "A System of Light before Becoming a Figure of Stone": The Phantasmagoric Prison. *Crime, Media, Culture* 7(1): 83–97.

Fili, Andriani. 2013. Women in Prison: Victims or Resisters? Representations of Agency in Women's Prisons in Greece. *Signs: Journal of Women in Culture and Society* 39(1): 1–26.

Fine, Michelle, and María Elena Torre. 2006. Intimate Details: Participatory Action Research in Prison. *Action Research* 4(3): 253–69.

Finkelhor, David, Richard Ormrod, Heather Turner, and Sherry Hamby. 2005. The Victimization of Children and Youth: A Comprehensive, National Survey. *Child Maltreatment* 10(1): 5–25.

Fleetwood, Jennifer. 2015. In Search of Respectability: Narrative Practice in a Women's Prison in Quito, Ecuador. Pp. 43–68 in *Narrative Criminology: Understanding Stories of Crime,* edited by Lois Presser and Sveinung Sandberg. New York: NYU Press.

Flores, Jerry. 2016. *Caught Up: Girls, Surveillance, and Wraparound Incarceration.* Berkeley: University of California Press.

Flowers, Shawn. 2010. *Employment and Female Offenders: An Update of the Empirical Research.* Washington, DC: National Institute of Corrections, U.S. Department of Justice.

Fowler, Loretta. 2001. *The Four Hills of Life: Northern Arapaho Knowledge and Life Movement.* Lincoln: University of Nebraska Press.

Freedman, Estelle. 1996. The Prison Lesbian: Race, Class, and the Construction of the Aggressive Female Homosexual, 1915–1965. *Feminist Studies* 22(2): 397–423.

———. 1981. *Their Sisters' Keepers: Women's Prison Reform in America, 1830–1930.* Ann Arbor: University of Michigan Press.

Gaarder, Emily, and Joanne Belknap. 2006. Tenuous Borders: Girls Transferred to Adult Court. *Criminology* 40(3): 481–517.

Gagné, Patricia. 1991. Appalachian Women: Violence and Social Control. *Journal of Contemporary Ethnography* 20: 387–415.

Garceau, Dee. 1997. *The Important Things of Life: Women, Work, and Family in Sweetwater County, Wyoming, 1880–1929.* Lincoln: University of Nebraska Press.

Garcia, Angela. 2014. Regeneration: Life, Drugs, and the Remaking of Hispano Inheritance. *Social Anthropology* 22(2): 200–212.

Garriott, William. 2011. *Policing Methamphetamine: Narcopolitics in Rural America.* New York: NYU Press.

George, Erin. 2010. *A Woman Doing Life: Notes from a Prison for Women.* New York: Oxford University Press.

Giallombardo, Rose. 1966. *Society of Women: A Study of a Women's Prison.* New York: Wiley.

Gilmore, Ruth Wilson. 2007. *Golden Gulag: Prisons, Surplus, Crisis, and Opposition in Globalizing California.* Berkeley: University of California Press.

Giordano, Peggy, Stephen Cernkovich, and Jennifer Rudolph. 2002. Gender, Crime, and Desistance: Towards a Theory of Cognitive Transformation. *American Journal of Sociology* 107: 990–1094.

Giordano, Peggy, and Jennifer Copp. 2015. "Packages" of Risk: Implications for Determining the Effect of Maternal Incarceration on Child Wellbeing. *Criminology & Public Policy* 14(1): 157–68.

Girshick, Lori. 1999. *No Safe Haven: Stories of Women in Prison.* Boston: Northeastern University Press.

Goffman, Alice. 2014. *On the Run: Fugitive Life in an American City.* Chicago: University of Chicago Press.

Goldberg, Rosalyn Negron, and Emma Brown. 2010. Gender, Personal Networks, and Drug Use among Rural African Americans. *International Quarterly of Community Health Education* 30(1): 41–54.

Goldenberg, Shira, Jean Shoveller, M. Koehoorn, and Aleck Ostry. 2008. And They Call This Progress? Consequences for Young People of Living and Working in Resource-Extraction Communities. *Critical Public Health* 20: 157–68.

Goodmark, Leigh. 2012. *A Troubled Marriage: Domestic Violence and the Legal System.* New York: NYU Press.

Gordon, Jill, Blythe Proulx, and Patricia Grant. 2013. Trepidation among the "Keepers": Gendered Perceptions of Fear and Risk of Victimization among Correctional Officers. *American Journal of Criminal Justice* 38: 245–65.

Gottschalk, Maria. 2014. *Caught: The Prison State and the Lockdown of American Politics.* Princeton, NJ: Princeton University Press.

————. 2006. *The Prison and the Gallows: The Politics of Mass Incarceration in America*. Cambridge: Cambridge University Press.

Grant, Kathleen, Stephanie Sinclair Kelly, Sangeeta Agrawal, Jane Meza, James Meyer, and Debra Romberger. 2007. Methamphetamine Use in Rural Midwesterners. *American Journal on Addictions* 16(2): 79–84.

Greer, Kimberly. 2002. Walking an Emotional Tightrope: Managing Emotions in a Women's Prison. *Symbolic Interaction* 25(1): 117–39.

Grounds, Linda. 2011. Forensic Psychological Evaluations of Women Who Embezzle. Accessed at www.drlindagrounds.com.

Hackett, Colleen. 2013. Transforming Visions: Governing through Alternative Practices and Therapeutic Interventions at a Women's Reentry Center. *Feminist Criminology* 8(3): 221–42.

Hall-Sanchez, Amanda. 2014. Male Peer Support, Hunting, and Separation/Divorce Sexual Assault in Rural Ohio. *Critical Criminology* 22(4): 495–510.

Haney, Lynne. 2010. *Offending Women: Power, Punishment, and the Regulation of Desire*. Berkeley: University of California Press.

Haney, Lynne, and András Tapolcai. 2010. Imagining the Self and Other: Women Narrate Prison Life across Cultures. Pp. 196–204 in *Interrupted Life: Experiences of Incarcerated Women in the United States*, edited by Rickie Solinger, Paula Johnson, Martha Raimon, Tina Reynolds, and Ruby Tapia. Berkeley: University of California Press.

Hannah-Moffat, Kelly. 2010. Sacrosanct or Flawed: Risk, Accountability, and Gender-Responsive Penal Policies. *Current Issues in Criminal Justice* 22(2): 1–23.

————. 2004. Losing Ground: Gendered Knowledges, Parole Risk, and Responsibility. *Social Politics* 11(3): 363–85.

————. 1999. Moral Agent or Actuarial Subject: Risk and Canadian Women's Imprisonment. *Theoretical Criminology* 3(1): 71–94.

————. 1995. Feminine Fortresses: Woman-Centered Prisons? *Prison Journal* 75(2): 135–64.

Heidemann, Gretchen, Julie Cedarbaum, and Sidney Martinez. 2016. Beyond Recidivism: How Formerly Incarcerated Women Define Success. *Affilia: Journal of Women and Social Work* 31: 24–40.

————. 2014. "We Walk through It Together": The Importance of Peer Support for Formerly Incarcerated Women's Success. *Journal of Offender Rehabilitation* 53: 522–42.

Heidensohn, Frances M. 2012. The Future of Feminist Criminology. *Crime, Media, Culture* 8(2): 123–34.

Heitzeg, Nancy. 2015. "Whiteness," Criminality, and the Double Standards of Deviance/Social Control. *Contemporary Justice Review* 18(2): 197–214.

Henne, Kathryn, and Emily Troshynski. 2013. Mapping the Margins of Intersectionality: Criminological Possibilities in a Transnational World. *Theoretical Criminology* 17(4): 455–73.

Herrschaft, Bryn, Bonita Veysey, Heather Tubman-Carbone, and Johanna Christian. 2009. Gender Differences in the Transformation Narrative: Implications for Revised Reentry Strategies for Female Offenders. *Journal of Offender Rehabilitation* 48: 463–82.

Herz, Denise, and Rebecca Murray. 2003. Exploring Arrestee Drug Use in Rural Nebraska. *Journal of Drug Issues* 33(1): 99–117.

Hochstetler, Andy, Heith Copes, and J. Patrick Williams. 2010. "That's Not Who I Am": How Offenders Commit Violent Acts and Reject Authentically Violent Selves. *Justice Quarterly* 27(4): 492–516.

Huebner, Beth, Christina DeJong, and Jennifer Cobbina. 2010. Women Coming Home: Long-Term Patterns of Recidivism. *Justice Quarterly* 27: 225–54.

Huey Dye, Meredith, Ronald Aday, Lori Farney, and Jordan Raley. 2014. "The Rock I Cling To": Religious Engagement in the Lives of Life-Sentenced Women. *Prison Journal* 94(3): 388–408.

Hughes, Susan. 2000. The Sheepeater Myth of Northwestern Wyoming. *Plains Anthropologist* 45: 171–83.

Hunter, Lori, Richard Krannich, and Michael Smith. 2002. Rural Migration, Rapid Growth, and Fear of Crime. *Rural Sociology* 67(1): 71–89.

Jacobsen, Carol, and Lora Bex Lempert. 2013. Institutional Disparities: Considerations of Gender in the Commutation Process for Incarcerated Women. *Signs* 39(1): 265–89.

Janisch, Roy. 2014. Native American Incarceration: A Neglected Problem? *Sociology of Crime, Law & Deviance* 19: 159–77.

Johnson, Ida. 2014. Economic Impediments to Women's Success on Parole: "We Need Someone on Our Side." *Prison Journal* 94(3): 365–87.

Johnson, Paula. 2003. *Inner Lives: Voices of African American Women in Prison*. New York: NYU Press.

Johnson-Webb, Karen, Leonard Baer, and Wilbert Gesler. 1997. What Is Rural? Issues and Considerations. *Geography of Rural Health* 13(3): 253–56.

Jonas, Adam, April Young, and Jennifer Havens. 2012. OxyContin as Currency: OxyContin Use and Increased Social Capital among Rural Appalachian Drug Users. *Social Science & Medicine* 74(10): 1602–09.

Kelly, J., M. G. Myers, and S. A. Brown. 2002. Do Adolescents Affiliate with 12-Step Groups? A Multivariate Process Model of Effects. *Journal of Studies of Alcohol* 63: 293–304.

Keyes, Katherine, Magdalena Cerda, Joanne Brady, Jennifer Havens, and Sandro Galea. 2014. Understanding the Rural-Urban Differences in Nonmedical Prescription Opioid Use and Abuse in the United States. *American Journal of Public Health* 104(2): E52–E59.

Kilty, Jennifer. 2006. Under the Barred Umbrella: Is There Room for Women-Centered Self-Injury Policy in Canadian Corrections? *Criminology & Public Policy* 5: 161–82.

Klein, Dorie. 1973. The Etiology of Female Crime: A Review of the Literature. *Issues in Criminology* 8(2): 3–29.

Klenowski, Paul, Heith Copes, and Christopher Mullins. 2008. Gender, Identity, and Accounts: How White Collar Offenders Do Gender When Making Sense of Their Crimes. *Justice Quarterly* 28(1): 46–69.

Knepper, Paul, and Sandra Schicluna. 2010. Historical Criminology and the Imprisonment of Women in Nineteenth-Century Malta. *Theoretical Criminology* 14(4): 407–24.

Krishnan, Satya, Judith Halbert, Keith McNeil, and Isadore Newman. 2004. From Respite to Transition: Women's Use of Domestic Violence Shelters in Rural New Mexico. *Journal of Family Violence* 19: 165–73.

Kruttschnitt, Candace. 2010. The Paradox of Women's Imprisonment. *Daedalus: Journal of the American Academy of Arts & Sciences* 139(3): 32–42.

Kruttschnitt, Candace, and Kristin Carbone-Lopez. 2006. Moving beyond Stereotypes: Women's Subjective Accounts of Their Violent Crime. *Criminology* 44(2): 321–51.

Kubiac, Sheryl Pimblott, Julie Hanna, and Marianne Balton. 2005. "I Came to Prison to Do My Time—Not to Get Raped": Coping within the Institutional Setting. *Stress, Trauma & Crisis* 8: 157–77.

Kunzel, Regina. 2008. *Criminal Intimacy: Prison and the Uneven History of Modern American Sexuality*. Chicago: University of Chicago Press.

Lawston, Jodie Michelle. 2009. "We're All Sisters": Bridging and Legitimacy in the Women's Anti-Prison Movement. *Gender & Society* 23(5): 639–64.

LeBaron, Genevieve, and Adrienne Roberts. 2010. Toward a Feminist Political Economy of Capitalism and Carcerality. *Signs: Journal of Women in Culture and Society* 36(1):19–44.

Leigey, Margaret, and Katie Reed. 2010. A Woman's Life before Serving Life: Examining the Negative Pre-incarceration Life Events of Female Life-Sentenced Inmates. *Women and Criminal Justice* 20: 302–22.

Lempert, Lora. 2016. *Women Doing Life: Gender, Punishment, and the Struggle for Identity*. New York: NYU Press.

Lempert, Lora Bex, Suzanne Bergeron, and Maureen Linker. 2005. Negotiating the Politics of Space: Teaching Women's Studies in a Women's Prison. *NWSA Journal* 17(2): 199–207.

Leonard, Elizabeth. 2002. *Convicted Survivors: The Imprisonment of Battered Women Who Kill*. Albany: State University of New York Press.

Lesy, Michael. 1973. *Wisconsin Death Trip*. New York: Pantheon.

Leverentz, Andrea. 2014. *The Ex-Prisoner's Dilemma: How Women Negotiate Competing Narratives of Reentry and Desistance*. New Brunswick, NJ: Rutgers University Press.

———. 2011. Being a Good Daughter and Sister: Families of Origin in the Reentry of African American Female Ex-Prisoners. *Feminist Criminology* 6: 239–67.

———. 2006. The Love of a Good Man? Romantic Relationships as a Source of Support or Hindrance for Female Ex-Offenders. *Journal of Research in Crime & Delinquency* 43: 459–88.

Linders, Annulla, and Alana van Gundy-Yoder. 2008. Gall, Gallantry, and the Gallows: Capital Punishment and the Social Construction of Gender, 1840–1920. *Gender & Society* 22(3): 324–48.

Linnemann, Travis, and Tyler Wall. 2013. "This Is Your Face on Meth": The Punitive Spectacle of "White Trash" in the Rural War on Drugs. *Theoretical Criminology* 17(3): 315–34.

Logan, T. K., Lucy Evans, Erin Stevenson, and Carol Jordan. 2005. Barriers to Services for Rural and Urban Survivors of Rape. *Journal of Interpersonal Violence* 20: 591–616.

Logan, T. K., Erin Stevenson, Lucy Evans, and Carl Leukefeld. 2004. Rural and Urban Women's Perceptions of Barriers to Health, Mental Health, and Criminal Justice Services: Implications for Victim Services. *Violence & Victims* 19(1): 37–62.

Lombroso, Caesar, and Guglielmo Ferrero. 2004 [1893]. *Criminal Woman, the Prostitute, and the Normal Woman [La Donna Delinquente]*. Trans. by Nicole Hahn Rafter and Mary Gibson. Durham, NC: Duke University Press.

Lopez, Vera. 2017. *Complicated Lives: Girls, Parenting, Drugs, and Juvenile Justice*. Camden, NJ: Rutgers University Press.

Lynch, Kellie, and T. K. Logan. 2015. Risk Factors in Arrest of Rural and Urban Female Victims of Intimate Partner Violence. *Violence & Victims* 30(3): 488–501.

Lynch, Shannon, Dana DeHart, Joanne Belknap, B. L. Green, P. Dass-Brailsford, K. Johnson, and E. Whalley. 2016. A Multisite Study of the Prevalence of Serious Mental Illness, PTSD, and Substance Use Disorders of Women in Jail. *Psychiatric Services* 65(5): 670–74.

Maharidge, Dale, and Michael Williamson. 2011. *Someplace like America: Tales from the New Great Depression*. Berkeley: University of California Press.

Malloch, Margaret, and Gill McIvor, eds. 2013. *Women, Punishment, and Social Justice: Human Rights and Penal Practices*. London: Routledge.

Manoogian, Margaret, Joan Jurich, Yoshie Sano, and Ju-Lien Ko. 2015. "My Kids Are More Important Than Money": Parenting Expectations and Commitment among Appalachian Low-Income Mothers. *Journal of Family Issues* 36(3): 326–50.

Marshall, Gregory. 2009. *Shaped by Stories: The Ethical Power of Narratives*. South Bend, IN: University of Notre Dame Press.

Martin, Philip. 2009. *Importing Poverty? Immigration and the Changing Face of Rural America*. New Haven, CT: Yale University Press.

Massey, Garth. 2004. Making Sense of Work on the Wind River Reservation. *American Indian Quarterly* 28(3/4): 786–816.

McAdams, Dan. 2013. *The Redemptive Self: Stories Americans Live By*. Oxford: Oxford University Press.

McCall-Hosenfeld, Jennifer, Sucharita Mukherjee, and Erik Lehman. 2014. The Prevalence and Correlates of Lifetime Psychiatric Disorders and Trauma Exposures in Urban and Rural Settings: Results from the National Comorbidity Survey Replication (NCS-R). *PLoS ONE* 9(11): e112416. doi:10.1371/journal.pone.0112416.

McCall-Hosenfeld, Jennifer, Carol Weisman, Amanda Perry, Marianne Hillemeier, and Cynthia Chung. 2014. I Just Keep My Antennae Out: How Rural Primary Care Physicians Respond to Intimate Partner Violence. *Journal of Interpersonal Violence* 29(14): 2670–2694.

McConnel, Patricia. 1989. *Sing Soft, Sing Loud*. New York: Logoria Books.

McCorkel, Jill. 2013. *Breaking Women: Gender, Race, and the New Politics of Imprisonment*. New York: NYU Press.

McDaniels-Wilson, Cathy, and Joanne Belknap. 2008. The Extensive Sexual Violation and Sexual Abuse Histories of Incarcerated Women. *Violence against Women* 14(10): 1090–1127.

McIntyre, Alice. 2013. The Value of "Silence" in the Lives of Post-Incarcerated Women. *Journal of Offender Rehabilitation* 52(1): 1–15.

McKell, Jan. 2009. *Red Light Women of the Rocky Mountains*. Albuquerque: University of New Mexico Press.

Messina, Nena, William Burdon, Garo Hagopian, and Michael Prendergast. 2006. Predictors of Prison-Based Treatment Outcomes: A Comparison of Men and Women Participants. *American Journal of Drug and Alcohol Abuse* 32: 7–28.

Meyer, Cheryl, and Michelle Oberman. 2001. *Mothers Who Kill Their Children: Understanding the Acts of Moms from Susan Smith to the "Prom Mom."* New York: NYU Press.

Michaelson, Venezia, and Jeanne Flavin. 2014. Not All Women Are Mothers: Addressing the Invisibility of Women under the Control of the Criminal Justice System Who Do Not Have Children. *Prison Journal* 94(3): 328–46.

Michel, Cedric, John Cochran, and Kathleen Heide. 2015. Public Knowledge about White Collar Crime: An Exploratory Study. *Crime, Law & Social Change* 65: 67–91.

———. 2014. Sociodemographic Correlates of Knowledge about Elite Deviance. *American Journal of Criminal Justice* 40: 639–60.

Miller, Jody. 2008. *Getting Played: African American Girls, Urban Inequality, and Gendered Violence*. New York: NYU Press.

———. 1998. "Up It Up": Gender and the Accomplishment of Street Robbery. *Criminology* 36: 37–66.

Miller, Jody, Kristin Carbone-Lopez, and Mikh V. Gunderman. 2015. Gendered Narratives of Self, Addiction, and Recovery among Women Methamphetamine Users. Pp. 69–95 in *Narrative Criminology: Understanding Stories of Crime*, edited by Lois Presser and Sveinung Sandberg. New York: NYU Press.

Miller, Jody, and Scott Decker. 2001. Young Women and Gang Violence: An Examination of Gender, Street Offending, and Violent Victimization in Gangs. *Justice Quarterly* 18(1): 115–40.

Miller, Susan. 2005. *Victims as Offenders: The Paradox of Women's Violence in Relationships*. New Brunswick, NJ: Rutgers University Press.

Miller, Susan, and Michelle Meloy. 2006. Women's Use of Force: Voices of Women Arrested for Domestic Violence. *Violence against Women* 12(1): 89–115.

Moos, R., and C. Timko. 2008. Outcome Research on Twelve-Step and Other Self-Help Programs. Pp. 511–21 in *Textbook of Substance Abuse Treatment*, edited by M. Galanter and H. O. Kleber. Washington, DC: American Psychiatric Press.

Morash, Merry. 2010. *Women on Probation and Parole: A Feminist Critique of Community Programs and Services*. Boston: Northeastern University Press.

Morris, Katy. 2017. "More Reputation Than She Deserves": Remembering Suffrage in Wyoming. *Rethinking History* 21(1): 48–66.

Morris, Monique. 2016. *Pushout: The Criminalization of Black Girls in School*. New York: New Press.

Mosher, Clayton, and Dretha Phillips. 2006. The Dynamics of Prison-Based Therapeutic Community for Women Offenders: Retention, Completion, and Outcomes. *Prison Journal* 86(1): 6–31.

Murakawa, Naomi. 2014. *The First Civil Right: How Liberals Built Prison America*. Oxford: Oxford University Press.

Naffine, Ngaire. 1996. *Feminism and Criminology*. Cambridge: Polity Press.

National Center for Frontier Communities. 2018a. Frontier Definitions List. http://frontierus.org/frontier-definitions/.

———. 2018b. Frontier Maps. http://frontierus.org/maps/.

Nofziger, Stacey, and Susan Williams. 2005. Perceptions of Police and Safety in a Small Town. *Police Quarterly* 8(2): 248–70.

Nuytiens, An, and Jenneke Christiaens. 2015. Female Pathways to Crime and Prison: Challenging the (US) Gendered Pathways Perspective. *European Journal of Criminology* 13(2): 195–213.

O'Brien, Patricia. 2001. *Making It in the "Free World": Women in Transition from Prison*. Albany: SUNY Press.

O'Connor, Christopher. 2015. Insiders and Outsiders: Social Change, Deviant Others, and Sense of Community in a Boomtown. *International Journal of Comparative & Applied Criminal Justice* 39: 219–38.

———. 2012. Agency and Reflexivity in Boomtown Transitions: Young People Deciding on a School and Work Direction. *Journal of Education & Work* 27: 372–91.

O'Connor, Patricia. 2015. Telling Moments: Narrative Hot Spots in Accounts of Criminal Acts. Pp. 174–206 in *Narrative Criminology: Understanding Stories of Crime*, edited by Lois Presser and Sveinung Sandberg. New York: NYU Press.

Okamoto, Scott, Stephen Kulis, Susana Helm, Christopher Edwards, and Danielle Giroux. 2014. The Social Contexts of Drug Offenders and Their Relationship to Drug Use of Rural Hawaiian Drug Youths. *Journal of Child & Adolescent Substance Abuse* 23(4): 242–52.

Omori, Marisa. 2013. Moral Panics and Morality Policy: The Impact of Media, Political Ideology, Drug Use, and Manufacturing on Methamphetamine Legislation in the United States. *Journal of Drug Issues* 43(4): 517–34.

Opsal, Tara. 2015. "It's Their World, So You've Just Got to Get Through": Women's Experiences of Parole Governance. *Feminist Criminology* 10(2): 188–207.

———. 2011. Women Disrupting a Marginalized Identity: Subverting the Parolee Identity through Narrative. *Journal of Contemporary Ethnography* 40(2): 135–67.

Otis, Melanie, Carrie Oser, and Michele Staton-Tindall. 2016. Violent Victimization and Substance Dependency: Comparing Rural Incarcerated Heterosexual and Sexual Minority Women. *Journal of Social Work Practice in the Addictions* 16(1/2): 176–201.

Owen, Barbara. 2017. *In Search of Safety: Confronting Inequality in Women's Imprisonment*. Berkeley: University of California Press.

———. 2008. *Gendered Violence and Safety: A Contextual Approach to Improving Security in Women's Facilities*. Washington, DC: U.S. Department of Justice.

Owen, Barbara, and James Wells. 2005. *Staff Perspectives on Sexual Violence in Adult Prisons and Jails: Results from Focus Group Interviews*. Washington, DC: National Institute of Corrections.

Pardue, Angela, Bruce Arrigo, and Daniel Murphy. 2011. Sex and Sexuality in Women's Prisons: A Preliminary Typological Investigation. *Prison Journal* 91(3): 279–304.

Park, Nicholas, Lisa Melander, and Shanell Sanchez. 2016. Nonmedical Prescription Drug Use among Midwestern Rural Adolescents. *Journal of Child & Adolescent Substance Abuse* 25(4): 360–69.

Parker, Karen, and Amy Reckdenwald. 2008. Women and Crime in Context: Examining the Linkages between Patriarchy and Female Offending across Space. *Feminist Criminology* 3(1): 5–24.

Patten, Ryan, Sarah Messer, and Kimberlee Candela. 2015. "I Don't See Myself as Prison Material": Motivations for Entering a Rural Drug Court. *International Journal of Offender Therapy & Comparative Criminology* 59(11): 1188–1202.

Patton, Tracey Owens, and Sally Schedlock. 2012. *Gender, Whiteness, and Power in Rodeo: Breaking Away from the Ties of Sexism and Racism*. Lanham, MD: Lexington Books.

Payne, Brian, Bruce Berg, and Ivan Sun. 2005. Policing in Small-Town America: Dogs, Drunks, Disorder, and Dysfunction. *Journal of Criminal Justice* 33(1): 31–41.

Pearce, Diana. 2016. *The Self-Sufficiency Standard for Wyoming 2016*. Washington State: Center for Women's Welfare. Prepared for the Wyoming Women's Foundation. Can be accessed at http://wywf.org.

Pease, Bob. 2010. Reconstructing Violent Rural Masculinities: Responding to Fractures in the Rural Gender Order in Australia. *Culture, Society & Masculinities* 2(2): 154–64.

Perkinson, Robert. 2010. *Texas Tough: The Rise of America's Prison Empire*. New York: Metropolitan Books.

Pickering, Kathleen, Mark Harvey, Gene Summers, and David Mushinski. 2006. *Welfare Reform in Persistent Rural Poverty: Dreams, Disenchantment, and Diversity*. University Park: Pennsylvania State University Press.

Pollack, Shoshana. 2007. Reconceptualizing Women's Agency and Empowerment: Challenges to Self-Esteem Discourse and Women's Lawbreaking. *Women and Criminal Justice* 12(1): 75–89.

Pollak, Otto. 1950. *The Criminality of Women*. Philadelphia: University of Pennsylvania Press.

Pollock, Jocelyn, and Sareta Davis. 2015. The Continuing Myth of the Violent Female Offender. *Criminal Justice Review* 30(1): 5–29.

Presser, Lois, and Sveinung Sandberg. 2015. *Narrative Criminology: Understanding Stories of Crime*. New York: NYU Press.

Raj, Anita, Jennifer Rose, Michelle Decker, Cynthia Rosengard, Megan Hebert, Michael Stein, and Jennifer Clark. 2008. Prevalence and Patterns of Sexual Assault across the Life Span among Incarcerated Women. *Violence against Women* 14(5): 528–41.

Rankin, Charles. 1990. Teaching Opportunities and Limitation for Wyoming Women. *Western Historical Quarterly* 21(2): 147–70.

Raphael, Jody. 2000. *Saving Bernice: Battered Women, Welfare, and Poverty*. Boston: Northeastern University Press.

Redding, Arthur. 2007. Frontier Mythographies: Savagery and Civilization in Frederick Jackson Turner and John Ford. *Literature/Film Quarterly* 35(4): 313–22.

Reisig, Michael, Kristy Holtfreter, and Merry Morash. 2006. Assessing Recidivism Risk across Female Pathways to Crime. *Justice Quarterly* 23(3): 384–403.

Renner, Lynnette, Leah Habib, Ann Stromquist, and Corinne Peek-Asa. 2014. The Association of Intimate Partner Violence and Depressive Symptoms in a Cohort of Rural Couples. *Journal of Rural Health* 30(1): 50–58.

Rhew, Isaac, David Hawkins, and Sabrina Oesterle. 2011. Drug Use and Risk among Youth in Different Rural Contexts. *Health & Place* 17(3): 775–83.

Richardson, Rebecca, and Shawn Flower. 2014. How Gender of Ex-Offenders Influences Access to Employment Opportunities. *Journal of Applied Rehabilitation Counseling* 45(4): 35–43.

Richie, Beth. 2012. *Arrested Justice: Black Women, Violence, and America's Prison Nation*. New York: NYU Press.

———. 2001. Challenges Incarcerated Women Face as They Return to Their Communities: Findings from Life History Interviews. *Crime & Delinquency* 47(3): 368–89.

Rierdan, Andi. 1997. *The Farm: Life inside a Women's Prison*. Amherst: University of Massachusetts Press.

Rockell, Barbara. 2013. Women and Crime in the Rural-Urban Fringe. *International Journal of Rural Criminology* 2(1): 53–74.

Rommie, Jamie. 2018. The Green River Pageant and the Americanization of the American Frontier. *Cercles* 19: 172–82.

Ross, Luana. 1998. *Inventing the Savage: The Social Construction of Native American Criminality*. Austin: University of Texas Press.

Roush, Karen, and Ann Kurth. 2016. The Lived Experience of Intimate Partner Violence in the Rural Setting. *Journal of Obstetric, Gynecologic & Neonatal Nursing* 45(3): 308–19.

Ryan, Jake, and Charles Sackrey. 1996. *Strangers in Paradise: Academics from the Working Class*. New York: Vintage.

Ruddell, Rick. 2011. Boomtown Policing: Responding to the Dark Side of Resource Development. *Policing* 5: 328–42.

Samenow, Stanton. 2014 [1984]. *Inside the Criminal Mind*. New York: Broadway Books.

Sandberg, Linn. 2013. Backward, Dumb, and Violent Hillbillies? Rural Geographies and Intersectional Studies on Intimate Partner Violence. *Affilia* 28: 350–65.

Sanderson, Nathan. 2011. "We Were All Trespassers": George Edward Lemmon, Anglo-American Cattle Ranching, and the Great Sioux Reservation. *Agricultural History Society* 85(1): 50–71.

Sanger, Andrew. 2007. Eugenics, Race, and Margaret Sanger Revisited: Reproductive Freedom for All? *Hypatia* 22(2): 210–17.

Schaffner, Laurie. 2006. *Girls in Trouble with the Law*. Piscataway, NJ: Rutgers University Press.

Scheffler, Judith. 1984. An Annotated Bibliography of Writing by Women Prisoners. *Prison Journal* 64(1): 68–83.

Scott, John, Kerry Carrington, and Alison McIntosh. 2012. Established-Outsider Relations and Fear of Crime in Mining Towns. *Sociologia Ruralis* 52(2): 147–69.

Sennett, Richard, and Jonathan Cobb. 1973. *The Hidden Injuries of Class*. New York: Vintage.

Sered, Susan, and Maureen Norton-Hawk. 2014. *Can't Catch a Break: Gender, Jail, Drugs, and the Limits of Personal Responsibility*. Berkeley: University of California Press.

Severance, Theresa. 2005. "You Know Who You Can Go To": Cooperation and Exchange between Incarcerated Women. *Prison Journal* 85(3): 343–67.

———. 2004. The Prison Lesbian Revisited. *Journal of Lesbian and Gay Social Services* 17(3): 39–57.

Sexton, Rocky, Robert Carlson, Carl Leukefeld, and Brenda Booth. 2008. Trajectories of Methamphetamine Use in the Rural South: A Longitudinal Qualitative Study. *Human Organization* 67(2): 181–93.

Shalinsky, Audrey. 1991. Images of Women in Twentieth-Century Wyoming Town Celebrations. *Plains Anthropologists* 36(134): 69–75.

Sharp, Susan. 2014. *Mean Lives, Mean Laws: Oklahoma's Women Prisoners*. Camden, NJ: Rutgers University Press.

Sharpe, Gilly. 2015. Precarious Identities: "Young" Motherhood, Desistance, and Stigma. *Criminology & Criminal Justice* 15(4): 407–22.

Shepherd, Judy. 2001. Where Do You Go When It's 40 Below? Domestic Violence among Rural Alaska Native Women. *Affilia* 16(4): 488–510.

Sherman, Jennifer. 2009. *Those Who Work, Those Who Don't: Poverty, Morality, and Family in Rural America*. Minneapolis: University of Minnesota Press.

———. 2006. Coping with Rural Poverty: Economic Survival and Moral Capital in Rural America. *Social Forces* 85(2): 891–913.

Shteir, Rachel. 2011. *The Steal: The Cultural History of Shoplifting*. New York: Penguin.

Shuman, Robert, Jeanne McCauley, Eve Waltermaurer, Patrick Roche, and Helen Hollis. 2008. Understanding Intimate Partner Violence against Women in the Rural South. *Violence & Victims* 23(3): 390–405.

Siegel, Jane. 2011. *Disrupted Childhoods: Children of Women in Prison*. New Brunswick, NJ: Rutgers University Press.

Sims, Victor. 1990. *Small Town and Rural Police*. Springfield, IL: Charles C. Thomas.

Slotkin, Richard. 1992. *Gunfighter Nation: The Myth of the Frontier in Twentieth-Century America*. Norman: University of Oklahoma Press.

Small, Jeon, Geoffrey Curran, and Brenda Booth. 2010. Barriers and Facilitators for Alcohol Treatment for Women: Are There More or Less for Rural Women? *Journal of Substance Abuse Treatment* 39(1): 1–13.

Smart, Carol. 1977. *Women, Crime, and Criminology: A Feminist Critique*. London: Routledge & Kegan Paul.

Smith, Catrin. 2014. Injecting Drug Use and the Performance of Rural Femininity: An Ethnographic Study of Female Injecting Drug Users in Rural North Wales. *Critical Criminology* 22(4): 511–25.

———. 2002. Punishment and Pleasure: Women, Food, and the Imprisoned Body. *Sociological Review* 50(2): 197–214.

Smoyer, Amy. 2015. Feeding Relationships: Foodways and Social Networks in a Women's Prison. *Women & Social Work* 30(1): 26–39.

Solinger, Rickie, Paula Johnson, Martha Raimon, Tina Reynolds, and Ruby Tapia. 2010. *Interrupted Life: Experiences of Incarcerated Women in the United States*. Berkeley: University of California Press.

Stamm, Henry. 1999. *People of the Wind River: The Eastern Shoshones, 1825–1900*. Norman: University of Oklahoma Press.

Standing, Guy. 2011. *The Precariat: The New Dangerous Class*. London: Bloomsbury Academic.

Staton-Tindall, Michele, Kathi Harp, Alexandra Minieri, Carrie Oser, J. Matthew Webster, Jennifer Havens, and Carol Leukefeld. 2015. An Exploratory Study of Mental Health and HIV Risk Behavior among Drug-Using Rural Women in Jail. *Psychiatric Rehabilitation Journal* 38(1): 45–54.

Subramanian, Ram, Kristine Riley, and Chris Mai. 2018. *Divided Justice: Trends in Black and White Jail Incarceration, 1990–2013*. New York: Vera Institute of Justice.

Sudbuy, Julia, ed. 2005. *Global Lockdown: Race, Gender, and the Prison-Industrial Complex*. New York: Routledge.

Sweeney, Megan. 2010. *"Reading Is My Window": Books and the Art of Reading in Women's Prisons*. Chapel Hill: University of North Carolina Press.

Sykes, Gresham. 2007 [1958]. *The Society of Captives: A Study of a Maximum Security Prison*. Princeton, NJ: Princeton University Press.

Tapia, Ruby C. 2010. "Introduction." Pp. 1–10 in *Interrupted Life: Experiences of Incarcerated Women in the United States*, edited by R. Solinger, P. C. Johnson, M. L. Raimon, T. Reynolds, and R. Tapia. Berkeley: University of California Press.

Thomas, William Isaac. 1923. *The Unadjusted Girl*. Boston: Little, Brown.

Turner, Frederick Jackson. 1994. Pp. 31–60 in *The Significance of the Frontier in American History, 1893: Rereading Frederick Jackson Turner*, edited by John Mack Faragher. New York: Holt.

———. 1893. *The Significance of the Frontier in American History*. Chicago: American Historical Association.

Turner, Jo. 2015. Female Prisoners, Aftercare, and Release: Residential Provision and Support in Late Nineteenth-Century England. *British Journal of Community Justice* 13(3): 35–50.

U.S. Bureau of Land Management. 2018. BLM Wyoming: What We Manage. www.blm.gov.

U.S. Congress. 1997. Adoption and Safe Families Act of 1997. Retrieved from https://www.gpo.gov/.

U.S. Department of Agriculture. 2016. Wyoming Agricultural Statistics. Cheyenne, Wyoming: U.S. Department of Agriculture Mountain Region, Wyoming Field Office. www.nass.usda.gov.

U.S. Department of Justice. 2016a. Correctional Populations in the United States. Retrieved from: www.bjs.gov

———. 2016b. Prisoners in 2016. Retrieved from: www.bjs.gov.

———. 2015a. *Female Victims of Violence*. Washington, DC: U.S. Department of Justice Office of Justice Programs. www.bjs.gov.

———. 2015b. Prisoners in 2015. Retrieved from: www.bjs.gov.

———. 2010. *Parents in Prison and Their Minor Children*. Washington, DC: U.S. Department of Justice Office of Justice Programs. www.bjs.gov.

U.S. Energy Information Administration. 2016. Wyoming: State Profile and Energy Estimates. www.eia.gov.

U.S. National Park Service. 2018. Yellowstone National Park: Total Recreation Visitors. https://irma.nps.gov.

Wacquant, Loïc. 2009. *Prisons of Poverty*. Minneapolis: University of Minnesota Press.

Waldman, Ayelet, and Robin Levi, eds. 2011. *Inside This Place, Not of It: Narratives from Women's Prisons*. San Francisco: McSweeney's Books.

Walker, Lenore. 2000 [1979]. *The Battered Woman Syndrome*. New York: Springer.

———. 1992. Battered Women Syndrome and Self-Defense. *Notre Dame Journal of Law, Ethics, and Public Policy* 3: 321–34.

Walsh, Avwyn Mae. 2015. Staging Women in Prisons: Clean Break Theatre Company's Dramaturgy of the Cage. *Crime, Media, Culture* 12(3): 309–26.

Walsh, Kate, David DeLillo, and Mario Scalara. 2011. The Cumulative Impact of Sexual Revictimization on Emotion Regulation Difficulties: An Examination of Female Inmates. *Violence against Women* 17(8): 1103–8.

Ward, Kyle, and Alida Merlo. 2015. Rural Jail Reentry and Mental Health: Identifying Challenges for Offenders and Professionals. *Prison Journal* 96(1): 27–52.

Websdale, Neil. 1998. *Rural Women Battering and the Justice System: An Ethnography*. Thousand Oaks, CA: Sage.

Weisburd, David, Elin Waring, and Ellen Chayet. 2001. *White-Collar Crime and Criminal Careers*. Cambridge: Cambridge University Press.

Weisheit, Ralph. 1993. Studying Drugs in Rural Areas: Notes from the Field. *Journal of Research in Crime & Delinquency* 30(2): 213–32.

Weisheit, Ralph, David Falcone, and Edward Wells. 2006. *Crime and Policing in Rural and Small-Town America*. Prospect Heights, IL: Waveland.

Wesely, Jennifer. 2006. Considering the Context of Women's Violence: Gender, Lived Experience, and Cumulative Victimization. *Feminist Criminology* 1(4): 303–28.

Wesely, Jennifer, and James Wright. 2009. From the Inside Out: Efforts by Homeless Women to Disrupt Cycles of Crime and Violence. *Women & Criminal Justice* 19(3): 217–34.

Willging, Cathleen, Gilbert Quintero, and Elizabeth Lilliott. 2014. Hitting the Wall: Youth Perspectives on Boredom, Trouble, and Drug Use Dynamics in Rural New Mexico. *Youth & Society* 46(1): 3–29.

Worrall, Anne. 1990. *Offending Women: Female Lawbreakers and the Criminal Justice System.* London: Routledge.

Wozencraft, Kim. 1993. *Notes from the Country Club.* New York: Trafalgar Square.

Wright, Patricia, Katharine Stewart, Ellen Fischer, Robert Carlson, J. Wang, Carl Leukefeld, and B. Booth. 2007. HIV Risk Behaviors among Rural Stimulant Users: Variations by Gender and Race/Ethnicity. *AIDS Education & Prevention* 19(2): 137–50.

Wyoming Department of Health. 2018. Wyoming Frontier Information. https://health. wyo.gov.

Wyse, Jessica. 2013. Rehabilitating Criminal Selves: Gendered Strategies in Community Corrections. *Gender & Society* 27(2): 231–55.

Young, April, and Jennifer Havens. 2012. Transition from First Illicit Drug Use to First Injection Drug Use among Rural Appalachian Drug Users. *Addiction* 107(3): 587–96.

Young, April, Nika Larian, and Jennifer Havens. 2014. Gender Differences in Circumstances Surrounding First Injection Experience of Rural Injection Drug Users in the United States. *Drug & Alcohol Dependence* 134(1): 401–5.

Zimmer, Lynn. 1987. How Women Reshape the Prison Guard Role. *Gender & Society* 1(4): 415–31.

Zimmer Schneider, Rachel, and Kathryn Feltey. 2009. "No Matter What Has Been Done Wrong Can Always Be Redone Right": Spirituality in the Lives of Imprisoned Battered Women. *Violence against Women* 15(4): 443–59.

INDEX

ABOUT THE AUTHORS

Susan Dewey is Associate Professor at the University of Wyoming, where she leads the national award-winning college-in-prison program Wyoming Pathways from Prison. She is the author or editor of eleven books and eighty papers and reports on the intersections among poverty, violence, and women's criminal justice system involvement.

Bonnie Zare is Associate Professor of Women's and Gender Studies at Virginia Tech. Her research focuses on discourses of identity, feminism, and activism in contemporary India; she also does ethnographic work with nonprivileged populations, including women in prison. Her most recent essay is "Indifference Is the New Black: Season One and the Violation of Women's Solidarity" for *Caged Women: Incarceration, Representation, and Media*, ed. Laurie Gordy and Shirley Jackson (forthcoming 2019).

Catherine Connolly is Professor and Director of Gender and Women's Studies at the University of Wyoming. She publishes in the areas of sexuality and the law, as well as public policy in Wyoming. She has served in the Wyoming House of Representatives since 2009 and currently serves as the House Minority Floor leader.

Rhett Epler is a fifth-generation native of Wyoming, where he is pursuing a PhD. His co-authored articles on the criminal justice system have appeared in *Psychology of Women Quarterly*, *Reviews in Anthropology*, and a special issue of *Wagadu* titled "Telling My Story: Voices from the Wyoming Women's Prison."

Rosemary Bratton has been involved in social justice and economic justice for disenfranchised women throughout her career. As founder of the Hilde Project, Rosemary pursues, with entrepreneurial zeal for practical and innovative solutions, empowerment for women, including incarcerated and formerly incarcerated women, and ending violence against women.